Finding a Path

Finding a Path

Stories from My Life

HARRY W. STRACHAN

iUniverse, Inc.
Bloomington

Finding a Path
Stories from My Life

iUniverse books may be ordered through booksellers or by contacting:

iUniverse
1663 Liberty Drive
Bloomington, IN 47403
www.iuniverse.com
1-800-Authors (1-800-288-4677)

ISBN: 978-1-4620-4199-2 (sc)
ISBN: 978-1-4620-4201-2 (hc)
ISBN: 978-1-4620-4200-5 (ebk)

Printed in the United States of America

iUniverse rev. date: 09/02/2011

Praise for *Finding A Path: Stories from My Life*

This shockingly authentic life story entertains, inspires and educates. The eldest son of American missionaries, Harry vividly captures the tragedies and triumphs of his life's unusual journey. From childhood in rural Costa Rica to Harvard Law School; from devastating earthquakes to failure at marriage, hopeful dreams collide with real world demons. By sharing wisdom through intimate stories, Harry offers us the courage to accept our own realities and imperfection—to traverse our own potholes—and discover our own unique path in life.

Thomas Tierney, former Managing Partner Bain & Company Chair of Bridgespan & author of *Give Smart*

Harry Strachan, whom I've known for many years, is a man of thought, compassion and action who has made a difference in Central America and Panama . . . at INCAE, a world class business school . . . later as a consultant and investment banker . . . and through the Strachan Foundation. You will read a very personal and honest story of his struggles. The issues that have confronted wise men of all religions throughout history—family, profession, social contribution, faith and reason—come into vivid light in the stories from Harry's life."

Ernesto Fernandez H., Chairman Grupo and Fundacion Uno

My first impressions of Harry Strachan as a young boy were his wide open face and eager eyes. Half a century later these same characteristics shine through in the honesty with which he write. This book is the story of his pilgrimage both professionally and in his faith after the untimely death of his father. Educated in two Christian schools he earned his law degree and then a doctorate at Harvard. With amazing honesty, Harry tells the story of his growth and success in the business world, his struggles of faith, his two marriages and the evolution of his thoughts throughout his life.

David M. Howard, Former President, Latin America Mission

The fascinating story of a bright young "M.K." who learned basic economics from his frugal missionary parents and went on to brilliant careers in education and finance.

John Stam, LAM missionary

Harry Strachan is one of the most remarkable people I've ever known. He has been a life-long friend whose path through sorrow and success has been a brilliant example to me of the 'examined life.' Written principally for his children, these stories will resonate with anyone who is willing to live outside the box.

Maestro John Nelson, Conductor

For my parents, Ken and Elizabeth.
They gave us life,
Showed us a good way—
How to love, serve, and live with integrity.

CONTENTS

INTRODUCTION

In a college literature course we read the play *The Skin of Our Teeth* by Thornton Wilder. As I remember it fifty years later (and I deliberately write from memory because it's what I've carried over the years), one of the characters, a fortune teller, leaves center stage and walks to the edge of the platform to address the audience directly:

> I tell the future!
> But who can tell the past?
> Yes, your past.
> You lie awake at night wondering what it meant,
> Wondering what it was trying to tell you.
> Yes, I tell the future—that's easy,
> But who can tell the past?

I could picture her on the edge of the stage talking directly to me. Her words struck deep. I was already having trouble aligning my own personal experiences with what my religion and society led me to expect. I was attempting to integrate my sexual and spiritual drives, my Latin American roots and my Anglo-Saxon heritage, my ambition to be successful in the secular world and my desire to do God's will. I had no clear idea of what career would fit my talents; the clues in my past were opaque. But I remember thinking, *If I ever learn enough from my life to write up my memoirs, I've found the quote that should go at the beginning.*

DELIVERING ON A PROMISE

It's a dark night in this my sixty-fifth year, 2007. I sit in my home looking out at the twinkling lights of the central valley of Costa Rica where I was born. Folders on my desk hold the weekly letters written home from high school, college, and law school that my mother faithfully saved. On the shelf, three-ring binders contain journal entries from my adult years, entries in which I wrestled with my life. I haven't re-read most of them since they were written.

In 1965, profoundly disappointed at not finding Dad's personal life among his papers, I determined to leave some written record of my own life before I died, should my children ever come looking for me. At this desk I'm trying to deliver on that promise.

Re-reading a sampling of the letters and journals has convinced me that, while they contain a record of events and people, many now forgotten, they do not contain the stories that most profoundly influenced me. These are not written down, but are carried inside me, jumbled like letters in an old trunk, all out of order.

The important stories in my memory trunk tell about heroic grandparents and parents whose missionary legacy I have run away from, yet somehow carried throughout my life. They come from childhood in Costa Rica, or tell of leaving the family cocoon for high school and college in the United States, and then of going on to graduate school and the army. They send out glimmers of meaning, like discarded bottles in an overgrown lot.

The early death of my parents is still painful, and grieving for them never seems to end. My life also seems to have had more than its share of medical traumas—"potholes" that nearly killed me, yet which paradoxically made my life much richer. The stories associated with my spiritual journey are complicated, and I see now that it's a journey that probably won't ever feel completed.

When I look back on my various careers, I marvel at the success of the teams to which I belonged. Work has been good to me. In teaching and consulting and investing, I found work that fit my talents. I saw INCAE, Bain, Bain Capital, and Mesoamerica grow large and reputable. Though money was never my chief objective, the financial rewards for my work exceeded expectations and permitted an endowment for the Strachan Foundation, set up in honor of my grandparents and parents.

When I tried to write a traditional autobiography some years ago, I became so bored, I thought, *This is going to kill me, and even if it doesn't, it will destroy my grandchildren's pleasure in reading.* So I put the project aside.

But some time later in a consulting case team meeting, seeking an indirect way to tackle a problem, I began with a story from another client's experience. Eyes lit up and the group's energy level increased. They laughed at the unexpected ending, but understood my point. *Stories are fun*, I thought, *I may not have the capacity to write an interesting autobiography, but I do have some good stories. Maybe that's the way to talk about my life.*

The stories from my years in teaching and administrative positions at INCAE, the graduate school of business in Central America where I started my academic career, were relatively easy to write. I gathered them into a small volume as a gift for the school when I retired from the board after thirty-seven years of involvement. Subsequently, INCAE published them privately in both English and Spanish.[1] The positive reactions of unexpected readers, like the administrative staff and spouses of the professors, encouraged me to keep writing.

A similar collection of stories for Bain & Co, also a retirement gift, was published in a pamphlet.[2] Again, unexpected readers convinced me that telling stories was the right approach. My daughter then insisted that I write my more personal and family stories, ones more accessible and of greater interest to those not involved in teaching or consulting.

In following the advice to visualize my audience, I've pictured the generation of my grandsons, thirty years from now. In my mind's eye they look similar to their parents, my nieces and nephews, and many of the young professionals with whom I work at INCAE, CALI, Bain, and Mesoamerica.

Like these young leaders from government, non-profit organizations, and the private sector, they are well-educated, have important jobs, are ambitious, and are enjoying successful careers. They are also, by and large, idealists who want to "do good" as well as "do well." They want their lives to count for something. In truth, they want it all: to be great parents, good spouses, and growing human beings. While playing society's game successfully, they don't want to "lose their souls." They wish to live with integrity and authenticity.

As I write for them, I recognize that I don't have a magic formula, but I do believe my experiences may be relevant. I want to encourage them all to believe that it is possible to be ambitious in their work and to

---

[1] *INCAE Memories, 1970-1982*, INCAE, Alajuela, Costa Rica, 2007.

[2] *Bain Stories from the Early Years: The Education of a Consultant*, Bain & Co, Boston, 2008.

be authentic. It isn't always easy to balance all the competing demands and the contradictions of life, but a creative synthesis often emerges from the effort. Inevitably they will hit their own potholes—major illnesses, divorces, getting fired, losses and disappointments—but if my experience is any indicator, these may be the most important sources of growth.

For that reason, the stories in this collection deal less with work and more with the journey into adulthood, through marriage, parenthood, and adversity. They cover significant stops on the path to health in its broadest sense, my definition of the spiritual journey. My own experience has convinced me that Carl Jung was right when he emphasized the importance of knowing, accepting, and integrating the many parts of oneself. I'm convinced it is a source of energy, it pays great dividends, and it is the key to a successful life.

THE SUMMER OF 1965

Where to start? Perhaps on a similar dark night in the summer of 1965.

That summer I was twenty-three and at the end of my second year of law school. I was sitting in the office provided by the Latin America Mission (LAM) on the second floor of the old seminary building in San Jose, Costa Rica. The desk in front of me was also covered with old letters and documents, circled in the light of the desk lamp. Their musty smell filled the cool night air. The ceiling light was dim, the building quiet, everyone in the surrounding offices having left for home hours before. In the far corner of the second floor, there was an apartment in which a single female missionary lived along with a pretty summer intern, but they were too far away for me to hear any of their sounds.

My Job

I was back in the land of my birth to collect my dad's papers, interview the missionaries who had worked closely with him, and gather materials for his biography. He had died five months earlier at the age of fifty-four from Hodgkin's lymphoma. In the preceding two years, I had watched him waste away, both from the disease and the chemotherapy.

His death left me awash in feelings I tried hard to control. In the immediate aftermath, I distracted myself with handling the practical details of moving his body from California back to San Jose for burial. I was in shock, so I focused on the nitty-gritty details and worried about my mother and younger brothers and sisters.

All of us flew to Costa Rica, I traveling out to fly with my mother and the younger children from Pasadena, where my father had been teaching at Fuller Theological Seminary while fighting the cancer. At the wake in the main chapel of the seminary building, as the oldest son, I stood next to my mother and tried with dignity and warmth to receive condolences from the endless line of people his life had touched. There were maids and taxi drivers, missionaries and ministers, businessmen and politicians, many with moving stories of how he had changed their lives. An old woman remembered him as a young boy living across the street. A prominent pastor described his seminary teaching and mentoring. A young missionary said that her call to the mission field had come as a result of his sermon in her church years before. Many just wept as they hugged us.

At midnight when the doors were shut and everyone had left, I sat in the empty chapel next to the coffin. Long after I had spent all my tears and run out of things to write in my journal, I stubbornly sat there refusing to go to bed for reasons I could not explain, even to myself. Maybe I was hoping I'd find some release from the deep anger I felt.

I was angry at the suffering and humiliation of his death. He had dropped to a hundred pounds, and his body was covered with boils. I was angry at the hope and guilt stirred up by well-meaning friends. Until the very end, many of his colleagues around the world were absolutely certain that God would not let the devil take this architect of Evangelism in Depth. "His work is too critical and still unfinished!" they said. One assured us that God had personally told him there would be a miraculous recovery. "The devil won't get this victory; we must claim this miracle with faith!" he declared. But the end had come just as the doctors predicted, and one of my sisters wondered if it was her lack of faith that blocked the healing.

I wrote in my journal, "God damn it! God damn his death!"

The next morning the funeral was held in the Templo Biblico, the downtown Protestant church built by my grandparents. The large building was crowded to overflowing. I no longer remember exactly what I said on behalf of the family in my part of the service, although I do recall that the intention of my remarks was to thank all those present and to honor his memory.

The family friend who was so sure of the miracle quoted Romans 8:28 at the funeral, affirming that "all things work together for good." But on the platform looking out over the crowd, I could see nothing good coming from this death, not for the mission, not for my mother, not for my brothers and sisters, and certainly not for me. The whole thing felt like an unmitigated disaster. It added to my growing sense that what I had been led to believe in Christianity "ain't necessarily so." While not fully admitting it to myself, I was angry at God for how He was managing the world.

Over the next few months, sitting in my room at the Harvard Law School, I would have the strange experience of feeling my father's eyes looking down at me from his picture over my desk. I'd break down in tears—tears of grief and something more, and I'd find myself talking to the picture saying, "I miss you . . . I'm doing the best I can." I remembered a dream I'd shared with him on his last visit to Boston in my first year of law school.

As we walked together on the Boston Common between his commitments at Park St. Church, I described the dream:

> The family is in Wheaton [Illinois] at the town swimming pool. I've been practicing the dives from the three meter board that you, Dad, have always done so well—the full gainer and the one and half forward pike. Through many painful flops, I've persisted and finally learned them. I swim over to you and ask, "Dad, would you check out my dives?"
>
> My first dive is the one and half forward pike. It's one of the best I've ever done, though I'm aware as I enter the water that my feet aren't exactly together. As I come up from the dive, I sense that it has been noticed by those around the pool, but I swim nonchalantly over to the board once again. My full gainer is also the best I've ever done. It causes only a minor

splash as I enter the water straight up. This time I hear gasps of approval from around the pool.

When I reach the edge of the pool, you come over, kneel down, and with a smile on your face say: "That was very good, Son. Now you want to make sure you keep your hands together and your toes touching."

You are, of course, correct, but a tidal wave of despair sweeps over me. I know I'll never be able to do it perfectly. I don't want you to see my despair, so I turn away and start swimming up and down the pool. I feel I am drowning. The choking that wakes me up is caused by the tears I just can't stop.

When I finished telling my father the dream, he stopped, looked me full in the face and said, "I'm sorry, so sorry, Harry. I was hoping I would not be an albatross around your neck." He went on to tell me of the pain he felt at never meeting his father's expectations, and he concluded, "I always wanted to make sure you did not have the same experience. I am so, so sorry!"

Hidden Objectives

The project that brought me to Costa Rica had multiple objectives. The main one, supported by the mission and my mother, was to collect materials for the biography everyone wanted to see written about my father.

I had two additional personal objectives. First, I hoped to learn more of my father's life, things like the relationship to his own dad that he had hinted about but never fully explained. I was looking for journals or personal letters that would give me a window on his interior life, so that I could find out if it resembled my own in any way.

Second, I hoped the project would help me recapture a faith I had been losing. This was the main reason I had been working throughout the summer like a man possessed. In his *Varieties of Religious Experience*, William James talks of searching for clear evidence of divine intervention in the lives of the people of religion he was studying. Without knowing exactly what it might look like, I was looking for evidence of the divine in my father's personal papers and in the lives of the missionaries I was talking to. I wanted the evidence—maybe miracles or saintliness—to be enough to rekindle my faith and give me guidance for my own career. My hope was that it would put me back on the path followed by my grandparents and parents, founders and leaders of the LAM. I was hoping to find, not just a lost father, but my faith and vocation.

It was for these reasons the interviews started right after breakfast, the collection of materials lasted all day, and the reading went late into the night. The intensity of work kept me from participating in the fun evening or weekend activities of the other interns. I spent most of my time alone, instead of with the seminary students who shared the dorm I was staying in.

Eroding Faith

The story behind "losing one's faith" tends to be as unique and personal as the story of "finding faith." The roots of my belief had taken hold in my home, and experiences in high school deepened and made the Christianity of my parents and grandparents my own. I entered Wheaton College planning on seminary and a life of Christian service, though seeds of doubt had already been planted.

In college, my faith eroded. The reasons were complex and included intellectual doubts about doctrines like the inerrancy of the scriptures or the creationist anti-evolution view. I felt alienated from the conservative political agenda of the evangelical community and the narrow ethics that made movies, dancing, and drinking sinful. There were probably elements of plain adolescent rebellion. But the main cause, it seemed to me, were experiences where the practice of faith had not worked out like I had been led to believe it would, experiences like that of selling books door to door one summer. To ignore the contradiction between what I thought Christianity promised and what I actually experienced raised issues of personal integrity. I felt forced to choose between the message of my experience and the teachings of the church and scripture.

By my senior year of college, my faith was neither clear enough nor strong enough to be shared with others. I was not ready for seminary, and in fact, I felt a strong need to learn more about how the real world worked. A full scholarship to Harvard Law School provided a nice solution. It meant picking up some useful skills for the ministry should that ever be my destination, and if not, a career that might fit my talents. The scholarship and decision would distress my mother, but perhaps make my father secretly proud.

So I entered law school with a hopeful metaphor taken from *The Pilgrim's Regress* by C.S. Lewis. If, like the protagonist in his novel, I left the island of my childhood faith and set off on a journey to find the truth, if I faced my doubts with integrity, sought to understand the world as it really was, paid attention to what worked, threw myself into the ocean of life, at the end I might find myself on a new island of deep authentic faith and to my surprise, discover that it was the backside of the same island I'd left, but now seen in a totally new way.

That was still my hope when I landed in Costa Rica in the summer of 1965. My intuition was that perhaps this summer project would help me not only get to know the man I most wanted to emulate, but also see the "good" that God had done through his death.

Evidence of the Divine

By this evening in 1965, the summer was coming to an end. Most of the interviews had been completed, and most of the documents and letters I'd found had been read. Unfortunately, it had not turned out the way I hoped. Yes, his letters and sermons contained some personal stories, but there were no journals or documents that shared his inner journey.

On one hand, the interviews had been far more successful than expected—many of my missionary "aunts and uncles" opened their lives to me. They shared their hopes, heartbreaks, frustrations, doubts, their faith in miracles, and their spiritual barrenness. But the clearer I saw their lives, the less it seemed to me to be clear evidence of the divine. What was most apparent was the struggle—the constant attempt to be faithful servants in frustrating, thankless jobs; to be responsible parents to rebellious teenagers; and loving spouses. I saw people trying to make sense of God's plan for them, straining for the experience of the divine in the everyday, not always successfully.

They were admirable people, committed and humane, among the best I have ever known. Yet their lives struck me as sad. It felt as if somehow on the road to maturity, I had passed some of them. Roles had been reversed. They were now seeking reassurance and guidance, hoping I could do for them what my father, their leader and mentor, had done. And I, who felt spiritually lost and empty, had nothing to give them. There was no satisfaction in this role reversal, only another illusion of childhood stripped away.

The Intern

There was a knock on the open door. I looked up, and the pretty college intern in the corner apartment was standing in the doorway. "You're working late," she said. "Am I interrupting?"

"No problem," I answered and wheeled my chair from the desk and indicated the black vinyl sofa where she could sit. She offered to help me if I'd tell her what I was trying to do.

I described my project, even though I couldn't think of any way she could help. She was eager to know more about the mission's roots and asked questions. She was easy to talk to, a good listener, so I told her about the tall, Scottish missionary grandfather for whom I was named. I knew him mainly from heroic stories: fearless boxer and long distance swimmer, self-taught scholar who memorized a page of the Spanish dictionary each day. He gave sermons based on the latest science in rented town halls across Latin America, often to hostile audiences. In the U.S. on fund-raising trips, he was an infectiously enthusiastic preacher who taught his audiences Spanish choruses. He was dogmatic in his faith, having personally experienced the "victorious Christian life" that frees and empowers. He was also certain of the error of Catholicism and the degeneracy of life as lived by most of the people in Latin America, and he was deeply convinced of their need to be evangelized and saved.

The intern was empathetic and interested. She asked about my grandmother, Susan Beamish Strachan, the founder of most of the works she had seen in Costa Rica—the hospital, the children's home, and the seminary. I told her about this short Irish lady with a great sense of humor and charm who built the buildings and ran the local ministries while her husband was away on evangelistic campaigns. She wrote the mission's news magazine and hosted a monthly salon in her house at which musicians and poets performed.

It was harder to talk about my father, Robert Kenneth, whose papers were scattered on the desk. He was a less commanding presence, shorter, more introverted. Though apparently popular at Wheaton College, where he was a star basketball player and accomplished diver, he was thrown out his senior year for playing cards. God rescued his life through Dallas Theological Seminary and marriage to my mother. He returned to work with his parents in the mission, but his style was very different from Grandfather's. He was less charismatic, yet more personal and warm. He attracted a talented group whom he actively involved in its leadership. The mission expanded into radio stations, a publishing house, schools, and into other countries. He managed Billy Graham's Caribbean evangelistic campaign, and then inaugurated more comprehensive campaigns under the banner of "Evangelism in Depth." He was far less dogmatic about the truth than his father, less certain about the boundaries of the true church, and more ecumenical than separatist. Though he felt he never measured up to his father, many of the missionaries who knew them both told me he was the more effective leader. Before his death, Wheaton College gave him the same honorary doctorate they had given his dad.

The intern also told me about herself, how she had come down for the summer to find out whether God was calling her to be a missionary. She spoke admiringly of the missionaries with whom she worked, but was perplexed that their work was not more exciting. She felt her true vocation was as a teacher, but wondered where. The summer had taught her a lot, but she still had no clarity as to what she should do.

In later conversations she showed particular interest in my mother, Elizabeth Walker Strachan, also a teacher. She knew Mother had helped start Colegio Monterrey, a K-12 school that became highly regarded as a private school accessible to poorer families. She had done this while managing to raise six children, teach classes, and be a marriage counselor. On top of that, she'd even written some books.

When the intern asked what Mother was going to do now that my dad was dead, I told her she was in the process of completing a master's in pre-kinder education. Returning to Costa Rica, she had a three-part vision: She was going to start a program in the national university to train teachers, establishing a model kindergarten at Colegio Monterrey to use as a laboratory. She was going to join with others to advocate adding kindergarten to the offering of public schools. Finally, she hoped to raise money for a program of daycare centers in some of the poorer sections of town, perhaps utilizing empty churches during the week. These would provide nutrition, parent training and schooling, in addition to caring for children of poor working mothers.

The intern mentioned, but didn't elaborate on, a boyfriend back home, and she knew I was writing a girl in Massachusetts, since her roommate brought me weekly letters. Neither of us seemed inclined to talk about these other relationships.

Nor did I share my spiritual doubts or why I had chosen law school instead of seminary or the discouraging results of my search for the divine. I was careful to avoid sowing any doubts in others, remembering my mother's warning, "Better a millstone is hung around your neck and you are sunk in the sea, than that you lead another astray."

Talking with her, I realized how much I enjoyed the way she thought and expressed herself. Our conversation was full of laughter, and, at least for me, a palpable attraction began to creep in.

One night I told her how during my childhood we played cowboys in the lumber yard near the seminary until we got chased out. I asked if she'd like to see it. It was a moonlit night. Walking across the railroad tracks, I offered her my hand as support, and felt a jolt as we touched. On the other side of the tracks, we came together like two magnets.

The next few nights, though the office was dangerously public, we'd end our talks sitting close together on the black vinyl couch kissing. The summer was coming to an end. There was no talk of love. Though I didn't visualize myself with her in the future, I felt strangely happy and free. We didn't "go all the way," but the hugging felt wonderful to me.

I must have felt some guilt about what we were doing, since I would have been mortified had anyone discovered us. Yet I mainly remember feeling perplexed about the lack of guilt. The affection we shared was what I wanted, even if there was no future to the relationship. Throughout the day I anticipated the evening, but I left the job of figuring out what it all meant until some later date. I knew I had to integrate what I was doing with what I thought of as my code of behavior.

The Stories I Took Away

The summer ended. I returned to Boston exhausted by my experiences, suffering chest pains, which concerned the doctors in the Harvard Clinic, and which turned out to be tension. In the years that followed, the summer of 1965 became a mythic junction in my life.

The summer had not answered my doubts, nor had it brought me to any island of faith I could recognize. In fact, I was further out to sea than ever before, and instead of regaining my childhood faith, I felt I had permanently lost it.

One immediate implication was that I could not write the biography that my mother or the mission wanted. Even if I had been a good writer, which I knew I was not, I no longer saw things the way a Christian publisher would demand in a missionary biography. I turned over the files, interview notes and tapes to my mother, and the mission asked Elisabeth Elliot to do the job.[3]

I knew a career as a pastor or missionary was no longer likely, so I would never measure up to what I imagined as Dad's expectations. But I didn't know if I was right in that assumption because his real life was irrevocably lost. I needed to find an alternative career, and that filled me with great anxiety. Law school was more enjoyable than I expected, but I wasn't enthused by the idea of being a lawyer. What if I never found meaningful work for which I was well suited?

I made no effort to stay in touch with the intern. My romantic life remained compartmentalized, and I buried my memories of her. Instead of asking what the experience told me about myself, I concluded that I was dangerously vulnerable to romance. If I didn't guard against temptation, I'd become sexually dissolute. To save me from myself, it was time to start thinking seriously of marriage.

Finally, I continued to believe that my father's death was a disaster for everyone. For many years I found no evidence to challenge this interpretation. I saw the reorganization of the LAM into multiple independent ministries led by local boards as a splintering due to ideological conflicts and financial pressure, which a strong leader like Dad could have helped resolve. My mother's continued deep sadness

---

3   The biography she wrote was *Who Shall Ascend: The Life of R. Kenneth Strachan of Costa Rica.*

until her own premature drowning and my siblings' struggles into adulthood seemed to me exacerbated by Dad's absence—all of which filled me with anxiety.

These were the stories about that summer that I told myself during the following forty years. It was only in writing them and others up, that I began to see the path of my life differently. But that's for the concluding chapters.

FAMILY TALES

GRANDPARENTS

Grandfather Harry Strachan

"Your grandfather, Harry Strachan, was a very tall, strong man. Before the Lord saved him, he was a boxer and long-distance swimmer in Scotland. He had deep convictions, enormous personal discipline, and great stamina.

"Once, on a campaign off the coast of Honduras, he went for a swim. He was miles from shore when he was stung in the leg by a giant ray. Friends helped him swim back to the beach. His leg was swelling from the poison, and there was no clinic or hospital nearby. Night was coming on. They built a fire, took a steel rod, and without anesthesia put it in the wound to cauterize the hole. The next day, they were able to get him to a hospital on horseback.

"Once high in the Andes, he was set upon by three robbers. He beat up all three and sent them fleeing down the mountain. On another occasion he was sitting in the corner office of the seminary, the one your father now occupies. He looked out the window down toward *Paseo de Los Estudiantes* (the boulevard). He saw some young men standing outside a bar blocking two student nurses who were on their way to the *Clínica Bíblica*. In a flash he was out the door running down the block; he picked two of the men up by the scruff of their necks, cracked their heads together, threw them in the gutter; then he picked up another and threw him back into the bar."

Here the story diverges. In the first version, he warns them that if he ever again catches them bothering the nurses, they'll get much worse. In a second version, he begins to preach the gospel.

Harry and Susan Strachan circa 1932 with children
Ken, Grace, and Harry Wallace

I am a little boy on the bed listening to my mother. I am looking at a picture of a smiling man with two little boys in his arms, myself and my cousin Paul. The man has white hair and a big white mustache. He looks very tall to me; I imagine him way over six feet tall, but find out years later he was my height, only five feet, ten inches. In those days, though, that made him a giant in Latin America. I have no clear memory of him, as he died at age seventy-two when I was four.

Over the years I learned the following about him: He always spoke both English and Spanish with a Scottish brogue, though he acquired a correct and extensive Spanish vocabulary. For some period of his life, he followed the daily practice of memorizing a page from the Spanish dictionary. He also had a notebook in which he collected colloquial sayings that he used to spice up his sermons.

In public his wife addressed him formally as Mr. or Dr. Strachan. Missionaries and members of the church in Costa Rica experienced him as a formidable, somewhat distant man. Grandmother Strachan described him as a "dour Scotsman," someone who didn't have the gift of small talk, but who prayed to become a warmer person. Then, confusing me, I was told that up at the Bible home with the orphan children, he would get down on the floor to play with them, and they would climb all over him, laughing. He was their favorite visitor, and their school was named after him.

He was famous for his evangelistic innovations. There were only a handful of Protestant churches in Latin America, and where they existed, Roman Catholics would not enter them. So he would rent the largest hall or theater available. Then he would put provocative advertisements in the newspaper designed to attract people to the meetings. The announced topics might have to do with science (something he apparently loved to read about) or marriage or raising children. Whatever the topic, it always ended up with the gospel and a call to conversion. One of his most successful was the "Night for Drunkards," and there is a family story about one of these events. The crowd gathered, loud and unruly, apparently having prepared for the topic with much drink. His colleague couldn't quiet them down for the introduction. My grandfather solved the problem by slowly and dramatically walking across the stage so all could see him. There was no drop in the volume of noise, so he came down the steps toward the front row. There was a slight pause in the din as the curious tried to figure out what he was going to do. Then he began speaking quietly to the people on the first row. Like a wave traveling back up the hall, quiet descended, as people strained to hear what he was saying. It was then that he looked up and began his prepared speech.

In the late 1980s, I flew to California on a business trip and visited my good friends Gary and Linda Bergthold. Linda wrote that when she mentioned my name to her minister father, he asked, "Is he by any chance related to the missionary in Latin America named Harry Strachan? If so, I must meet him and tell him a story."

This is the story he told me, imitating my grandfather's brogue in the appropriate spots:

> I was a young minister in my first small rural church. Your grandfather came as a missionary speaker. He first taught us a chorus in Spanish and had us sing it till we had it memorized. I still can sing it to this day. He had us laughing and standing and happy. Then he told the story of his conversion—how he had been raised in a religious family but left the faith, how in a Billy Sunday meeting he accepted the Lord and came home, and how for three days and nights he literally danced around

his room in great joy, filled with the Holy Spirit, freed from so much bondage in his life. He described his call to the mission field, how God steered him from Africa to Argentina, and then of his vision for evangelism throughout the continent of Latin America.

It was wonderful; he was so charismatic! Later in the parking lot outside the church, we talked for hours—one of the most important evenings of my life. Before he left he said, "Arvid, whatever you do, never stop preaching the filling of the Holy Spirit!" And I never have.

My mother's stories and descriptions seemed to me to juxtapose my grandfather with my father, perhaps unintentionally. Grandfather Strachan was tall and strong and liked individual sports like swimming and boxing. My dad was short and athletic and excelled in team sports like basketball and baseball. Grandfather was extroverted and charismatic, and his presence filled any room he entered. Father was more reserved, didn't compete for center stage, yet he had a quiet presence that suggested much depth. Grandfather was certain of the truth, fearless in his opinions, judgmental, and probably dogmatic. Dad was more tolerant and ecumenical, prone to give others the benefit of the doubt. My grandfather was successful from the start of his career, his leadership abilities never in doubt. My father was something of an underperformer in high school and college. His capacity as a missionary was doubted by the mission board at the start of his career. Yet by the time I was old enough to hear the stories, my dad's special talents for attracting good people, his strategic vision, his balanced judgment, his personal humility, and his skills as a speaker had made him one of the most influential missionary leaders of his generation. My mother's admiration and loyalty made it clear that if I were forced to choose between my grandfather's or my father's traits, I should choose Dad's.

The truth was that I felt I didn't measure up to either of them. If I could have chosen a name, it would have been my father's, but the struggle to name me was long over by the time I was born. Mother wanted to name me Robert Kenneth after my dad. Her family tradition was that the firstborn always carried the father's name. My father was in the Scottish tradition, where firstborn names alternate down the line, and he wanted me to be given my grandfather's name. But his real reason, and the one that made him inflexible in the disagreement with my mother, was that he'd vowed at his younger brother's death bed that his first son would be given his brother's name. Harry Wallace had died from malaria, or typhoid fever, or the medicine for them, in a Florida hospital, and my father felt he'd failed him in some important way, which he never shared with us.

I often wondered what Grandfather Strachan had really been like. How would we have gotten along if he had lived? I knew he had died from heart problems, so in the aftermath of my own heart attack and triple bypass, I sensed that we might have more in common than I thought. As part of my visualization therapy following the heart attack, I decided to "talk" with him to discover what in my life needed changing.

One day during my medical sabbatical when I was fifty, I visualized myself traveling back in time from Newton, Massachusetts, to Costa Rica. I entered the apartment at *La Finquita* (The Little Farm) where my grandparents spent their last years. I found him alone in the living room, sitting in an easy chair, reading. He looked as he did in his pictures with white hair and full mustache. I approached him, expecting someone serious, perhaps dour, but was surprised when he greeted me with a big smile and a twinkle in his eye. As we talked, I found he had a much greater sense of humor and fun than I had been told. We talked about his life and his faith. He was as certain and strong and vibrant as ever, but listening to his story I realized that his faith had freed him and enriched his life greatly. Though he led a strict Scottish Presbyterian lifestyle, his "letting go and letting God" opened up a life of great abundance and joy. He was much less judgmental than I expected. I was also impressed by his curiosity; he seemed deeply interested in everything—science, politics, even business. I could see that he read a huge amount, and the books around him showed his varied interests. As with many self-educated men who wished they could have completed more formal schooling, it seemed he imagined he'd missed out on more than, in fact, he had.

As our imaginary meeting was coming to an end, I asked him, "Grandfather, if you had your life to live over again, what would you do differently?" This was one of the critical questions I was asking myself. With the very kindest of looks, a look that brought tears to my eyes, he gave me a totally unexpected answer. "Harry, I don't have a lot of regrets, but if I could, I would have been less disciplined."

I puzzled over his answer for many days because I have always felt I was deficient in discipline, though I can be quite "driven." I decided Grandfather was warning me that my inherited promoter tendencies—the way I can become obsessed, even to the detriment of my relationships—was something I needed to learn to manage.

Grandfather William Walker

In contrast to Grandfather Strachan, still a grand presence in the Costa Rica of my childhood, my grandfather William Walker was a shadowy figure as I grew up. I knew he had been a "beloved" Southern Baptist minister, but he had died when my mother was a little girl. Her direct memories of him were hazy. In the one picture I remember of him, he was bald, close to fifty, a good-looking man with even features. I was told he was beloved because he had such a sunny, happy, infectiously enthusiastic personality.

Clara and William Walker circa 1925

In family lore, my sister Clare and I were by body and temperament categorized as "Walker," while the others were more "Strachan." Though I desperately wanted to be "Strachan" (because in my ignorance I didn't fully appreciate that other inheritance), I knew I was probably more "Walker."

When my son Ken, a happy towhead full of infectious enthusiasm, was about two years of age and running around our house in Managua, Nicaragua, I thought with surprise, *Maybe those Walker genes are what I'm looking at in this little boy. I should have learned more about that side of my family. Perhaps I owe Rev. Walker more than I think. If, as some friends have suggested, "optimistic enthusiasm" is one of my traits, especially in certain crisis situations, maybe it comes from that side of the family.*

Grandmother Susan Beamish Strachan

Though I begin with my grandfathers, the under-appreciated truth is that our family has always been a matriarchy, full of strong and accomplished women. This is true of my grandmothers, my mother and aunts, and it comes down to present-day sisters and cousins, where the women of the family have tended to achieve more than the men.

The following story is told about my grandmothers. My sister Cathy, tiny and active, was bossing around the older girls in her pre-kinder play group. One of the mothers laughingly pointed this out to Mother and another missionary. This other woman, who had studied at Columbia Bible College under Grandmother Walker and who now worked under Grandmother Strachan, quickly replied, "Well, what do you expect? She has two five-star generals for grandmothers!"

Susan Beamish Strachan was small—under five feet tall. In supposed contrast to her husband, she could be warm and charming, had a quick wit, was a good writer, and was very energetic. While Grandfather traveled around the continent holding campaigns, she organized the seminary, to which he sent converts for training. She also started a women's clinic in her home, which eventually became a nursing school and the *Hospital Clínica Bíblica*. She edited the mission magazine, kept in touch with donors at home, and held the position of "Co-Director" of the mission.

Grandmother Strachan circa 1945 with Grace and
Dayton Roberts with Susie and Evie, Harry and Paul
behind, Ken and Elizabeth with Robin and Cathy

Everyone told me Grandmother Strachan would have been a
fabulous businesswoman. She loved to buy property and apparently
had a Midas touch for choosing sites that would appreciate in value. She
enjoyed building things and was good at it. She was frugal, negotiated
hard, but bought and built for the long run. While the seminary was
under construction, she pushed the contractor hard to reduce costs. He
brought her a money-saving suggestion to substitute a single door for
the double door at the entrance. She stepped back from the building,
no doubt visualizing the impact of the change on the functionality and
dignity of the building, estimating these intangibles versus the savings
and other factors; however, she mentioned none of this in her answer
to the contractor. She simply said, "No, God wants us to have a double
door."

One day high in the mountains a hard horseback ride above Barva,
she came around a bend to see below a picturesque coffee and dairy
farm. God told her, "This is the place for my Bible home for the
children that I have placed in your heart."

There was one slight problem with this plan, however: the strictly Catholic owner of the farm had sworn he would never sell to *protestantes*. No problem, Grandmother was sure she'd heard God's message. Then either God changed the owner's heart or my grandmother charmed him into selling it to the mission at a very good price.

She was also a firm and effective hands-on administrator. There is a great photo of her in this role taken at the farm. She's wearing a wide-brimmed hat, dressed in a long riding skirt, sitting straight on a big black horse called Cholo, her regular mount for supervising the coffee and dairy activities.

She was very loyal to Cholo, a handsome spirited stallion. Dr. Cameron, the medical director of the hospital and her companion on trips to dispense medical services, rode a white gelding named Boy. Dr. Cameron thought Cholo was mean and dangerous, and she kept trying to get Grandmother to find a new horse. One day the expected happened, Cholo threw my grandmother, breaking a number of bones, but even that didn't convince her to replace him.

One story about Grandmother Strachan puzzled me as a teenager, but also filled me with pride. In those early years of the mission, Grandmother turned her living room into a once-a-month literary salon. She began a "Night of the Arts," where musicians, poets, and writers would gather to play the piano or read their pieces. She loved archaeology and was a supporting member of the British Archaeological Society.

This picture of my grandparents didn't square with much of what I saw in the fundamentalist evangelical world in the post-World War II era. It seemed to me that the church group to which I belonged, with its zeal to maintain orthodoxy, had became increasingly anti-intellectual and withdrawn from the world. It only made sense to me when I saw the movie *Chariots of Fire,* whose protagonist was a member of my grandfather's religious group, and when I read *The Call* by John Hersey, a missionary kid from China of that same era. I realized that to my grandparents, as well as to most of the founders of the Ivy League schools, being a Christian meant a commitment to excellence in all aspects of life: being the best scholar, the best athlete, as well as the best Christian. It meant solving problems in the world and translating your faith into service, particularly for the poor.

Grandmother Clara Bigham Walker

Clara Bigham Walker physically towered over my other grandmother in the pictures in our family album. She wore long straight dresses that hung down over a stiff girdle I could always feel when as a little boy I hugged her around the waist.

My mother was a high achiever and probably high-strung, and family stories suggest that she was as strong-willed as her mother. As a result, their relationship was more conflictive than that of her sisters. It seems that on an early visit to Costa Rica, Grandmother Walker made a number of suggestions on how I should be raised that greatly upset Mother. For this or other reasons, I sensed and internalized the tension between them, and this led me to have a somewhat formal relationship with Grandmother Walker. Although several of my brothers and sisters remember her as warm and nonjudgmental, I felt an unspoken disapproval, though this may have been my fault rather than hers.

That she was a truly admirable lady, though, was undeniable. Her first husband had died shortly before my Aunt Florence was born. Grandmother went back to teaching. Then nine years later, both she and Florence were courted by a highly regarded Baptist minister, William Walker, whom she married. Three more children were born: my Aunt Catherine, my mother Elizabeth, and finally my Uncle Bill. Twelve years after marrying, Rev. Walker died of a heart attack, leaving no estate and Grandmother with the job of raising the children. My mother was nine at the time.

Grandmother Walker, without giving up her strong Southern Baptist loyalties, gravitated into work with the Victorious Life Movement headed by Robert McQuilken. For many years, she was Dean of Women, among other responsibilities, at Columbia Bible College (now Columbia International University) in South Carolina.

She earned very little, but was a superb manager of money, saving enough for a home at the summer campgrounds called Ben Lippen outside of Asheville, North Carolina. She invested in good stocks, which permitted her to take care of herself all her life without any help from her children.

Grandmother Walker circa 1946 with Harry
and Cathy

I remember being told that she was one of the first women graduate students in mathematics at a Mississippi university (though I have never confirmed this) and that any mathematical aptitude I had was inherited from her. Education was in her blood. Three generations of her grandfathers had apparently been superintendents of education. I remember her taking a long list from the grocery store, reading down the list once, and adding up three and four digit numbers as she read. She taught me how to do this, but while I got fairly good at estimating the total, I was never as fast or accurate as she.

On retirement she moved to Wheaton, Illinois, to be near her oldest daughter, Aunt Florence. Her other three children were overseas as missionaries—Uncle Bill in Japan, Aunt Catherine first in China and then Indonesia, and my mother in Costa Rica. She lived in her own house, rented rooms to college students, taught a Bible class at her Baptist church, drove a 1956 Chevy far too carefully for my impatient tastes, and kept up with a large number of women who considered her their mentor. The summer before I entered Wheaton, she gave me room and board, and for part of that year kept my younger brother Johnny with her.

Use of Genetic Heritage

Physically more Walker than Strachan, inwardly wanting to model myself on my father, I grew up wondering who I really was at the genetic level, feeling genes determine a lot more than we're willing to admit. I was therefore both curious to know and fearful of finding out what genes I had failed to receive from my four grandparents and two parents.

This fear of insufficient genes has disappeared over the years. I feel that even if I didn't inherit certain traits, I have become more and more like my father in ways I wanted to emulate. We all have capacity for development. If it's true that we're pretty much stuck with our basic personalities, it's amazing the new behaviors we can learn.

Today I find it useful to tell myself (even if agnostic about the science of it) that the genetic traits of my grandparents, locked away in my DNA, are like shelves in a store. When I am in need of a certain trait or skill, I can go into the storeroom and find it in the DNA of one of my ancestors. Each of these different people, admirable in his or her own way, has much to give. My job is to find that quality, activate it, and actualize it until it is mine. It's also my responsibility when a behavior is getting out of hand, to control its excesses.

My Niche in the Family Ecology

The family, I've read, is a complex ecology. Each member tends to occupy a particular niche. Later children find their older siblings have already occupied certain niches from which they refuse to be dislodged. To survive, the younger ones gravitate to other niches. If the older sibling gets approval for being a good student, the next child may focus on sports. If the older gets attention by what he accomplishes in work or studies, the younger might find her niche in social activities. If the oldest wins rewards for being "good," the younger might even decide he is better off being the "bad" one.

I grew up in a dense tropical ecology, crowded with a large number of brothers, sisters, cousins, some blood relatives, and other "aunts and uncles" by community.

My immediate ecology was dominated by my two towering parents. I was the oldest of six, and we had arrived in rapid succession; by the time I was ten, I had five brothers and sisters. I was rewarded for being good in school, doing chores, setting a good example, and for being someone to whom Mother could talk to when Dad was away on long trips. I was given the role of "leader," and tended to be the one to design the games we played and write the plays we put on.

Ken and Elizabeth circa 1949 with children Robin,
Clare, Cathy, Johnny, and Harry

As my mother struggled to cope with a growing family, she put all of us to work on chores at a very early age. Cathy and I, as the oldest, got the heaviest jobs. When there were six of us, we were organized into three work teams, and I was paired with Marie, the youngest. Each team had jobs at each meal. Cathy and I would often compete to see who was fastest at getting done. Both of us got a lot of positive reinforcement for working well and fast, a real advantage when we later worked our way through high school and college.

Strachan sibs circa 1951: Clare, Cathy, Harry holding
Marie, Robin, and Johnny

From early on we became babysitters. Several of Mother's friends feared she was both endangering the family and forcing us to grow up too early, but I think she was proud of what she got us to do. She happily described how on one of our earliest stays in the U.S., when I was about five, she bought a two-wheeled cart to carry groceries home. She would pin an envelope inside my jacket with the grocery list and enough money to pay for the items. Then I would walk the three or four blocks to the supermarket, at one point crossing a four-lane highway. She had trained me to be defensively watchful of cars that might violate the laws. Inside the store, the clerk would unpin the envelope and fill the cart, then put the checked-off list, the receipt, and the change back in the envelope and re-pin it inside my jacket. I would drag the cart back home, often finding it almost too heavy to pull.

Whatever their inner doubts, my parents projected great confidence in our ability to take care of ourselves in tough situations. "Strachans know how to land on their feet!" they would say. I vaguely recall a Sunday when Robin, the middle brother who was about eight at the time, was left at church by mistake. (This was not as negligent as it sounds, since Sunday was the day on which some of us brought home friends while others ate lunch at their friends' homes.) He was not missed until he appeared at home on his own, having walked across town, probably a good three miles. He was praised greatly for his self-reliance, and whatever consternation Mother felt, she kept to herself.

As the oldest child, Mother would sometimes tell me our family's money problems. "Harry, because of the visitors we had at the beginning of the month, we're going to run dry on our food budget this month. I'm planning on cutting back on the meat and having a number of banana-based meals toward the end of the month. I don't want you complaining about this. I want you to make the other kids feel we're having a treat."

At the end of the month, I'd obediently fake enthusiasm for bananas, but this news of our precarious finances and my own helplessness to do anything about it filled me with anxiety. I've wondered if it may have made money more important to me than it should have been. Later in life, I developed an almost obsessive determination to avoid financial dependence on others, not to mention an abiding ambivalence about bananas.

I won't attempt to describe the niches filled by Cathy, born fifteen months later, or Robin, Clare, Johnny, and Marie who completed the family. I'll only say that each did find a special niche in the family, each grew into a person I love and admire, and each has had a productive life worth its own book of stories.

Interpenetrated with my immediate family ecology was the family of Aunt Grace, my father's sister, and her husband, Uncle Dayton Roberts. They also returned as missionaries with the LAM after studying in the US. The six Roberts cousins were closely paired with us in age. Paul was seven months older than I. He and John Nelson, son of other LAM missionaries, were my two closest childhood friends. He was followed by Susie, Evie, Gracie, Bary (initially Buddy for William Dayton Jr.), and Betsy. When both families were residing in Costa Rica, we were constantly in each other's homes. Our families vacationed together, and it was as if we were a single family unit.

Betsy, Gracie, Bary, Susie, Paul, Evie with Aunt Grace
and Uncle Dayton circa 1980

A Darwinian would say we all competed for resources, and among the scarcest was the attention of our busy parents. We certainly competed in sports and card games and no doubt in many other ways. My mother even organized contests for memorizing verses. My memory, however, is that we nourished and cared for each other more than competed. Certainly in adulthood I have thought of each of the Roberts more as brothers and sisters than cousins. Though we live all over the world, we look for opportunities to vacation together and have family reunions. Their children are nieces and nephews whom I love and in whose lives I take a personal interest.

The extended Strachan-Roberts family was embedded in a larger "mission family" that was also a part of my ecology. Before the LAM grew too large, the other adult missionaries were called "aunt" or "uncle," and they thought of themselves as such. The group was close, united by a common calling and also by their separation from the worldly culture they had come to change. The Nelsons, Headingtons, Fentons, Hoods, Paines, Kinches, Solts, Longworths, Gays, Howards, Foulkes, Stams, Stevens, Garcias, Cruz, Cabezas, Gonzalez, Pretiz, Dr. Cameron, Milre Lisso, Miss Neely, and Miss Thor, among others, were more present in our lives than blood aunts and uncles in distant lands. Their children were among our closest friends. Unfortunately, we lost touch with many of them once we went off to high school and college in the States.

Our extended family outside Costa Rica included the McKellins, my mother's oldest sister, Aunt Florence, with her family in Wheaton; Uncle Bill Walker and his family in Japan; and Aunt Catherine Walker in Indonesia. Every week Mother wrote a "family letter" to them as well as to Grandmother Walker. She'd often read sections from their letters at the dinner table. When possible, we visited them in the States, but differences of age and geography meant that we were not as close. Late in life, I've gotten to know some of them better, and we have discovered a special bond.

With Walker Relatives: Aunt Catherine, Aunt Florence (McKellin), Uncle Bill and Aunt Mary

CHILDHOOD SNAPSHOTS

Back Seat Criticism

One of my earliest memories is being in the car with Mother, sitting in the back seat with my cousin Paul and good friend John Nelson. I was so small I could only look up through the window at clouds and blue sky. For reasons totally forgotten, at that particular moment, I was the one on the "outside" and the other two were saying mean things, like "Harry is the smallest," criticisms that stung me deeply. I was trying hard not to cry, perhaps out of a desire to give them no satisfaction, and I looked out the window and pretended I wasn't listening.

To my surprise, this pretense worked. I entered a zone of quietness and peace. I still could hear the gibes, but they felt far away; somehow I was insulated. I thought, *So this is what it means when people say, "Sticks and stones can break my bones, but words can never hurt me."*

Dealing with strong emotions was always a challenge for me, as I suspect it often is for children. I could hardly bear to lose at sports without wanting to cry or strike out. I intensely anticipated weekend *paseos* (outings), and if they were canceled, the disappointment was so great that over time, I tried hard not to have any expectations. I remember fights in which I felt such a murderous rage that I wanted to kill someone.

In self-defense, therefore, I looked for an interior place to which I could withdraw to avoid the strong passions that would otherwise carry me away. That is probably still my pattern. Hurt or angry, I withdraw. I bottle up my feelings as much as possible until I've figured out what I'm going to do. This can be very adaptive if you're a leader who cannot afford to lose your cool, but it's not as useful in certain intimate relations or where the expression of spontaneous emotion is appropriate.

El Descanso and Camp Roblealto

We anticipated the annual family vacations with almost unbearable excitement, and many of my favorite snapshots relate to these events. Any place we visited more than twice became a childhood tradition, and one of those places was *El Descanso* (the Rest House). It sat high in the mountains above Barva, on the farm purchased by my grandmother for what we called the "orphanage," today the *Hogar Biblico*, a residence for children from dysfunctional homes who need long-term care and counseling. It was also the site of *Roblealto*, the Christian camp grounds.

In the earliest years, it was reachable only by horseback. Our parents would drive the car as far as Barva where they met horses brought down for them to ride the rest of the way. By the time we children started going, the journey could be made by car on a dirt road, but it was so steep, it could only be traveled in the dry season, and even then, we often had to get out and walk certain slopes.

El Descanso was on the high ground near the entrance and was used by the missionaries for vacations. It looked down over pastures and coffee fields toward the Central Valley in the distance. The whole scene was framed by distant blue-gray mountains. A hundred yards down the road were eight or so green wooden homes with red tin roofs, each holding eight or twelve children and the house parents. There was a little chapel that served as the school during the week. Beyond that, in the center of the houses, stood the administrative building that housed the kitchen and dining hall with its shiny wooden floors. It was a treat to eat at the long tables with the children and to play with them afterwards, but I never lost the feeling of being an outsider, a "gringo," lucky in some special way to be living with both my mother and my father.

I would wake up just as it was getting light outside, the ground generally wet with dew, a mist rising from the pastures and the hills around. I'd put on my rain boots and clothes and run down to help milk the cows, marveling at how they always headed to the same stall and voraciously ate the pasture grass mixed with chopped banana trees and sprinkled with molasses. My fingers still remember the technique I was taught for milking—squeezing from the top down while pulling on the nipple—and seeing the thin stream of white milk whip into the pail set near the back feet of the cow. The older boys and men who cared for these cows seemed amused by my many questions, and I was awed by their esoteric knowledge.

At the bottom of the farm was *Roblealto*, the camp used by the mission for its camp ministries and church retreats. There were cabins in the woods full of bunk beds and a small swimming pool fed by water from the stream that ran through the farm. Crossing the stream meant jumping from rock to rock. These were slick and wet, and a slip led to tennis shoes and pants full of water. There was a big pasture that also served as a soccer field, and there were several horses we were sometimes allowed to ride.

Once while home from school in the United States, I wrote a "Western" play, which Robin, Johnny, Bary, and I enacted in this pasture. We had three saddled horses, one of which was white, and several Western hats, one of which was also white. We rotated the role of the hero, but he always rode the white horse and wore the white hat. We had a Brownie camera with a roll of film. The rough script involved a number of important scenes: a mugging of the fair damsel by two bad guys, a gun fight in the corral, a chase on horseback with the hero jumping from one horse to the other, and another where the hero jumped from the tree onto the two bad guys riding underneath. Fortunately, no one was maimed in making our snapshot movie.

In his youth, my father had also loved to roam the farm on horseback. One morning in the 1930s, my father rode out on Boy, Dr. Cameron's beloved white horse. Though older, Boy nevertheless pressed at the bit and tried to gallop up the hill to a pasture high above the farm. When they got to the top, my father stopped to let Boy catch his breath, hooking his leg over the saddle and looking back over the valley. Without warning, Boy sighed and collapsed under him, dead from a heart attack. Deeply shaken, my father realized there was nothing he could do except to leave Boy there to be buried later. He took off the saddle and carried it back to the farm on foot. This story played an important role in a visualization I had following my triple bypass.

Puntarenas and Pirates

We also vacationed at another mission rest home in Puntarenas, the Pacific port town. Puntarenas was connected to San Jose by a narrow gauge railroad. We boarded the train from a station three or four blocks from the seminary and hospital.

We always left in the early morning for the half-day trip, climbing into the cars and sitting on wooden benches facing each other. The train had a special clickety-clack sound. Its whistle was blown at the crossings, and warm air washed over us through open windows. The poles that provided the electric current for the train were so close that arms stretched out the window might get whacked off. The doors stayed open, and teenagers would daringly stand on the bottom step, hold on to the hand rails, and lean out to look up the track at the engine.

At stops along the way in Atenas or Orotina, women carrying baskets of fruit and *tamales* on their heads would board the train and walk up the aisles selling their wares. You could buy Coca Colas from buckets filled with ice if you had the money. The scenery was spectacular. Initially the train made its way through coffee plantations and the small towns of the Central Valley. Then the vegetation changed to tropical forests as the train twisted down the mountain, crossing narrow trestles over deep gorges, coming into flatlands covered with banana plantations and sugar cane fields. When we crossed the wide river, we could see the ocean in the distance. Finally, with the sea on the left, the train moved onto a long narrow spit of land to Puntarenas.

The mission's house sat across the road by the ocean, a wooden building on stilts that rose up out of the sand. A porch ran all the way around the house. There were four high-ceilinged bedrooms with open lattices at the top to encourage ventilation. Underneath the porch and house between the stilts was cool, dark sand, where we played when we had to stay out of the midday sun. When the Strachan and Roberts families vacationed together, each set of parents took one of the four bedrooms. The five boys were in a room full of canvas beds called *tejeretas,* and the seven girls piled into the fourth room.

We'd play on the beach and in the ocean in front of the house most of day, sometimes diving for snail shells that glowed with a phosphorescent light (these we'd later stow in our bedroom, and after three days they'd lose their shine and smell quite badly). At noon we'd stop for lunch and the mandatory siesta, which of course never involved much sleep. Mother generally had us do some project, like reading books or memorizing poems or verses in the Bible in exchange for a prize. One prize I remember was little tins of condensed milk.

A wide cement walkway ran alongside the beach all the way to the large pier that jutted into the bay and onto which cargo for Costa Rica was unloaded. A favorite after-dinner ritual, particularly if our fathers had joined us on the vacation, was to walk down the walkway to the pier. People would be fishing; vendors would be selling *granizados* (sweet syrup on shaved ice). We'd walk arm-in-arm the three or four blocks, enjoying the evening breezes and feeling that we were a close family, many of the scuffles and tensions of the day left behind.

Back on the front porch in the early dark, we would beg my father to tell us stories of Puntarenas when he was a boy, particularly about the pirate caves he'd explored near beaches linked to the mainland.

There was a true story of how my father and grandfather had once gone for a hike among the caves. Miscalculating the incoming tide, they were caught on the rocks and slammed by the strong waves. They were nearly killed; at one point my dad catching my grandfather by the arm just before being sucked into the sea. This served as a warning of the hidden dangers, even in what appeared to be a benign ocean.

Other stories described caves my father had explored with his Boy Scout troop. These were always full of skeletons and pirate treasure, which, for one reason or another, the boys were never able to take out before some mishap closed the cave. Another of our favorite stories was about the time he went fishing in the river close to where it emptied into the ocean. He was sitting in the center of the railroad trestle we'd crossed over en route to Puntarenas, so he could drop his line in the deep water. Then he noticed a shark circling his line in the water. This so distracted him that he didn't hear the train starting to cross the trestle until it was too late to make a run for it. His only means of escape was to hang from the beams of wood under the tracks, while the train rumbled overhead shaking everything, the shark waiting patiently for him to fall into the water below. The train gone, arms aching from holding himself up, he still had to find the strength to pull himself up onto the trestle, and with shaking steps walk the open planks back to the river bank.

Another story involved going on an evangelistic tour on the mission boat up the Magdalena River of Colombia deep into the remote equatorial jungle. Seeking relief from the oppressive heat, Dad went under the cool trees on the river bank and lay down to take a nap. He dreamed he was in quicksand, his feet sinking deeper and deeper, and he was unable to free them. Waking, he looked down to see a boa constrictor that had already swallowed his feet all the way up to his knees. He struggled mightily, but the backward-slanting teeth of the snake made it impossible for him to free himself. The snake gradually worked its way up past his waist to just under his arm pits. In desperation, Dad wrapped his arms around two trees and blocked the snake from further progress. This led to a stalemate. It was only broken when the snake said, "Okay, I'll let you go if you promise not to tell any more snake stories in your sermons!"

Years later my own children would ask for stories. With no shame, I would steal my dad's stories as if they had happened to me. Friends have berated me for telling young children scary tales, and perhaps they are right. But these stories as we lay rapt and bundled together under the dark, starry sky, helped create a deep sense of family.

Mother the Educator

Other snapshots bring my mother, the constant educator, into sharp relief. No matter how small our homes, she insisted that she and my father have a big double bed. In the late afternoon or evening, we would gather to listen to a story on that bed, five or six of us packed around her like sardines in a tin. My favorites were fairy tales and stories from the Arabian nights. They seeded my own imaginary world and were remembered with greater vividness than much of what happened in my world at school.

Fearful that we weren't getting much of an education, Mother gave up eating breakfast with us for a time and instead sat on a stool above the table. Largely ignoring the rush and chaos of getting multiple children fed and ready to go to school, she would read to us from Time magazine or give us quizzes from Reader's Digest's "Increase Your Word Power."

She put great emphasis on becoming a lifelong reader. She had strong opinions about what was good to read and what was trash. "Constructive reading" started with the Bible and Bible stories, included history, biographies and other works of non-fiction, and the classics of great literature. "Trash" included the Westerns I loved, comic books, romantic novellas, and even the mysteries she and Dad adored.

She had no qualms about bribing us if it got us to read more, study better, or memorize Bible verses, and looking back, she got some great bargains. A project that took me most of a year when I was around ten was to read the entire Bible. I did this for about fourteen *colones*, the equivalent at the time of ten dollars. When I tried to negotiate my way out of the interminable "begats," the complex instructions for the Temple, and the baffling visions of Revelation, she refused to reduce the reading load. It was all part of God's inspired Book.

Mother also had strong opinions regarding music. Classical music was "good" music, and semi-classical was "okay." I recall feeling a poignant sadness one summer afternoon as I listened to the strains of Claire de Lune and the pounding rain on the tin roof while reading *The Brothers Karamazov* and *Dr. Zhivago*. Though few of us had much talent, at least two years of piano lessons were mandatory. Hymns were Mother's favorites and were sung not only at church, but during our family prayers before bedtime. Popular music, especially rock and roll, was "bad," and we were not allowed to listen to it on the radio.

She reluctantly accepted Western novels and the violence portrayed in them, but watching violence on TV was prohibited. She was a great believer in the power of thought. "As a man thinketh, so is he," was one of her favorite sayings. A corollary of this proposition was that one should not fill one's mind with lustful thoughts nor watch ads for liquor and cigarettes. We only once had a TV in our home during a two year stint in New Jersey, and Mother made us read an hour for every half hour of TV viewing. We were not allowed to go to movies since they tended to glorify immoral behavior and immoral movie stars.

Mother was my first "case method" teacher. "I can't tell you the names, Harry, but your daddy is facing a difficult decision. A single missionary nurse working at the *Clinica* came into his office today to tell him that she believes the Lord is calling her to go to Guanacaste (a rural province on the coast). The other directors feel she really belongs in San Jose since she is doing a great job in the nursing school. How do you think Daddy should handle this situation?"

I would screw up my brow, go off to think about it, and return to share my advice. She'd listen carefully, then say, "That's very good, Harry," and then describe what Dad had done, including both his decision and how he went about implementing it. She always stressed his careful attention to the feelings of others.

School grades were very important, though A's were quickly passed over and much attention was devoted to the C's and, God forbid, anything lower. Grades, however, were private and were not discussed in front of other brothers and sisters. "None of your business; comparisons are odious!" Mother would say if I asked what grades Cathy or Robin had gotten. "The important thing is not the grade. The real question is, 'Did you do your best?'"

By the time I was midway through grade school and doing reasonably well, Mother apparently stopped worrying about me and focused her attention on some of my brothers and sisters who were having more trouble. I got my homework in on time, my friends were "good influences," and, according to my aunt, I was liked by my teachers for my enthusiasm. My memory, however, is that there were always others in my class who got better grades and were the leaders of the class. I was smaller than anyone else in my class, whether boy or girl, and something of a loner. I loved to read, and I raced through my schoolwork in order to do other things. On the long walks to and from school, I spun out elaborate daydreams.

Money Management

My parents' attitudes and practices toward money, though not mainstream, were a superior way of managing finances. It is the paradigm I've tried to adapt to my own situation and one I'd love to see passed down in our family.

Both my parents had the talent, higher education, and leadership abilities necessary to be successful entrepreneurs. Though they were responsible for managing thousands of dollars in the mission, their personal income was always low. In the Latin America Mission, each missionary, no matter what position in hierarchy or tenure, received the same salary. It was called an "allowance" and was determined by the number of people in the family. While I was growing up, the monthly living allowance, which came from churches abroad, was $100 per adult and $25 per child. Our annual family income in the 1950s, therefore, was $4,200 a year. In 2010 dollars that is equivalent to around $35,000 a year. Our family of eight lived on that—food, rent, clothing, education, vacations. Unexpected gifts, which sometimes came at Christmas, probably added a bit more and were used for special treats or for gifts to others.

My folks' approach to finances was the following: 10 percent of income was "tithe." Even though they were already giving their time to help others, they believed the Bible teaches the first 10 percent belongs to the Lord. Most of it, I recall, didn't go to the church, but to others with greater needs.

Another 10 percent went into a "savings account" for emergencies and education. When I received a scholarship for high school in the United States, my plane ticket to the States used a significant portion of those savings.

The rest was divided into envelopes, my mother's way of budgeting. The food envelope was designed to make sure we always had plenty of milk (the "perfect food") even if at the end of the month the bananas in our backyard replaced meat.

The envelope for rent and utilities was emptied at the beginning of the month to ensure we didn't fall behind. The education envelope was next in priority to cover school fees, books, and uniforms, if necessary. The clothing budget was minimal and was supplemented by gifts of hand-me-downs that rarely thrilled us. Most travel was by bus. In the early 1950s, we used a car we were given, but later, we had to sell it because we couldn't afford the insurance, gas, and repairs.

On our birthdays or at Christmas, each of us got to request one gift within a predetermined price range, around ten dollars. One memorable gift was my first baseball glove, a left-handed one so I could share it with my cousin Paul who was left-handed. This is probably the reason I am close to ambidextrous. I still throw with my left hand and write with my right. Another much requested gift, which required a huge amount of lobbying on my part as well as a supplement from my own savings, was a BB gun.

Mother usually persuaded us to share many of the Christmas gifts we received from others with poorer families in the neighborhood. We would fill bags with food and buy small gifts, then deliver them on Christmas Eve before going for *tamales* at the home of friends.

Debt was not an alternative, either in our personal lives or in the mission's finances. If we purchased anything, it was because we had the money. We paid our obligations on time. Mother was emphatic about the maxim "Neither a borrower nor a lender be."

College was a "must." There was no question of stopping after high school, but we knew that we'd have to get scholarships and work to make ends meet. Every one of us not only finished college, but got masters or doctorate degrees.

We grew up knowing money was scarce and you had to be careful with it. You didn't, however, let it rule your life. "Love of money is the root of all evil." You made your decisions based on other values. Compared to most of our friends in the United States, we were poor, but compared to most people in Costa Rica, we were well off and could afford to be generous. We were taught that God provides what is needed, but also that God takes care of those "who take care of themselves and others." He counts on us to be good stewards of what we're given—out time, our talents, and any money that comes our way. "To whom much is given much is required."

My Ranch

Early in childhood I fell in love with Westerns and books like *My Friend Flicka* and the *Black Stallion* series. In the States I contrived to be playing at a friend's house in the late afternoons when the half-hour Westerns were on TV. Though I noticed that the inevitable chase scene covered the same ground over and over again, this did not bother me. It only increased the pleasure of watching the hero in the white hat overtake the villain in the black hat, jump across his horse, and drag him to the ground. At night, my head under the covers and the radio turned low, I would listen to *The Lone Ranger*, imagining his magnificent white stallion Silver and loyal partner Tonto.

Soon most of our neighborhood games were about cowboys and their adventures. I learned to crawl on my stomach, jump out of the cherry tree in the back yard onto the imaginary horse and rider passing underneath. When I was eight, my mother reluctantly (probably due to my father's intercession) gave me a dual holster with two pearl-handled cap pistols as my requested Christmas present.

When I was around thirteen years old, I got to spend two weeks on Dr. Oreamuno's ranch Tenorio on the side of a volcano in Guanacaste. Dr. Oreamuno was a prominent doctor at the *Clinica Biblica* and a friend of my father's, and he invited me to join in the annual roundup on his ranch.

Fantasizing about my ranch

Our job was to find the wild cattle in the deep brush and gullies and bring them into a wooden pen where they were pushed through a chute into a pool of black oily liquid to kill ticks. Then the calves would be branded. We wore leather chaps to protect us from the thorn bushes. I was assigned two horses, which I used on alternate days. It was sunup till sundown in the saddle. At night we had to do a full-body dip in our own vile oily substance to kill the ticks picked up during the day. This was followed by a soap-and-water bath and a meal of *tortillas*, rice, beans, and meat, which I was almost too tired to eat. The cowboys bedded down on wooden slats in a long low bunkroom away from the big house. To my disappointment, I had to stay in the guestroom.

The first week I was with the cowboys, they mainly talked about the coming weekend dance with marimba. The second week the talk was all about what had happened at the dance. Dr. Oreamuno's apparent instructions were that I was not to be taken to a dance, as *evangelicos no bailan* (evangelicals don't dance), and he had probably promised my parents that I'd not be exposed to this. I somehow persuaded them to allow me to at least watch.

There was a long marimba played by four men at the head of the large room with rough wooden floors. On either side of the marimba along the wall were simple benches set facing each other. All the women from grandmothers to little girls sat on one side. Across from them were all the men, grandfathers down to young grandsons. At the start of the music, as if launched by the starting shot of a race, each man or boy would rush over to the women's bench, take the hand of his partner, and lead her to the center of the room for a brisk four-step repetitive dance.

I watched in fascination until a commotion attracted my attention. I went outside to find one of the cowboys with a deeply cut leg that bled so profusely, he later died. He'd been in a machete fight, which not only shocked me with its violent end, but seared into my consciousness that the real world I was so well-protected from, was full of mysterious and dangerous things I understood only dimly.

That insight, however, did not detract from the thrill of this adventure. Even the long, uncomfortable ride home in the back of a jeep squeezed alongside a young girl, did not dim the memory of the week, but rather added a strange erotic twist to everything that had happened.

I returned to school from that fabulous vacation with visions of having my own ranch some day, and I soon sold the dream to my brother Robin. We found a large map of Guanacaste (the Wild West of Costa Rica). We put it on the wall of our room above our wooden desks and marked out the two thousand *manzanas* we envisioned having been given (one *manzana* being around two acres).

Then we drew a larger, more detailed map of our property, including the streams running through it, what land was in forest, what was covered with wild brush or native grasses, and what we could use as pasture. Robin had found a huge old Dickensian ledger in a trash can, still with many blank pages. We carefully inventoried our small band of native cattle, our horses, some pigs and chickens, and the tenant families that had come with the land. We estimated the sources of money coming in and budgeted for the expenses going out. This was done in long lists, as we had no knowledge of accounting for debits and credits.

Walking to and from school, I thought about all the things we were doing on the ranch. It was an elaborate daydream that moved through my head like a novel. At home we'd study the options and plan our next moves and then document them on the maps and in the ledger.

From an old *Book of Knowledge* encyclopedia, we read about the different pasture grasses, the various breeds of cattle, and the environments in which they thrived. One of the deacons in our church, don Elias Azofeifa, worked in a bank as an appraiser of ranches. I asked for an appointment with him, and he received me in his bank office. I described my imaginary ranch and some of the options I was studying. He said he agreed with my analysis that if we were going to upgrade our herd, it was probably best to import Brahmans for that part of Guanacaste, as they handled heat and disease better than other breeds. He also confirmed that *estrella* grass was nutritious for cattle and defended itself well against wild grasses. He confirmed the ratios I was using for number of cattle per acre, gave advice on the best sizes in which to divide the fields, as well as on the amount of salt, minerals, and medicines each cow needed. Although this must have been one of the weirdest consultations he ever gave, he never laughed at me.

So we pretended to import Brahman bulls from Florida to upgrade our stock, and we put the tenants to work upgrading the pastures with *estrella* grass, being careful to leave woods around the streams. We read the newspapers for the price of young castrated males that were sold to be fattened and also for the price of heavier cattle taken to slaughter. We calculated the calves that were born and listed them in our ledger. We sold many of the young males, keeping the females to build up our herd. Our estimates had to be wildly optimistic because within one year we were making obscene profits, as well as growing the herd and rebuilding the ranch.

With our profits we rebuilt the fences, planted *jocote* trees, which we strung with barbed wire, and then we moved on to more ambitious projects. These included a dam across the river and an electric power plant. After more sessions reading about hydropower plants in the *Book of Knowledge*, we made detailed architectural drawings of the power plant with its water canals and turbines.

Then we built houses for the workers, again having made architectural drawings. Each house had a vegetable garden, and we helped our industrious tenants create a cooperative to sell their surplus in the nearby town.

We also built a K-12 school and a small hospital capable of serving not just the needs of the ranch, but of surrounding neighbors as well. We set aside a plot for a small lovely Protestant church.

I vaguely remember that by the end we'd begun to diversify into related activities like a factory for curing hides and our own slaughterhouse. Each of these ventures had to be researched and each was imagined in living color over many miles of walking to and from school. Then the idea was transferred into drawings, with the estimated revenues and expenses recorded in the ledger book. The project came to an end for two reasons. When I asked my partner Robin what he was going to do with his share of the earnings, he showed me his drawing of a large asphalt racetrack and the cars he was buying to race on it. Somehow his noisy cars and the wide racetrack felt like a violation of my bucolic ranch. Also, about this time my sisters and their friends discovered what we were up to. They spread the word and teased us unmercifully.

Did I seriously think that ranching might be my vocation? No, it didn't cross my mind. While I had no clear idea what I'd do in life, I envisioned it as something that would require a lot of education. Perhaps I would follow in my father's footsteps and be a missionary.

Looking back now, I wonder if with more self-awareness I could have seen seeds of my later vocation, consulting. Business stories interest me, probably more so than theology, science, medicine, or politics, though I enjoy reading about all these areas. What I like about business is that to do it well, you have to be eclectic, learn about many different things, and master a great variety of skills. Business also has measurable financial feedback. You know whether you win or lose, whether your dream corresponds to reality or misses it. It requires right-brain analysis based on accurate data collection, financial models, evaluations, but also the left brain's intuitive capacity to put the elements together in time and space. Another wonderful thing is that if you are successful, it creates jobs for people and these jobs provide them with both income and education. Last but not least, you often end up with enough money for financial independence and helping others.

There is an interesting postscript to my boyhood ranch. Near the age of thirty when I was again living in Central America, I taught business classes at INCAE. An early promotion pushed me into the position of academic director involving management duties I was not very good at. When particularly frustrated at having to manage a bunch of academics, my dreams of a ranch revived. I would take an afternoon off to drive through ranches around Lake Nicaragua. I even collected some maps of the future highway system and found some fertile land across the border in Costa Rica through which they planned to build a new highway. I considered buying a piece of land cheap enough for a professor in that isolated, lush section, figuring I could develop it slowly until the new highway made its exploitation profitable and increased the value of the land.

One day, teetering on the edge of implementing my plan, I suddenly realized what a stupid thing I was about to do. It was not that the business ideas weren't solid or the strategy feasible. But the truth was that an imaginary ranch allowed me to choose which problems to solve and to solve them in an imaginary way. If I bought an actual ranch, I'd suddenly find myself dealing with the sort of administrative problems I so disliked. Rather than being a source of relaxation and relief, the ranch would become one more headache from which to escape.

Even now, driving through rural areas provokes imaginings about what could be done with the land. I recently floated the idea with some friends of buying a ranch where I could bring my grandchildren for summer vacations or that could be used as a retreat center. The response was immediate: "Harry, are you crazy? Your tolerance for administrative hassles is very limited. Don't complicate your life with the real world. Imagine it. Read about it. Write about it. That suits you much better!"

Faith of our Family

Christianity ruled every aspect of our lives and religious training began very early.

Every meal started with holding hands, bowing our heads, closing our eyes, and giving thanks to God for our food. Each of us learned at a young age to say the blessing, always ending with "in Jesus' name,

Amen." Once Marie, my youngest sister, who'd just learned how to do it, got a bit carried away. After asking for God's blessing on the food, she went on, "And God please bless Harry and please bless Cathy . . ." and so on down through all the kids. She was starting in on our cousins, when Dad stepped in to say "and in Jesus' name, Amen." We all laughingly joined in on the "Amen."

Many of the rules we lived by derived from our Christianity. Some were sacrosanct like the Ten Commandment prohibitions against lying, stealing, and so forth. Others were derivatives from "love one another," like no fighting at the table or criticizing each other. Keeping the Sabbath holy meant no swimming on Sunday or playing normal games. As we entered our teenage years, rules included not dancing, drinking, smoking, or going to movies. The strict observation of these made us feel very different from the rest of society.

Faith, though, was more than rules. Nothing in the world was as important as knowing God and loving Him. The everyday material world we could see was only a relatively insignificant part of a much greater spiritual realm. And in this larger universe there was a cosmic battle going on between God and Satan.

One got intimations of this larger world through Bible stories. Among the things Mother read to us was a large book with colored pictures that fascinated me. We soon knew by heart the stories of Noah and his ark of animals. Heavy with mystery was why God wanted Abraham to sacrifice his son Isaac, or why God chose Jacob, the cheater, over his brother Esau. In fact, we found many of the stories and pictures memorable and vivid: Joseph, a dream interpreter who became prime minister after his brothers sold him as a slave to Egypt; Moses and the burning bush; Gideon culling his army by how the soldiers drank water from the stream.

The most fascinating stories were about the boy who slew the giant Goliath and became King David, displacing his good friend Jonathan as King of Israel. He later stole the wife of one of his important generals, and his life ended in terrible heartbreak over his own son Absalom. David seemed more alive to me than almost any character in the Bible, even Jesus. He apparently delighted the Lord, yet he seemed to violate all the rules. From David I got the sense that, while rules were important, a spirit of courage, gratitude, and yes, penitence was more important. Life and morality were more complicated than simple rules.

Years later I read The Book of J, a translation of what scholars believe is the oldest layer of the Pentateuch, and a literary critic's speculations regarding it. Harold Bloom's thesis was that the author of this part of the Bible probably was one of David's daughters, who, in his opinion, joined Shakespeare as one of the two greatest writers ever to live. This part of the Bible was certainly the most powerful for me. I've been sorry, even a little guilty, that I never provided my children with the same experience of a childhood steeped in these Bible stories.

Stories in the Gospels about Jesus were almost as fascinating as those of David, but since we thought of Jesus as God rather than a mortal, he never seemed as real and alive to me as David. I sensed the power of the parables, and I loved the picture of Jesus beside the woman caught in the act of adultery, stooped down drawing letters in the sand while the accusers drifted away, convicted by their own guilt.

When at ten years of age I finished reading the whole Bible for the first time, motivated by Mother's bribe, I was surprised that I didn't feel transformed. I'm sure now, though, that the sediment laid in my psyche by the Bible and its stories shaped my imagination and perceptions.

Sunday was spent at Sunday school and church in the *Templo Biblico*. We were taught that going to church was an important part of being a Christian and that it was critical for us Strachans to set a good example. I found it boring and sensed that for my parents, religion was more about developing a personal relationship with God than something external like going to church. We were taught that the gate into that relationship came when you "accepted" Jesus as your Savior, asked for his forgiveness, and dedicated your life to him. That first happened for me at an evening campfire during a summer Christian camp at *Roblealto* when I was about seven.

When I think back to my childhood religion, it is not rules and stories or even that first experience of "being saved" that has had the most influence on my life. What has stayed with me like the cosmos background radiation is a paradigm of the great importance of everything in life. It was communicated in the idea that I had been chosen before the world began to be a "son of God." He had given me a secret name. He had a plan for my life. He'd sent his very own son Jesus to save me. His Holy Spirit was at work in me and in the world. This gave life great significance, though it didn't necessarily make it fun. This was why it was important to do everything "with all your heart, soul, and mind."

People often talk of the "Protestant work ethic" as something that pushes many people to be high achievers, even after turning their backs on the specifics of their childhood faith. I suspect it's not so much the ethic, which many other cultures share, as an ingrained sense that everything matters profoundly. Everything mattered because everything was part of God's plan for my life. Mother drove that point home time and time again. When I proved to her that I had been unfairly graded by a teacher, she acknowledged the mistake, but then asked me, "What do you think God is trying to teach you by this, Harry?"

Questions like this didn't take the sting out of life's setbacks, but they firmly shut the door on feeling victimized. They steered me away from blaming others for my problems. Long after I'd ceased to believe that God intervenes in the natural order to manipulate events and outcomes, I still practiced the habit of looking for the lessons in everything that happened, a habit I now see as having great adaptive value when I went away to school.

LEAVING THE FAMILY COCOON

HAMPDEN DUBOSE ACADEMY

I went to the United States for the tenth grade at Hampden DuBose Academy (HDA). My scholarship to the school was made possible by two women, Mrs. Biggers and Mrs. Winters, whose generosity changed my life.

HDA was a small school of two hundred students, located on an elegant estate with a lake in the orange groves near Orlando, Florida. The school was based on a fundamentalist Christianity that affected all activities. Only intramural sports were played, and the administration was proud that the school was unaccredited.

HDA was my seventeenth school. Before arriving, I had attended sixteen schools in Costa Rica and the U.S., not one of them for a two full years. This was the result of our family's many moves, the lack of public schools in Costa Rica that didn't require Catholic religious training, and Mother's ceaseless efforts to improve our education within the financial constraints of our budget.

I was small for my age, sensitive about my size, very late entering puberty, socially insecure and naïve, yet strangely confident that God had a great destiny in store for me.

John's Sport Coat

I knew from what I had heard that Hampden DuBose was going to introduce me to a new world of manners. I needed a suit for church on Sunday and a sport coat and tie to wear to supper each night. My friend John Nelson, who had been attending the school for two years, explained that we'd be seated boy-girl at the table, be taught how to help seat the girls and make good conversation. There would even be events where we'd have to ask a girl on a date.

His mother, Aunt Thelma, took both of us shopping in St. Petersburg. To help stretch my small clothing budget, she gave me a cream-colored sport coat flecked with brown specks. John, a head taller than me, had outgrown it the year before, and it fit me well. Then she taught me how to tie a tie, and John's grandmother, in whose home we were staying, inspected us. She said I looked quite "spiffy" and that we were among the handsomest boys she'd ever seen.

Leaving for HDA, 1956, with John and Peter Nelson, and I in the cream sport coat

When we arrived on campus, John made it a point to introduce me to some of his friends that I would be joining in the sophomore class. I recall standing in a circle with six or so of them, shaking hands and trying to remember their names. John's best friend from the prior year reached out to feel my sport coat and laughingly said, "Oh, that's John's old sport coat, isn't it?"

I felt mortified, not sure whether he was being sarcastic and cruel or just making a comment, and said nothing. But I soon noticed that the "in crowd" loved to make witty, often sarcastic comments, a style of talking unknown to me. I watched and mimicked them that first year, and when summer came, I went home to try out this new patter on my brothers and sisters.

After about twenty-four hours, we were at the dinner table and my father interrupted me. In a dry, matter-of-fact tone he said, "That's a pretty artificial way of talking, Harry—in addition to not being kind." I immediately knew he was right and determined to give it up. My mother reinforced his point with one of her favorite quotes, "Be kind, my son, and let who will be clever!"

Cleaning Azaleas

Everyone in the school had daily chores along with making their beds and cleaning their room. These included tasks like sweeping the walks, serving the tables, washing dishes. They were assigned and rotated on a weekly basis, and some, like guest waiting, were of greater prestige than others. On Monday (our day off, as we had classes on Saturday) we cleaned up the grounds.

One Monday I joined several others, and we were given toothbrushes and told to go out and remove the dead blossoms from the azalea bushes. It was boring, boring work and the spring day was also beastly hot. The task felt pointless as the gardens held thousands of azalea bushes we'd never reach in the allotted time. I seriously considered speeding sloppily through the work, rather than carefully and gently brushing away the dead blossoms.

On further consideration, though, I decided, *No, I'll do the very best I can.* This wasn't because I knew God was watching and wished azaleas to have help dropping dead blossoms. Instead, the decision arose from a message to us from Doc DuBose, the headmaster.

> An act becomes a habit, a habit becomes your character, and your character becomes your destiny. It may not seem important, but when you throw a gum wrapper on the ground, you're building your character. When you don't complete your homework, you're building your character. And when you do a task in a sloppy fashion, you're building your character.

His advice rang true for me. And so, though the job was pointless, I diligently applied my toothbrush to those poor bushes—for my character's sake.

Later in life I came to believe it was important to balance Doc's dictum with another one known as The 80/20 Rule: "Focus on the 20 percent that has 80 percent of the impact, namely, what is really important. Either don't do or do quickly those tasks that don't make a difference." I still believe, however, that it pays to over—rather than under-invest in the quality of one's work.

Bolts from the Blue

HDA had morning chapel and an evening vesper service each day. We sang hymns and there was generally a sermon, often given by outside speakers. They would expound on scripture and tell interesting stories from their own or others' experience. The service usually ended with an invitation to ask God for forgiveness or to make a renewed commitment to do His will. I responded positively to most of these messages, taking them as personally directed to me.

My repentance and commitment to a new life were sincere, even if not always effective. Often the experience was euphoric and filled me with a sense of optimism and meaningfulness, and this aligned with my childhood religious training. I was discovering for myself the Christianity of my family, and these experiences validated truths I had been taught.

Mrs. DuBose, the headmistress of the school, regularly gave the entire student body a spiritual "booster shot," an impromptu scolding to keep us from getting complacent. It was not uncommon for it to be triggered by a misdeed that had come to her attention. If there was no obvious infraction at hand, then she would simply deliver a sharp criticism like a bolt from the blue, such as, "Harry, you know I'm talking to you! Don't pretend you don't. You know you have PRIDE in your heart!"

Being on the receiving end of this bolt, madly trying to figure out how her message applied to me, caused me to flush, and the mortification her words caused me were proof that my heart really was full of pride. Even if I couldn't put my finger on it, I knew there was much sin in my life. Even when her arrows were shot at someone else, they effectively struck me.

My peak humiliation at her hands came during a rehearsal of the Easter Cantata before graduation our junior year. The large chorus of seventy or so people was arrayed four rows deep. As the smallest boy, I was on the first row out on the right wing with several other first tenors. I was doing my best to hit the high notes standing by Jim Howard, my senior friend and the best of the tenors. Miss Hill was leading the choir. Mrs. DuBose was sitting in the middle of the auditorium supervising the rehearsal, her large florid fan going back and forth to keep cool.

Suddenly she snapped the fan shut so loudly we could all hear it. Smashing it down on the chair in front of her, she stood up and started walking to the front. Pointing to our wing of the choir at Jim and me, she said, "No, no, no! Jim, you move over to the other side of the stage. Can't all of you hear that?! Costa Rica, Harry, whatever your name is, you're pulling Jim flat!"

Declaiming to a Tree Stump

Perhaps to encourage me to be a preacher, my mother once told me, "Harry, you have an amazing gift for speaking in public that the Lord is going to use."

Exactly what it meant to have the gift of public speaking, though, was a mystery to me as I left for school. If asked, I'd have assumed it meant talking loud enough to be heard, perhaps enunciating words clearly, not forgetting what you meant to say.

My first real insight into public speaking came in the woods behind the bowling alley in the spring of my sophomore year. Once a year everyone in the school had to give a declamation from memory. The one I'd chosen from the stack of potential speeches was about four paragraphs long, entitled "It's Always Too Soon to Quit."

Giving the declamation scared me. My name would be called out. I'd have to leave my seat in the audience, walk up the aisle with everyone's eyes on me, climb the steps to the platform without tripping, walk to the middle of the stage, turn to face the audience, and stand naked, as it were, with no lectern to hang on to. When I thought of facing an audience of over two-hundred teachers and students, I got a panicky feeling in my stomach.

Out in the middle of the woods, excused from class to practice, however, I was mainly feeling bored. I had repeated the piece so often, I had it memorized forward and backward. Facing the stump, my audience, I began to goof around. I started exaggerating the punch line, shifting the emphasis in dramatic fashion to a different word with each repetition, taking the pitch up or down, changing the pacing. "IT is always too soon to quit! It's ALWAYS too soon to quit! It's always too soon to QUIT!"

This turned out to be great fun. As I experimented, I discovered to my surprise that there really were many different ways to say the same words. I also noticed that in the process of using my delivery to add layers of meaning, I tended to lose the self-consciousness and paralyzing fear. I began to concentrate much more on the message rather than my terror of making mistakes.

Declamation Day arrived. I didn't trip on the steps. When I looked out at the audience, I could see individual faces with clarity, and I gratefully focused on the one or two that seemed eager to hear my message. I didn't forget any of the words, and the applause as I returned to my seat was gratifying. *That wasn't so bad*, I thought. *Actually, kind of fun, though I can't admit it to anyone.*

To my surprise, I was chosen as one of the five finalists in the Junior Division for sophomores and freshmen. Several weeks later at the finals, a formal evening event with outside judges, each of us finalists, dressed up in our suits or evening dresses, repeated our speeches. Though too nervous to eat anything at supper, I found that when my time came, my jitters turned into adrenalin, and as I walked up the aisle, I felt alive and happy.

I repeated a mantra I have since used to control my fear of public speaking: "God has not given us a spirit of fear, but of love (focus on others), joy (be enthusiastic) and a sound mind (pay attention, think clearly)!" I concentrated on my message, which fortunately was one I deeply believed, and it seemed to me that energy flowed through me to the audience. The experience was exciting and satisfying, a real "high."

At graduation I received the Declamation Medal for the Junior Division, and I began to feel accepted into the school and my class. That success led to more opportunities to do readings and skits. I was chosen to represent our class in debate, which later led to debating at Wheaton. Years later at Harvard Law School, my biggest success was winning the award for "Best Oral" in moot court.

Not all my public speaking was successful. I once was fired from a student play at Wheaton. A student friend, the director, had asked me to speak God's lines over the loudspeaker. At the rehearsal the drama teacher got a great laugh when he said, "This will never work! When that voice comes over the loudspeaker, everyone in the audience is going to say, 'That's not God. That's Harry'!"

I never became Mother's "famous preacher." Despite the best efforts of my speech teachers, I never became a polished speaker. I often failed to finish sentences and made many grammatical mistakes. But in teaching and consulting I have had numerous opportunities to speak in public. Any success I've had, I believe, goes back to the lessons I learned from the stump: focus on the message, get self-consciousness out of the way, let the enthusiasm flow, and let the delivery emphasize the most important parts of the message.

Blessing Roommates

In the first semester of my senior year, Mrs. DuBose's daughter, who was part of the administration, told me that I was being put in Hazel Hall with three roommates to "help them spiritually." I can't recall how she described the students, but they were among the students I least liked, "losers" in the slang of a later period.

About this time, a visiting preacher challenged us to take our daily spiritual practices to a new level—to make the Word of God a part of our life, not just by reading, but by memorizing the Bible. He encouraged us to take prayer seriously, to get up and kneel on the hard floor, to wrestle with God, not just lie in the warm bed and pray in a sleepy daze. I committed to his program at the start of that semester. I started getting up half an hour early. I would read an entire book of a book of the Bible. Then I would kneel on the cold, wooden floor and pray.

At the top of my prayer list was that God would help me "love" my roommates and "be a blessing to them." Each night after a day of frustrating interactions with these guys, I would kneel on the same floor and pray for forgiveness. I didn't even like them, much less love them. It was also clear that I was having no positive impact on their lives.

One of my roommates was sarcastic and hated having been sent to this school by his parents. Another was big and blubbery with pimples he couldn't control. He spent an inordinate amount of time in the bathroom, probably masturbating according to the sarcastic roommate.

The third was timid and on the edge of flunking out. I got very little help from any of them in trying to keep the room halfway clean.

This went on without much change for about a month and a half. One cold evening, in the midst of the prayer for forgiveness, I realized that this was not working. My knees hurt. Although I had memorized Ephesians, it hadn't transformed me. And it was clear that my relationship with my roommates was cold, strained, and thoroughly unpleasant. I told God that I was through trying to love my roommates, that He'd have to find another way to "bless" them, and that I was just going to be decent and try to understand them. The next morning I didn't get up half an hour early, instead I had a shorter Bible reading, and stayed in my warm bed for morning prayers.

Over the next two months when the opportunity presented itself, I'd ask them about themselves. I was genuinely curious about how they'd ended up at HDA and about their experiences. I listened without any attempt to give advice. I stopped cleaning up after them and told them to do it themselves. I came to like the sarcastic one, and we worked on football plays together. The pimply one told me about his broken home. It saddened me to think of coming from a family with lots of money but no love. The third began to talk about how lost he felt in class, and in talking seemed to lose his "deer in the headlights" look. I don't recall any of their lives being changed, and the third one still flunked out. I do remember, though, that the atmosphere in our room lightened. We began to laugh together, we began to like each other, and they seemed genuinely sorry when we got separated the following semester.

This experience didn't destroy my faith, but it did make me skeptical about dogmatic preachers and abstractions like "love" and "being a blessing." I began to pay more attention to my own experiences and the feedback life was giving me.

Looking back on my years at HDA, I see a little boy entering puberty, a contradictory bundle of insecurity and excessive arrogance. I was prone to enthusiasms, took everything too seriously, was willing to pontificate critically about the larger secular world—its music and movies, politics and business—things about which I was almost totally ignorant. I was deluded about the school's academic excellence and willing to overlook the way in which favoritism damaged the esteem of its least successful students.

Yet HDA was a wonderful gateway out of my home in Costa Rica to the larger world of the United States. Life was packed tightly, every "adjoining of time" put to good use. My summers at home were slow and boring by comparison. It was as if, when I returned to the crowded ecology of my large family and under the shade of my towering parents, I lost energy and focus. When I was at school, I experienced euphoria, times of depression, tastes of success and humiliation. It was a period of aliveness and discovery. At HDA, I woke up, became self-aware and self-motivated.

ON TO WHEATON COLLEGE

If high school was a time of awakening, college was a time, both literally and figuratively, of growth and adding muscle. I was 4 feet 11½ inches tall and weighed less than one hundred pounds at the start of my senior year of high school. By the end of my first year at Wheaton, I was my current 5 feet 10 inches and sixty pounds heavier.

I applied to Wheaton College because both of my parents were Wheaton graduates, as were most of my aunts and uncles, plus it had the reputation of being the best Christian college academically. One had to sign a pledge not to drink, smoke, dance, or go to movies, but that was no hardship since the same rules had applied at home and at Hampden DuBose. There were no vespers or common meals at Wheaton, but there was a mandatory chapel service every morning in a large auditorium. I loved the majestic booming organ, the wonderful acoustics, and two thousand students singing hymns with great gusto.

Wheaton turned out to be superb academically. I enjoyed the motivating, dedicated teachers, the exposure to a wide variety of disciplines, as well as writing papers, completing demanding exams, and a workload far heavier than I'd ever had. To the extent that a spotty education in sixteen schools and an unaccredited high school can be repaired, Wheaton did that for me. At the end of college, instead of the normal decline, my LSAT and GMAT scores were an average of one-hundred points higher than the SAT taken four years earlier.

Courses that Fit My Mind

I tended to judge people on a simple-minded continuum, smart to dumb, with similar scales for athletic and musical abilities. What I learned about myself in college, though, made me receptive to later research showing multiple types of mental, emotional, and physical intelligence. Almost everyone is smart at something and almost no one is smart at everything. Some subjects fit my mind well. I understood them intuitively, and they stayed with me after one reading. Other disciplines didn't stick no matter how often I reviewed them.

Foreign languages didn't stick. Two years of Greek convinced me I had no aptitude for languages. Every six weeks I had to go back and re-memorize all the vocabulary.

Rote courses, like ROTC and geology, were easy but boring. I signed up for ROTC (Army Reserve Officer Training) because I shared my dad's view that a minister should not be exempt from the obligations of normal citizens. I hated the early morning drills and dull classes, but thanks to ROTC, at the height of the Vietnam War I spent my military tour in the Army Medical Service Corps in Stuttgart, Germany, as a well-paid officer.

Geology consisted mainly of memorizing different types of rocks and geological formations. Tectonic plates had not yet become the accepted theory, and Wheaton avoided the debate about evolution. Later, after the 1972 earthquake in Nicaragua, I became fascinated by geology and read a number of popular science books about it.

Philosophy courses were among the most demanding at Wheaton, and Professor Holmes one of the best teachers. I took all of his courses, wrote many papers, but was never at the top of the class. I could tell other students had minds better suited to logic and philosophy (similar to my later experience in the study of law).

In courses for which I had some facility like math, the deficiencies of my high school background were such that I couldn't take the advanced materials. Surprisingly, given later interests, I took no courses in economics or political science. I did take "Introduction to Accounting" as a senior, and like high school geometry and algebra, it fit my brain. I quickly grasped the concepts and could use them for problem-solving.

My introductory course in psychology with Professor Dolby offered a new way of seeing the world. It explained many phenomena I had, up until that point, thought of as "spiritual." Professor Dolby, who was also an active therapist in the Wheaton community, oriented the course more toward clinical psychology than to the behaviorism of Skinner. In his course, Abnormal Psychology, I discovered that I had all the different neuroses, even those that were mutually exclusive.

I was so taken with this field of study that I decided to switch my major to psychology. I assumed that Dr. Dolby would be flattered and pleased with this decision. When I told him my intentions, he suggested I come over to his house to discuss things before finalizing the change.

I was greeted warmly by his wife and ushered into his office. We sat down, and he asked me to explain my thinking about switching majors. I was prepared and gave him what I thought was an eloquent argument: psychology was a powerful way to look at the world, and a wonderful means to help people. He listened thoughtfully, probably in his best therapist fashion. I expected his response would be encouraging. Instead he began, "You know, Harry, most of a therapist's work is listening silently to patients. A good therapist doesn't give advice. Are you sure this fits your personality? I have the sense that you really enjoy talking and tend to have strong opinions."

His comment stung, but I knew immediately that he was right. I wasn't a good listener, however much I valued that trait. I wasn't naturally accepting and compassionate. I wanted to solve any problem I saw, quickly and efficiently. I'd be a disaster as a therapist, probably bite my tongue in half trying to keep quiet.

So I remained a literature major. Wheaton's lit department was one of the best. Dr. Kilby and Dr. Batson were great teachers who became friends and mentors. I had no "ear" for the music of good writing and different styles, and grammar was always something of a mystery. These deficiencies were liabilities for a lit major, as I was unable to spot authors or poets through their style of writing. The reading load was greater than I was used to, but I learned to read fast, an advantage throughout the rest of my life.

Fortunately, these professors taught literature for its stories and ideas. Their courses focused on what was most compelling in the novels, plays, and poetry we read: ideas, human experiences, myths, insights. In the great literature of the Western world (the content of our classes), I felt I was being exposed to the "distilled experience" of multiple generations, being forced to empathize with all sorts of people, some quite nasty. I was assimilating more life than I could ever live directly in my short time on earth.

In the early 1960s, Wheaton experimented with an honors program for its best students. This consisted of classes with heavier reading loads and more papers. My freshman grades made me eligible for this group, and with sixty others, I took a survey course of world history covering the globe (Europe, Middle East, India, China, Japan, and the Americas) from ancient to modern times. A typical assignment involved sixty pages dense with battles, laws, and geography, and packed with names and dates. We covered the entire history of a civilization every week.

Professor Murk was young and enthusiastic; a stickler for learning accurately the names of important leaders, geographical places, and dates. His exams were diabolical, and we never had enough time to do a good job. He'd give us a mixed list of events or incidents from all periods of history and all geographies and ask us to arrange them in chronological order. Or, he'd give us a list of dates and ask us to name and describe the important incident that occurred on that date.

I was sure I'd failed the first semester exam, as I'd had to guess at more than half of the items and I barely finished on time. But to my surprise I had almost perfectly arranged the chronological items. I received the top grade in the class, an experience that began to give me a healthy respect for the unconscious. Something down there was clearly smarter than my conscious mind.

Discovering Writing

During my second year I took a creative writing class. My writing professor, unlike any English teacher I'd ever had, was largely indifferent to my weak spelling and grammar. Her focus was on whether the writing was interesting, vivid, and clear. One of the course requirements was to write something every day in a journal. At the end of each week we'd give her our brown notebooks, and she returned them on Monday of the following week. We could write about anything and in any style. She made no attempt to correct our grammar or spelling, but sprinkled enthusiastic comments in the margin of pieces she liked. On Monday, without revealing the author, she would read a couple of the journal entries from the class that she had really liked.

At first, finding something interesting to write about was very stressful. This led me to experiment with all sorts of crazy ideas like writing up dreams, reporting on imaginary conversations, or even poetry.

As soon as I began recording my dreams, they went from boring black and white to vivid Technicolor, loaded with action and dialogue. It was as if my unconscious, the moment it got attention, began to show off. One of the dreams captures my sense of being an outsider and was the first hint I had that, even if I didn't fully fit in, I could still make a positive contribution.

> I am a pitcher for the Yankees pitching in a World Series game in Yankee Stadium. The stands are full; the sun is out, the field a vivid green. What is unusual is that I am a spider about four or five feet tall. I'm a successful pitcher, because unlike human pitchers, I can rotate from one foot to another to another so that my fast ball hurdles out of my hand at higher speeds to the plate. The game is going our way; I'm striking out the opposing batters, gaining more and more confidence in my pitching motion and control of the strike zone.
>
> Suddenly a giant rocket ship descends to settle in center field, and a great fear grips us all. We know without being told that we are being invaded from outer space. The invaders are giant spiders five or six times my size. At their side is a beautiful icy human queen who has persuaded the spiders that if they don't preemptively invade earth, earth will invade them. Political leaders quickly arrive and the President tries to convince the spiders that Earth has no hostile intentions. The queen, however, is successful at portraying these protestations as sinister deceptions.
>
> I have a brilliant idea. Going up to the group, I address the leader of the spiders, "Sir, I assure you Earth has no evil intentions toward you. I am a spider like you and know this to be true. This queen is using you as a naked power play. Trust me, not her; I'm a spider like you." The world is saved!

I experimented with other forms of telling a story or talking about ideas, like the following poem, which I wrote in 1961:

No Parking

In early spring I walked the damp warm road
That rested weary rut-holes in the therapeutic sun,
And saw green shoots of lily stalks lift up
And shake their stubby heads in love of life
      And read with wonder a metallic sign
      That said, "No Parking Any Time."

This dark warm bed was overlaid with brittle stalks
Whose rusty blades lay still—a previous summer's fallen giants
Unmummied kings disintegrating midst decaying leaves
Who never again would feel the surge of life,
      And yet in death obeyed the sign
      That said, "No Parking Any Time."

I couldn't help but wonder what the new shoots thought
When they viewed the wreckage of a winter they had never known,
And saw ancestor's fate. Did it mirror their own?
Or did they only feel the tender sun and thrill of life
      And maybe puzzle as they read the sign
      That said, "No Parking Any Time."

My guess: that knowing clearly of their end,
They still believed God's winter would be good,
And until then would grow and bloom
Thrust up at first by love of life
      And then because in God's design
      There is No Parking Any Time.

That poem has stuck with me over the years. An imaginary conversation between the young Harry of 1961 and one nearly fifty years older might clarify:

OLD H: Where did that poem come from?

YOUNG H: It's something I actually saw as I walked to campus from our rooms.

OLD H: And what was most meaningful to you about the poem?

YOUNG H: I remember a certain excitement as it came together, a feeling almost of joy at the cleverness of the refrain, at teasing out the multiple meanings in the "No Parking" sign. By the way, what about the poem has caused you to remember it?

Old H: Well, I've always liked it—thought it one of your best poems. I remember that in writing it, you were mainly trying to capture the on-going surge of life. Death and loss, though mentioned in the poem, weren't much on your mind. In the intervening years since you wrote the poem, however, there have been numerous times when death and loss have come into my life, and the phrase "God's winter will be good!" has been a helpful message. I've always felt the poem had wisdom in it beyond anything you knew at the time. While much about you in college—your naïveté, brashness, and lack of empathy for others—embarrasses me, things like this poem show a redeeming side.

Life Packed Tight

A friend once said, "Harry is forever trying to pack ten pounds in a five pound sack." It's probably a habit that started with Mother's emphasis on using the "adjoinings of time." She could not abide wasting any of it. And that orientation has probably been reinforced by a fear of missing out on anything that looks interesting, fun, or important.

In retrospect, it's amazing to me the activities I crammed into my college years—not just an extra heavy academic load, but also a full set of extracurricular activities, plus a job to help pay expenses.

A typical course load was sixteen hours per semester, with a maximum of twenty if your grades permitted it. After my freshman year, my usual load was eighteen to twenty hours a semester.

Extracurricular activities included some that directly related to my religious life. The first year I taught a Sunday school class of fourth graders at my grandmother's Baptist church. I learned quickly that if I was not going to lose control of the class, I had to find exciting ways to make the Bible stories come alive. So I transposed these into modern settings and got eleven-year-old boys to act out the parts.

The next year I gave up the Sunday school class to lead a church service with the Spanish migrant workers in Elgin. It was a tough decision, but I considered the workers a needier group, and it forced me to use my Spanish. I also participated in the Foreign Mission Fellowship, a group on campus for those who envisioned missionary work in their future and wanted to promote it.

I went out for debate my freshman year. My partner, Harry Cawood, was a very polished speaker with a lot of experience from high school. Debate took us on a number of weekend trips around the Midwest, to contests in front of one or two judges in stark classrooms in the middle of largely empty buildings. Our team had increasing success, winning a number of tournaments in our division. By the end of the second season, we had made it to the junior finals held at West Point.

My junior and senior years I gave up debate in order to play soccer. My motivation was partly the need for more exercise, partly the camaraderie of the soccer team, but also the thought that in debate I might be cultivating more argumentative traits than was healthy. Coach Baptista was wonderful, and his strategies helped us win more games than we deserved. I loved the practices in the cold late afternoons of fall.

Work also filled up my time at school, as well as my summers during vacation. My summer job selling books door to door not only gave me a mythic spiritual story; it changed many of my ideas. I realized that people often failed to tell the truth, and that, indeed, they might not know themselves what they wanted. The stereotype of a salesman as a manipulator, who gets people to do what they don't want, turned out to be false. I learned that successful salesmen are efficient at helping people understand what's for sale, deciding if they really want it, and if so, figuring out how to get it. I also discovered that I had to manage my emotional ups and downs better to overcome that dreaded first call of the day.

Fitting soccer into a full life

Indirectly, selling did wonders for my self confidence. At the end of the first summer I thought, *Harry, you'll never in your life have a job this difficult. You've been through purgatory and emerged on the other side. You're going to be survivor!*

During the school year, the extra money from selling permitted me to put more time into other activities like school politics and to cut back on my job, but I continued to work about thirteen hours a week at Scripture Press. The company gave me a key to the building and let me come in late at night or on the weekend. The mindless typing in a dark empty building was a pleasant change of pace, and the extra money permitted me to help my family and build up some savings.

Work and extracurricular activities added to my quiver of experiences and forced me to be efficient. Conventional wisdom for college students seems to be "Focus on studies, minimize extracurricular activities, let nothing interfere with getting the best grades possible." My advice is somewhat different. I say, "You have to get good grades, but get involved. Do some sort of social service. Play sports and exercise. Don't be afraid of a part-time job. All of these activities will be as valuable as the academic work in developing your skills and capabilities."

Political Ups and Downs

At the end of our freshman year, we elected class officers for our sophomore year. The most coveted job for a sophomore was class representative to the student council, a platform that could position one to run for student council president at the end of the junior year, which was the most prized political position on campus.

At HDA individuals were "drafted" to be class officers. There was no self-promotion, no campaigning, and no promises offered. At Wheaton we had to run for an office, which included promoting ourselves, bragging about ourselves, and making promises—things I found distasteful. Some friends, however, persuaded me to run for student council representative. They wanted a candidate who did not belong to the "in crowd."

There were twelve candidates in the primary. In the first round, the large field would be winnowed down to four for the final election of two representatives. During the campaign a number of classmates told me I had become their candidate because, like them, I worked hard and I treated everyone the same. This made me uncomfortable for I felt I'd been given a public persona I hadn't earned. But it was exhilarating when the ballots were tallied that I had not only garnered the most votes in the primary, but enough to be elected representative on the first round.

The opposite happened at the end of my junior year when I ran for student council president against my former debate partner Harry Cawood. In this campaign I was a lightning rod for those reacting against the school. I was pigeonholed as the "loyal Wheaton Christian," while Cawood was more the "liberal rebel," even though we both knew that the opposite was closer to reality. We were good friends and spoke of each other only with great respect during the campaign. His supporters, however, (and probably mine) turned the election into a slinging match of bitter criticisms. Some scathing comments left me traumatized. The school paper added fuel to the fire, and the result was a close race, which I lost by ten votes.

I learned several things. First, people paste "personas" reflecting their own passions onto public figures. Second, the media reinforces them. Third, it requires a thicker skin than I have to be a good politician.

Friendships at 339 Jefferson Ave

One of the negative side effects of an obsession with the "adjoinings of time" was that it made me very task-oriented. I worked on such a tight schedule that if friends weren't ready to go to dinner, I refused to wait even ten minutes so we could eat together. I avoided bull sessions as a waste of time. I undervalued friendships until my experiences at 339 Jefferson Ave., my home for three years, began to open my eyes to their importance.

At the end of my first year in the freshman dorm, two friends from the year ahead of me, Jim Howard and Steve Savage, invited John Woodbridge and me to join them in rented rooms close to campus. One thing we had in common, among other things, was that we all came from religious families and had revered fathers or grandfathers as role models.

Each of us was busy and had an independent life, but living together caused us to intertwine in new ways. Several of us were active in social ministries or student government. Others of us played soccer together. Several had steady girlfriends who fixed the others of us up with blind dates. In the late evenings, we sometimes got into bull sessions on topics covering theology, politics, careers, and women.

Jim Howard was a natural artist, adept at drawing. He became a minister in the far North, partially supporting himself with his art. He had a great memory for poetry and humorous readings, loved Robert Service, and taught us scraps of poems, one of which I still quote when one of my brilliant suggestions is totally ignored:

Bad medicine," cried Tom the one-eyed
And made for to jump in the lake,
But when no one gave heed
To his little stampede,
He guessed he'd made a mistake.

Steve Savage was one of Southwestern's top salesmen, my team leader in selling, and he went on to a successful career in business. He was an incurable optimist. We'd awake with bleary eyes to find him out of bed, doing calisthenics, and singing happy hymns. Our immediate impulse was to strangle him for waking us, but he'd often end up persuading us to get up to join him.

Johnny Woodbridge went on to get several doctorates and teach in seminary. He was tall, thin, good-looking, and attractive to the girls. His dates tended to be the really hot girls, those who consciously or unconsciously radiated great sexual appeal. He'd come home from a date all aglow and immediately begin to tell us about this "wonderful spiritual woman" he'd met and how nice and intelligent she was. I'd mercilessly tease him about how he couldn't tell the difference between sexy and nice nor between physical and spiritual attraction. He'd protest vehemently, and who knows but what he may have been right. I'd call in my roommates for their quips and jokes, and as it got sillier and sillier, we'd all be laughing, genuinely fond of each other.

As one or the other graduated or moved out, others would join the rooms. We welcomed Guy Wilcox and George Huttar, one became a successful medical doctor and the other a masterful translator of the Bible into Indian dialects. My childhood friend John Nelson moved in for our senior year. To save money one semester, John and I decided to cook our own meals. We had one pan into which we'd pour a can of peas along with the juice. Then we'd add uncooked hotdogs. Our hot plate only had one working coil, so we could never quite get it to a boil. It was pretty awful, and we finally decided to return to the Wheaton cafeteria before we died of malnutrition.

John was a music major who was aiming at Julliard for graduate school. This required him to memorize reams of Bach, Beethoven, and other giants of classical music. He'd put a record on the phonograph, sheet music on a stand, climb up on the big easy chair, resting his butt on the back and his feet on the spring that stuck out of the seat, one hand waving the baton, the other rapidly turning the sheet music. I didn't particularly like classical music and was trying to study for my own comprehensive exams, but soon found that his music actually helped me concentrate. John went on to an illustrious career as musical director of orchestras and choirs around the world.

Today I recognize that I should have invested more time in these and many other Wheaton friends. What they taught me was often more important than what I learned in class. They made college fun. One of the pleasures of old age has been reconnecting with many of them and realizing what great people they are. I just wish I'd done so sooner.

Letting Go and Letting God

The summer before college, I lived with my grandmother in a basement bedroom she rented out during the school year. The room was damp, and I came to hate it. I was working as a typist in a complaint department typing up cards, sitting in a bay with four or five elderly (to me) ladies. It was boring and repetitive. In the late afternoon, I would go to the town swimming pool to swim and dive. I had no friends my own age. Sunday Grandmother and I went to her Baptist church, which I didn't much like. It wasn't a happy time, but I was only dimly aware of my unhappiness and loneliness.

One night I started reading a book about Robert McQuilken. I knew that he was the founder of Columbia Bible College and Ben Lippen School and had been a surrogate father to my mother. He was also a close friend of my Grandfather Strachan and an early supporter of the Latin America Mission.

The book was about the "victorious Christian life." It described how hard and fruitlessly most Christians work at their faith, finding little satisfaction because they've missed the point. Christianity is about "letting go and letting God." We are saved by grace, not works, and there is a huge gift of the Holy Spirit that God is eager for us to have. He came that we might have Life with a capital "L" and have it more abundantly. The book illuminated the barrenness of my own spiritual life and the potential of a more complete and joyful life.

Suddenly I felt a wind sweep into the basement room with a sound I would later recognize as that of an earthquake. It rushed through my body from top to bottom, and I found myself weeping copiously. It was as if all the inner sludge was being washed out. I felt clean and light and tremendously happy. I felt relaxed, calm, alive, and tingling with power.

The next day at work, my hands flew over the keys. I talked to the ladies with a new freedom, and they teased me. Our little corner of the office became a place of laughter. They told me about their families and lives with a new intimacy. Riding the bike back to town and down to the pool, I could see light splashing from every leaf. The hot, humid air had a special summer smell to it. I swam extra laps, my dives had never been better. I began to notice the people around the pool and get to know them. In the evening I stayed talking to my grandmother instead of bolting for the bedroom. Her "stop and start" driving when we went for groceries stopped bugging me.

The rest of the summer was transformed. It seemed like I had special radar for reading what the people around me were thinking and feeling. I felt a power flow through me, using me for its own purposes. I could almost see it. I seemed to be able to say just the right thing, and I got into deep conversations with strangers in unexpected and unforced ways.

Reading in my room in the evenings, I had a sense of peace, of comfortable emptiness. The room felt cool, not damp. I stopped worrying about myself. In fact, I stopped thinking about myself. I felt I had gotten "out of myself" and that the boundary around me was illusory. I let go and let God. Experiences like this strengthened and deepened my faith in the importance of the spiritual dimension, even as other experiences began to erode my confidence in what I thought I'd been taught.

The Baffling Answer to Prayer

At the end of my sophomore year, I made the momentous decision to give up my typing job and sell door-to-door. To do this I had to borrow money from a bank (with my uncle Jim McKellin's co-signature), buy a Volkswagen Bug, go through sales school, and join a team selling in the South.

I prayed a lot about this decision; the right action wasn't at all clear. If I were successful at this commission selling, my net earnings would double, making it possible to cut back on my twenty-three hours per week of work and get more involved in college life. It would be possible to play tennis and soccer, do more extracurricular activities, and handle a full academic load.

Failure, on the other hand, would mean dropping out of school for a year to pay off the car and make up the lost money. When I compared myself (an intense, insecure, unsophisticated, out-of-it missionary kid) with some of the others on Steve Savage's sales team (extroverted, self-confident, natural salesmen), the risk of failure seemed very real. The more I prayed about it, however, the more I became convinced that God was telling me to do this.

My used VW got me to Nashville, Tennessee, for sales school. I studied the assigned materials far more intensely than I did my college books. I wrote copious notes on everything the top salesmen told us in their lectures. I practiced my sales pitch endlessly in front of the mirror. After a week of training, we headed for the town in Kentucky that would be our summer home, rented rooms in an elderly lady's home, and started selling Bibles, dictionaries, and reference books door-to-door.

The start was okay, my sales in the first two or three days averaging around forty dollars a day. Our instructions were to call on every house on a road, no matter how rich or poor. If we worked efficiently, we could make twenty to thirty calls and demonstrate our books to some seven to ten people in a twelve-hour day. Success meant closing on two to four of these, taking a deposit (which we would then live on), and delivering the books at the end of the summer.

On Thursday of the first week, I worked my full twelve hours, but didn't sell a single book. At dinner with the others on the team, I felt a little humiliated. After supper I reviewed all the sales materials and determined to get an early start the next day. But Friday was another day with no sales in spite of going thirteen hours at full throttle. I felt doubly humiliated and ate supper alone.

On Saturday my team leader and friend, Steve Savage, came with me for a few hours to make sure the instructions were being followed.

"You're doing it right; just keep working." he said as he peeled off for his own territory.

So I worked. I made myself run up the walk to the porch with my satchel of samples. I knocked confidently on the door, not too loud, not too soft. I tried to keep it light when some timid-looking woman answered the door bell. "You don't shoot salesmen do you?" My demonstration was enthusiastic, crisp, and dramatic: "Notice how strong the binding is" while holding some pages and shaking the book vigorously. The close was confident: "This book sells for $9.95 and I do business one of two ways, I can leave it with you today or I can bring it at the end of the summer, whichever you prefer!"

Nevertheless, after another twenty-five calls, I still hadn't sold a thing. That evening, shocked and discouraged, I began to wonder why God was letting this happen. Our sales manager, Ted Welch, told Steve that no one in the history of the firm working as diligently as I, had ever gone this long without a sale.

After church on Sunday, I drove to a nearby park. I opened my Bible to random passages looking for a message, but nothing jumped out. "What might God be trying to teach me?" was the question I asked.

A sermon from high school emerged from memory. "Most people's prayers are so vague that anything that happens can be interpreted as God's answer. They don't really know if God answers prayer, because they don't talk to Him the way they would to their own father. When you pray, be specific. God answers specific prayers. There won't be any doubt." A light dawned in my brain! This is what God wants to teach me. *Pray so that there can be no doubt when He answers.*

In a flood of emotion, I took out a piece of paper and wrote out my prayer. The first paragraph described how I felt led by God to sell that summer. The next paragraph covered the list of things I would do to fulfill my part of the bargain. The third paragraph was my specific request: an average of $500 in sales per week for the entire summer. This was an audacious goal, one that would put me in the top twenty of over one thousand first-year salesmen. It meant sales averaging almost $100 per day. The last paragraph was a promise of what would be done with the extra time back at school and how God would be given all the glory. A deep sense of peace and happiness came over me. God was going to do this and my faith would be strengthened.

I went out eagerly on Monday and worked all day, but did not get the answer I was expecting. Instead I failed to sell a single book. Shaken, that night I repeated over and over again "Lord, I believe. Starting tomorrow the sales will come and hit $500 by Saturday. You're testing my faith. 'Lord, I believe, help Thou mine unbelief!'"

The next day was another thirteen hours and another twenty-five calls, but not a single sale. There was virtually no chance of $500 that week. I went to bed numb and desolate. Lying on my back in the dark, tears ran down both sides of my face and into my ears.

In spite of my despair, the next day I got another early start. It was pouring rain, and, within an hour I was soaked, but I didn't stop. By noon my shoes were squishing with every step. It seemed nearly impossible to get into a house to make a demonstration. At five o'clock with two or three hours of daylight left and zero sales, chilled in my wet clothes, I quit.

In the car driving back to town, it was impossible to see the road for the water. I pulled over to check why the windshield wipers weren't working and discovered it wasn't the wipers, but the tears that would not stop.

Getting back into the car, I was suddenly furious. Impulsively, I said out loud, "Enough! God, I don't want your help! I'm going it alone! Forget it! You're not going to hear another prayer from me about selling!"

This outburst shocked me. It seemed to come from some deep, hidden place inside. Would a bolt from the blue strike me for the blasphemy? Then in my mind, but still determined, the thoughts continued. *God, how do you expect me to continue believing in prayer after something like this? I'll call you back at the end of the summer.*

The next day, hitting the pavement once again, the sales began. I worked hard and became a better salesman. I didn't pray the rest of the summer and when my deliveries were completed and the results tallied up, my total sales had averaged $501 per week. I received a "Top Twenty First-Year Salesman" trophy. After selling the VW and repaying the bank loan, my net summer earnings were three times what they would have been in my old job in Wheaton.

I was aware of the amazing coincidence between the $500 request and the $501 actually earned. There were Christian friends who took that as proof that God had answered my prayers. For me, though, the lesson I took away was quite different. If God had in fact helped me, then what was the Lord really trying to teach me? "Stop praying about everything?"

And if the $501 at the end of the summer was pure coincidence and if He wasn't there at all, well . . . ?

So when I "called" God back at the end of the summer, God as I imagined Him had changed. He, She or It, I suspected, intervened far less to manipulate the world to our prayer requests than some imagine. If personally interested in me, God was probably more like a good father encouraging self-reliance and independence. Maybe the lesson to be learned was that God wanted me to figure out what worked using my own intelligence. Maybe the Lord wanted me more skeptical about sermons that purport to know His mind and ways.

Settling on Law School

By my senior year, I decided to attack these doubts directly. A number of complex factors like the selling experience and questions about certain doctrines had eroded my childhood beliefs. The required Bible courses did little to buttress my faith, so I tried to persuade one of the deans to allow me to undertake a tutorial with Professor Jerry Hawthorne whom I greatly respected. My plan was to do a paper on each of the doubts bothering me. I hoped that if I faced my skepticism of, for instance, the "inerrant inspiration of the scriptures," if I read widely and deeply about the subject, then I'd see the truth and recapture my faith. The dean refused to excuse me from Apologetics, but I began writing the papers on my own anyway. As it turned out, the opposite of what I hoped happened. As I studied what Christian scholars said about how the Bible had been written and assembled, I realized that other Christians had also left behind much of the doctrinal baggage of fundamentalist Christianity. This only reinforced my doubts.

By this time, however, theological issues were less important to me. I became comfortable leaving them in the limbo of agnosticism. I no longer believed there was a way to prove the truth of Christianity. For me the real test of a religion had become whether it "worked." The question to be answered was: "Does the faith and the practice of a religion bring health, energy, love, and effectiveness into life?"

When I looked at others and into my own life, the answer was mixed. For many, their faith narrowed them and made them intolerant. Others seemed stunted by excessive superstition. Yet I saw many who were liberated, saved from destructive tendencies, given courage and compassion. My faith in high school had been part of a wonderful awakening to a bigger world. In college it seemed that more growth came from doubts.

I asked myself, *If there is a clash between my experiences and the teachings of the Bible, am I going to believe the Bible or my experiences?* And I answered by saying, *Don't be arrogant, Harry. First try to accurately understand the cumulative wisdom of a two-thousand-year-old religion. But if you can't resolve it any other way, you must follow the authority of your own experience. Otherwise you'll become schizophrenic and cut off your only direct channel to God.*

This loss of faith did not lead me to a materialistic view of the world, as it did for some of my classmates. There were many writers who persuaded me of the deep wisdom in myths. They reinforced my sense that there is a spiritual realm, deeply important and real, and that our limited understanding of it should keep us humble. C.S. Lewis was one of the writers I discovered. I read virtually all his books, liking his novels and science fiction and the Narnia series even more than his apologetics. I found his feel for other dimensions of reality much more compelling than his linear logical arguments.

For these reasons and perhaps others of which I was not completely aware, I reached the end of college knowing I couldn't go to Fuller Theological Seminary. I was not ready to say Christianity wasn't true, but I knew I could not preach a gospel that didn't "click" for me. I decided to try a secular environment and learn more about the world.

I first considered a one-year master in business, similar to the one at Michigan State where Steve Savage had gone. Wheaton professors convinced me that it was worth an extra year to go to a more demanding program like the Harvard Business School. So I applied and was accepted there.

Then one day Professor Volkman, my accounting professor, said, "Harry, C students go to business school, A students go to law school. At law school you'll learn both about business and society and compete with the best." To help convince us, he drove a number of us to interview at Yale, Columbia, and Harvard during spring break. I was accepted with a full scholarship to both Northwestern and Harvard. Northwestern even offered an additional $2000 stipend for living expenses. Surprisingly, Professor Volkman, a Northwestern graduate himself, persuaded me to go to Harvard. "It's the best. You'll never regret it."

He was right; I have never regretted the decision. Many times since, I've marveled at my luck in having such a wonderful and generous professor who cared enough to push me into a top school.

INTO THE SECULAR WORLD

HARVARD LAW SCHOOL

Mother's Fears

When asked to share something of my background, I sometimes tell people "I have the only mother who wept and was sure the devil had intervened to lead her son astray when he was given a full scholarship to Harvard Law School." A friend once laughingly added, "And she was right!"

I think of the five years following college, three in law school followed by two in the army, as my introduction to the secular world. There is no doubt the Harvard Law School (HLS) started me on a very different road from the one I'd have traveled if I'd gone to seminary. But the story is probably unfair to my mother, even if true to my subjective experience. Though she never said so explicitly, I don't doubt that she was proud that I was accepted at Harvard and was going on to graduate school, but she also let me know that my decision to abandon seminary for law school deeply troubled her. I suspect she feared this would lead to a loss of faith and secular behaviors that she knew I no longer considered sinful. She feared that I was setting an example, as I shared doubts and defended new behaviors, that would exacerbate the trouble she was already having with my siblings. Our discussions about this tended to leave us both feeling bad.

But a movie of my life from the outside during law school would suggest that I made no dramatic breaks with my past. Rather the inner changes that began at HDA and Wheaton continued to accumulate. At HLS I presented a persona of a practicing Christian. I attended church every Sunday, joined the Park Street Church as an associate member, and became active in their collegiate/grad group. I valued church in part for the music, the stimulation of the sermon, the opportunity to reflect, but even more as a great place to meet attractive young ladies.

I helped organize a reading group that met once a week to read religious books. I recall being impacted by a book by Bonhoeffer, a liberal theologian killed by Hitler. The group included several practicing Roman Catholics and two Jews, one from a Reformed background, the other strictly Orthodox. I was fascinated by the similarities and differences that faith played in their lives and noted, as we discussed tough issues, that the conservative members of each religion shared more in common with conservatives of other faiths than they did with the liberals of their own faith.

I started my meals at Harkness Commons by bowing my head and saying grace silently, virtually the only one doing so. I liked the reminder to be thankful for what had come my way and was willing to be publicly known as someone of faith. Some of my dorm mates, determined to introduce me to alcohol and teach me to dance and to lose my virginity, would tease me about this practice, but toward the end of the first year, one told me he liked eating with me because of this custom.

After my father's death, deeply angry at God and feeling estranged from the Christian community, I still started my meal with bowed head and closed eyes, even though I did not pray. I was motivated by a perverse arrogance. My unbelief still honored the importance of the spiritual dimension, and I didn't want it confused with the "secularism" of my classmates. I felt many of them had chosen unbelief without reflection, out of ignorance. My doubts were different, and I still hoped to find a deeper, truer faith.

Terror in the Classroom

The stereotype I had of a typical HLS student was that he or she was a graduate of a private prep school and an Ivy League college. While some students fit that description, most of my class, certainly those in Story Hall, seemed to have come from Midwestern state universities like Michigan, or from Maine, or from City College in New York. Like me, many doubted they belonged at Harvard. As I got to know them, I found each had an interesting story, often about overcoming significant obstacles to get into law school.

Harvard Law School did little to rid us of our insecurity. We were told that the dean of the law school had until recently welcomed the incoming class saying, "Gentlemen, please look at the person on your right and the one on your left. By the end of the year, one of you will be gone." While this was no longer statistically true, nevertheless we were made to believe that HLS was a school with ruthless standards designed to weed out the dumb and lazy.

We were divided into sections of about eighty students, each with a common mandatory first year of tort, contracts, property, civil procedure, and criminal law. There was also group work on trial tactics and legal research linked to the moot court in which we all participated. Each course was taught by the case method, and often the case book used had been assembled by our professor.

Most of the classes were in Langdell Hall. We entered wearing our sport coats and ties (we were one of the last classes to have to dress up for class). The professor's desk was in the pit at the front of the class with blackboards behind it. A semi-circle of desks and chairs ascended toward the back of the room, each row rising above the other in the form of an amphitheater. The giants of law looked down on us from their portraits on the walls. Some were famous English judges with white wigs; others were Supreme Court Justices and professors from earlier eras.

Class began with the professor calling on a student to summarize the facts of the case and the decision of the judge. I prepared by reading the cases and underlining the important parts. Then I'd take a piece of onion-skin paper and type a summary of the facts and findings and paste it at the front of the case, ensuring that I'd be ready if called on.

With the preliminaries out of the way, the professor would then ask a student about the logic of the findings. Were they consistent with past precedents? Did he or she agree with the reasoning of the judge? No matter how good the answer, the professor would ask follow-up questions designed to trap the student into an inconsistency or to change his mind. It was like watching a rapier duel, except that at any moment the professor might turn his sword on another unsuspecting student and bring him into the discussion.

Once the main precedents were established, the professor would modify the facts. "Suppose instead that the facts had been . . . ?" In this way he'd try to get the student's articulation of the law to appear more and more unjust. If a student decided to modify his position, the professor would march him into another corner. It was both nerve-wracking and exhilarating, and we lived in awe of the brilliance of most of our professors.

One of my courses was with a famous, very short professor known for his gigantic ego. He would lock the classroom door in order to make it impossible for anyone to enter late. We were warned about him with this story:

In one class he called on Mr. Smith to state the facts. Mr. Smith replied, "I'm sorry, Professor Casner, but I am not prepared as my parents arrived unexpectedly last night, and I wasn't able to read the case."

Without pausing Prof. Casner responded, "And what was the finding of the judge in that case, Mr. Smith?"

"I'm not sure I was clear, Professor, but I am unprepared . . ."

"And what do you think of that finding, Mr. Smith?"

Silence. Silence throughout the classroom so tense you could cut it with a knife. Mercilessly Professor Casner continued to pound on the student, and when he got no answers, he walked over to where Mr. Smith was sitting, reached into his pocket, pulled out a dime, tossed it to him and said, "Here, Mr. Smith, go phone your mother and tell her you'll never be a lawyer!" He then folded his arms and watched steely-eyed while Mr. Smith gathered his books and walked to the door.

As Mr. Smith turned the handle, he looked back and said, "Professor Casner, you're a son of a bitch!"

Casner immediately replied, "Come back, Mr. Smith, that's the first lawyer-like thing I've heard you say!"

Stories like these were a part of the culture. The law school prided itself not only on being tough, but on being a "meritocracy." Few knew and no one cared what your background was—Wasp, Black, or Jew. Your exams were graded blind. You were ranked by your grade point average from first to last. If you were in the top 3 percent of the class, there was a good chance you'd make Law Review and clerk for a Supreme Court justice or come back some day as a professor. If you weren't in the top 3 percent, you sensed you didn't count for much, though you'd probably go on to make a lot of money as a lawyer or corporate executive or something else.

Whatever our success had been as undergraduates, we knew the deck was stacked against us. In my class we had about fifty college valedictorians. These "geniuses," with their perfect LSAT scores, worked as hard as anyone and could be found in Langdell Library studying until midnight. My first-year average barely put me in the top half of the class, but, while never in danger of making Law Review, I managed to hold my own in class discussions thanks to my debating experience.

Despite the pressures, law school was more fun than I expected, and to my surprise, I also learned a surprising amount of business and economics, particularly in the second year corporate and tax courses.

I don't second-guess myself about whether an MBA would have been more useful, because law school helped me develop a very important skill—the ability and habit of looking at every problem or conflict from all sides. If you made a particularly impassioned and effective argument for a certain position, it wasn't uncommon for the professor to say, "Okay. Now take the other side and make your counter-argument." At first this was very difficult, but in time, it helped me think on my feet and made me less dogmatic and more flexible. I also found that giving inner voices to contrasting positions helped me analyze tough decisions. Also, the extra years studying law may not have been strictly necessary from a career point of view, but they gave me more time to grow up socially.

Exploring More of Life

I arrived for registration thoroughly frustrated. After a long night's drive up from selling, I hit Boston's cow path pre-turnpike roads without signs, and was soon thoroughly lost. I was late for registration and assumed that meant only leftover classes. Instead, I found that registration was a mere formality; I had already been assigned to all my classes as well as to a single room in Story Hall. It was the first time I had ever had a room to myself, and it looked opulent.

I expected to have trouble making friends, but actually found it easier than in college. Perhaps because I had so little in common with my classmates, I was fascinated by their stories, each unique. Though they loved to tease me because I was openly religious and didn't drink, we had great conversations. Even if an odd duck, I felt accepted and genuinely liked. I was even elected as a representative on the Dorm Council. Since the Council's main job was putting on mixers, I protested that I was the least qualified for that position, but to no avail.

For exercise I took up squash and swimming. I also began to attend movies and plays at the Loeb Drama Center. I became a big fan of Bergman and Fellini. I loved the gung-hosity and lack of pretentiousness of most students. I witnessed these traits in action during exam week at the Brattle Theater. The tiny theater was packed for the annual showing of the movie *Casablanca*. From the opening credits, people were lustily cheering or booing. They knew the names of the screenwriters and producers as well as the actors. During the singing of the *Marseillaise*, the crowd stood and joined in. At the end, when the cynical French officer says, "Round up the usual suspects," the crowd went wild, all of us on our feet shouting and clapping. It was not cool, cynical cheering or booing. It was an uninhibited, genuine enthusiasm that I loved and with which I felt very comfortable.

The Dorm Council's mixers were designed to permit our largely male class to get to know women from surrounding schools like Radcliffe, Wellesley, and Simmons. While deafening music thumped through the loud speakers, men and women paraded past each other in small groups. It seemed to me a rather brutal meat market, but I was fascinated by the dancing, watched it closely, and began to try some. It was less difficult than I expected, and I discovered that I greatly enjoyed it.

While I avoided drinking at Story Hall, one Friday night toward the end of the first year, some friends in the Divinity School invited me to their rooms for a party. They were intent on introducing me to alcohol, and I was interested in finding out more about it. This was not easy to do as I'd already decided that beer and wine tasted dreadful and hard liquors even worse. However, I found that a Tom Collins of vodka and lemonade was really tasty.

I was soon saying "I'll drink to that" with some frequency, and my friends were mixing refills with double shots. When I got to my room and tried to lie down, I knew I was going to be really sick, so I walked to the shared bathroom and threw up repeatedly. Then I took a shower and fell into a deep sleep.

The next morning, Saturday, we had classes. I woke up without an alarm and though tired had no hangover; actually felt sort of cleaned out. I remembered thinking, *Getting drunk is something I want to avoid in the future, but I'm at least glad that I'm a happy drunk, not a mean one.* After class I visited my entrappers to find them all nursing dreadful hangovers. No one could believe I had come out so unscathed. I never told them I had thrown up most of the poison before going to bed.

Dad's Illness and Death

In March of my first year in law school, 1964, I received a phone call from Mother asking me to come to the mission headquarters in New Jersey. When I got there, she and Dad informed me that his medical tests at the Mayo Clinic had finally identified the source of a malaise that had been plaguing him the previous few years. He had a serious cancer, Hodgkin's disease. The only hope was chemotherapy.

Ken and Elizabeth circa 1960 with Johnny, Robin, Cathy, Harry, Marie, and Clare

The rest of that school year the family made plans to move to California. While teaching a course on missions at Fuller Seminary,

Dad would undergo chemo. Johnny and Marie would live with them in Altadena. The rest of us would continue in our respective schools, I returning to Harvard for my second year.

The reports from California were not encouraging. All of us made plans to travel there for Christmas. By the time we arrived, it was clear that the therapy hadn't worked. If anything, it was making things worse. My pain was not just that Dad was dying, but that he was being destroyed by both the disease and the "cure." His weight was drastically down and his body was covered in sores. We realized we had come home to tell our father a final goodbye.

Back in Boston in early 1965, I wrote extra mid-week letters to him. Rereading them, I notice a gentle and caring tone, but they skirt any discussion of his coming death, its anticipated impact on all of us, or the deep grief I was already feeling.

February 24, 1965, I wrote in my journal:

> 2 a.m. It seems as if the final countdown is on. In a phone call, Mother just reported that Dad won't last through the night. Why this strange feeling of distance between me and reality? Why this feeling of great detachment when that which I dreaded, when that which would wake me up in the middle of a dark night, covered with sweat and sobbing, is about to happen?
>
> Oh God, the distance evaporates and this great bitterness that I have tried to confess returns. It seems like such an insult, such a humiliation. It's bad enough to go in a flaming crash or stoned by a mob, or at the end of an Auca spear, but why a death of slowly consuming sickness? Why do You send him into the final round weighing 114 pounds, with lungs full of liquid, and wild itching that displaces any other thoughts? Deeper still, I am bitter because it was Your work that killed him—the responsibilities, the travel, the recurring sense of inadequacy for the job."
>
> 5a.m. The phone rang and Mother told me that Daddy is dead. She seemed so quiet. I lay back on my bed feeling a personal sense of loss. Before it was always in terms of the mission or Mother, or Johnny, but now it's me. Then the

tears were running down the outside of my face and almost unconsciously I was clenching my fists and saying 'God damn it!'

The only verse I can think of is that one where the man asked Jesus to let him go and bury his father and mother and Jesus answered "Let the dead bury the dead. Follow me. For no man having put his hand to the plow and turning back is fit for the kingdom of God."

I flew out to California and participated in a memorial service held at Fuller. I thanked those assembled on behalf of the family. Then with Mother and the younger children, we flew to Costa Rica with the casket for the wake in the *seminario sala* and the huge public funeral at the *Templo Biblico*.

I have a very difficult time remembering much of the period after the funeral. I suspect I was in shock. The chest pains I had had since grade school in periods of tension returned with a vengeance, and I was treated in the Harvard Holyoke Medical Center. The doctors diagnosed these as spasms of muscles around the esophagus. It was hard to concentrate on studies. I interpreted the verse "let the dead bury their dead" as, *Harry, don't ever forget the heritage Daddy gave you, but he's buried. Now get off your duff and do what I've given you to do.*

I wrote my brothers and sisters with greater frequency, but did not mention the waves of sadness that sometimes swept over me as I sat in my room studying. Mother and my siblings did the same. Our letters described what was happening in our lives and sounded upbeat. Each of us avoided burdening the others in the family with our feelings of overwhelming loss. But it was as if the lattice of the family had been broken.

I was more determined than ever to take care of myself and try to support Mother. In a letter written in 1968 to my sister Clare who had gone to live with Mother, I added a postscript:

Thanks for your Halloween letter . . . Mother in her letters is so proud of you and glad you're out there. Sometime as a surprise come up behind Mother and give her a big kiss and hug and say, "Harry asked me to give you this and say he thinks you are an A+ mother and he is very grateful for you."

There is another letter answering a request for advice on colleges from my youngest brother, Johnny, who was in high school. He was an A student, president of the youth group at church, and on the high school swim team. I include excerpts from the letter because the tone reflects the correspondence among us and throws some light on my thinking at that time.

Dear John,

Received your letter regarding college and was flattered that you would ask my advice. Will follow your outline.

<u>Academic</u>. I think you are right to be shooting for a top liberal arts education. Swarthmore or Harvard or Yale or Princeton would all be top notch in this area. Among the Christian schools, Wheaton is the best. I have not felt at all disadvantaged here at Harvard for having gone there. The quality of a school academically is closely correlated to the quality of students. It is their competition and interaction which you will find will help spur you to do your best. I'll just add that I've found that from college on, one's education is largely in one's own hands. The school makes possible the opportunity and may help stimulate you, but what you learn preparing for classes is only a part of what you need to know as you go on to the next level. So random personal reading is a good thing to keep up.

The letter goes on to evaluate the non-academic aspects, the Christian angle, and prestige. It makes the point that finances should not be a factor and that John should "shoot for the best school as you see it." I offer financial help if he needs it.

I haven't talked much of seeking the Lord's will. Personally I think there is way too much emphasis given to this so that one begins to think that advance planning is unnecessary. I think God uses much more natural means. Nevertheless, as you go through these factors, you'll realize that you can only know about 5% of the relevant factors and you'll feel your own limitation of knowledge. Here's where I think you can pray that

God, who sees further and sharper than you, will protect you from the wrong decision, perhaps by shutting a door, perhaps by shifting the relative weight of various factors in your mind. Doing all this there can be no disappointment if one school should not accept you and a sense of confidence as you come down to the point of final decision.

John I know these next few years are going to be great for you and think you're heading the right way. I'm real proud of you and I love you. If this sounds didactic, please forgive.

Your brother, Harry

Over years following Dad's death, my brothers and sisters struck out on their own paths, some rebelling more openly than others against Christianity. Each one faced the normal problems and disappointments of college and graduate school, the pressure of finances, and the heartbreak of romances. To my mother and me it felt that we were unraveling as a family. Mother didn't know what to do and would call me to talk about the issues, often weeping on the phone. To have written books on how to raise children must have added a sense of humiliation to failure. She talked of how deeply she missed my father.

I tried to help her see that some of the rebellion was a natural and important part of growing up; unfortunately, with Dad gone, the brunt of it fell on her. In our conversations and in my letters I told her that she had been and was a superb mother. But privately, her situation filled me with a deep sense of despair because nothing was going to bring Dad back, and there was nothing I or anyone could do to fill the holes in her life.

I tried to encourage her, not just to get on with her work life where we all felt she was doing an admirable job, but also to consider another romantic relation. She was still a very attractive woman, the sort that men gravitate toward, but she adamantly refused to even consider it and was upset with me for suggesting it. Though I felt I should be doing more to help everyone in the family, I knew I couldn't fill the vacuum my dad had left, and I barely had the psychic energy needed for my own life.

Deirdre and Marriage

With my nuclear family imploding, I took the first steps toward marriage and the start of my own family. At the time it felt like I was doing only what was natural and expected of any young man approaching the age of twenty-five, but looking back now, I wonder if there was a hidden need pushing me in this direction.

During the spring of my first year of law school, I went to a Saturday picnic sponsored by the Park Street Church college and grad group. Playing volleyball, I noticed a tall, statuesque girl I had not seen at any of the Sunday evening events. She had long, gorgeous auburn hair and radiated a natural innocent sexuality that attracted all the young men. She wasn't a polished athlete, but played volleyball enthusiastically. I found out she was a freshman at Mt. Holyoke, one of the seven sister colleges located in central Massachusetts. She had come to the picnic with the club for evangelical Christians on campus, a group in which she'd discovered an ardent, meaningful faith. During the twilight campfire service, we sat next to each other.

She told me later that what most attracted her about me was the way I humorously used Bible quotes in the conversation and knew all the words to the songs that we sang. She figured I must be religious, the sort of man she was looking for.

In my letter home that week I described meeting her in the volleyball game and wrote

> We teased each other and I was impressed by her quick wit, but even more the unselfconscious way she played and her natural ease and poise. When a group of us went for a five-minute walk to get something to drink, we walked together and after supper sat together at the meeting and had one of those improbable romances which are always very exciting, but rarely lead to anything. It was only as we were walking back to the car that I found out her father was a professor at Harvard in the English Department, and she found out I went to Law School. Her Celtic name is Deirdre Dunn.

By the end of the evening, I was infatuated, and she had invited me up to South Hadley for a picnic the following Saturday. I earned some notoriety in Story Hall for driving up there while everyone else madly prepared for finals the following week, exams which would determine our entire grade. We had a wonderful picnic up on a mountain, and I returned even more in love.

Wedding escort with bagpipes from Quincy House

Thus began a romance that lasted on and off throughout my law school years. Deirdre came home every few weeks for the weekend, and we exchanged regular letters. Unlike earlier infatuations in college, I believed from the beginning that Deirdre would be an ideal wife and that, by the end of law school at twenty-five, I'd be ready for marriage.

Besides her beauty and physical attraction, she appreciated my evangelical background, having had her own religious awakening in high school and college. She was smart and ambitious and expected to have her own career, similar to the women of my family. She was well-organized and efficient; I thought she would be a great mother. She was affectionate and was particularly supportive around the death of my dad. I liked her taste in clothing, art, and interior decorating, and also the fact that she was majoring in art and religion. She had what the Spanish call *mundo*, a presence and upbringing that would make her comfortable in any setting, no matter how high class. I envied the way she was clear about what she wanted and decisive in going after it.

As I came to the end of law school and she entered her last year in college, I was convinced the time had come for me to make a commitment. I was fearful that if I went into the army single, I'd become dissolute and promiscuous and not focus my energies on personal growth and work. Knowing how attractive she was to other men, I was also certain that if I didn't propose until after I returned from the army, she would not be available. In love with each other, believing that we fit together well, we decided to tie the knot as soon as she graduated. I brought her an engagement diamond and asked her father for her hand in marriage. We set the date for immediately after her early graduation from Mt. Holyoke. Our plan was to start married life together in Germany where the army was sending me.

Sibs hamming it up at my wedding: Clare, Robert,
Marie, Cathy, and John

In February of 1967, I returned from Germany to Cambridge for our wedding. It was held in the Divinity School Chapel, and bagpipers escorted us back to Quincy House for the reception. The parade attracted a great crowd of undergraduates, and the Scottish country dancing was a success with my friends and family. Deirdre and I left the next day for Spain and our honeymoon on the Malaga coast.

THE ARMY AND GERMANY

You Really Put the Fear of the Lord in Them

At the end of law school, the U.S. was still deeply enmeshed in the Vietnam War. My active duty could not be delayed. The partners in the New York firm where I'd worked while studying for the bar exam, had advised me against the Judge Advocate General's Corps (JAG). Law in the army would teach me precious little of use for a law career in New York, and it was not worth the extra year I'd have to give. So when the army asked for my preferred branch of service, I listed the Medical Service as number one, ahead of infantry and armor and the other options because of pacifistic (or more precisely, Vietnam) qualms. To my great relief, when my orders came in the spring of 1966, I found I'd be going to Germany instead of Vietnam.

When I arrived in Germany at the 5th General Hospital, my assignment was to be Assistant Registrar. I would report to Major Waters, a career officer who was plump and sported the sort of mustache British officers have in the movies. He and his friendly wife took me under their wing, and he was soon delegating most of the work to me. About six months later, a third officer, Lt. Bob Fisk, also a lawyer, joined our office. Our desks were crowded together in a room next to the large pen of open desks for the army of clerks responsible for processing medical records. We also managed six ambulances and a group of a dozen enlisted men who drove and took care of them.

The enlisted men and women we supervised were all about eighteen years of age, most just out of high school. I suspected that we got the bottom of the barrel talent-wise, with the army taking the smartest enlisted people for other critical jobs.

I noticed that the quality of effort of my clerks tended to deteriorate with time. So about every three weeks, I would wait for a particularly stupid error, then storm into the large room acting furious, threatening punishment or extra work. As Maj. Waters instructed, "You have to put the fear of the Lord in them."

When a German woman who claimed to be the wife of a big black sergeant came to deliver their baby, we found out that six months earlier another "wife" of his had come to deliver a baby. Army benefits, though generous, weren't supposed to be that generous, so we had a dilemma. After discussion, we decided we'd make an exception, but assigned our junior officer the job of making sure the sergeant understood that this was unacceptable and could not happen again without dire consequences.

Bob reported back that he had had an excellent interview that really "put the fear of the Lord into him." The sergeant was repentant and grateful for our decision. He swore he'd never do it again. When nine months later, a third German "wife" appeared at the hospital to deliver his baby, we laughingly teased the junior officer, "Yep, you really put the fear of the Lord in him!" This phrase served to remind us how little power the bars on our shoulders gave us.

There was a polite young ambulance driver from the mountains of Kentucky. He was shy, but always willing to do extra work. He struck me as having unrealized potential, so I sent him to courses to improve his skills. One night he got drunk, stole one of the ambulances from the car pool, and went on a joy ride that ended in a wreck. To make matters worse, he fought with the MPs who arrested him. Sober and deeply contrite, he told me he didn't know what got into him when he got liquored up. My options were limited and though I hated to do it, I had to recommend a court martial and dishonorable discharge.

First Lieutenant Strachan, Army MSC, Germany

Troubleshooting for Col. Miller

The 5th General Hospital had a strong pecking order among officers: doctors were at the top of the heap, followed by nurses and medical specialists, with the administrative medical service officers at the bottom. When I went into the army, I had decided to try out a new persona. I didn't tell anyone I had gone to Harvard Law School or was a missionary kid, and I thus avoided the awkwardness either piece of information introduced into the conversation. It was a good strategy. I fit in quickly and was happy to be part of the lowly MSCs. But three or four months into my assignment, someone in the personnel department leaked that I had gone to Harvard Law.

This led the commanding officer of the hospital, Col. Miller, a surgeon, to start using me as his trouble shooter. This increased my relative status and fortunately, didn't create awkwardness since most of my colleagues had accepted me as a personal friend. One of Col. Miller's first assignments was to advise him on what to do with a gynecologist caught molesting several enlisted men's wives during their medical visits. I can't remember how we defused the lawsuit, but the doctor was quickly reprimanded and shipped out.

Col. Miller also gave me the first consulting assignment of my life, namely the job of solving the financial problems of the Hospital Officers Club. It was going bankrupt for the third time; the underlying problem was that as the U.S. military presence in Germany was drawn down to supply troops to Vietnam, it became harder for officers clubs to survive on the dues and shrinking volume of business.

My first steps in designing a strategy were collecting a set of historical financial statements and interviewing a representative sample of older and younger, married, and unmarried officers regarding their preferences. I also picked the brain of the club's manager, a genial senior staff sergeant.

My conclusion was that the club really had three separate businesses: a restaurant, a hotel, and a bar. The restaurant lost a lot of money. Every time there was a crisis, it closed. Then it was invariably re-opened on the arrival of a new commanding officer. The hotel, the Visiting Officers Quarters (VOQ), had about a dozen low-cost rooms with a very low occupancy rate. The only money-making business was the bar and its slot machines. I noticed that the reported receipts from the slot machines went up when the staff sergeant was on leave.

Col. Miller accepted my strategy which was first, to close the dining hall to stop the losses and sell off all the dishes, tablecloths, and silverware. This would prevent a later administration from re-opening it, and the proceeds could cover some of the past deficit. Second, we'd offer touring bands a 40 percent discount to increase the occupancy rate at the VOQ. My hope was that after their gigs, they would come back and bring officers from other clubs. We would also push back the closing hour of the bar so that the bands could have a night cap. Occasionally, we hoped, two bands might even have an impromptu jam session that would encourage more participation.

Finally, I set up a system to correlate the slot receipts with those of the bar. I began to arrive randomly at closing time to empty the slot machines. I mentioned to the sergeant that I had some troubling evidence from the past, but wasn't going to report it unless the monitoring system showed that someone was robbing us. The slot receipts bounced up and stayed up. The sergeant supported me fully in implementing the new strategy.

Never having gone to night clubs, I believed the sexy young women singers and the hard smoking and drinking band players were far worldlier than I. One night, one of the groups invited me to have a drink. They told me about their homes in the South, and I realized that they weren't at all cynical and jaded, but rather naïve and a bit lonesome in Germany. When they found out I was a missionary kid, one took out his guitar, and we began to sing hymns. As we sang, the girls began to cry, messing up their mascara. I was deeply touched.

The Vienna Opera

After Deirdre and I married and moved into an apartment on the economy in Stuttgart, we wanted to take advantage of being in Europe, and Deirdre began planning weekend trips. As an art history major, there was much that she wanted to see. We bought a red Opel Cadet and a tent that fit into the trunk, and we'd drive to our destination with another couple, like the Colemans or the Fisks. We'd arrive Friday evening, set up tents on the outskirts of a town, put up folding lawn chairs, and have happy hour with a good Riesling. Then we'd change into our civilian best, mine being a three-piece dark suit with tie, and go to a good restaurant or concert. Other times, we'd just stay in the tent eating bread and cheese and playing bridge by lantern light.

One weekend in Vienna, we went to an opera. We had box seats on the right hand of the stage looking down on the singers. Toward the end of the opera, a large-bosomed soprano was taking an awfully long time to die. Watching the spectacle I thought, *This is too much! It's like a maudlin soap opera. Whatever makes people consider opera high art?*

Then I noticed the person sitting on my right. He was gazing down, arms folded on the rail. From his clothing and gnarled hands, he looked like a farmer who had come into the city for this event. The tears were streaming down his cheeks, and it was obvious that he was deeply moved by the music and story.

My mood instantly changed. I thought, *This man has learned to appreciate opera while you, Harry, have not. In a place deep inside of himself, he is being touched. In your ignorance, you haven't earned the right to judge!* I went back to listening with greater care.

In the years since, when I see an Indian Bollywood film or hear music from another culture, I try to remind myself of the lesson I learned in the Vienna Opera—I have no right to criticize until I have learned enough to appreciate.

Freedom to Be Happy

I did not expect to enjoy the army. I figured my challenge would be to go with the flow; to do my undemanding job well; to get along with my superiors, fellow officers, and the enlisted men I was to supervise; to take advantage of all the free time to read; and to do self-improvement projects.

To my surprise, however, I thoroughly enjoyed army life. My work was more challenging than I expected, and the extra assignments and college teaching I did added skills to my quiver. There was time for travel and vacations and enough money to enjoy it. My colleagues were interesting and unpretentious; I became fond of many of them. I did not have time for a lot of extra reading, nor I suspect, was there much self-improvement. All in all, it felt more like a low stress, happy summer vacation.

Several years later, I spent an evening in Quincy House with my father-in-law, Charles Dunn, and several of his colleagues, full professors in English at Harvard. We were spending the night so as to get to our classes in spite of a snow storm predicted to paralyze the city. With the snow whirling outside, we drank single malt whiskeys and talked. At one point I asked them when they had been happiest. To my surprise, they all believed it was in the military during World War II and the Korean War. One was a tail gunner flying in the Pacific theater. Another was responsible for supplying the army with tennis balls in Africa. None of their jobs had anything to do with their academic training or life's work. Nevertheless, in spite of the danger and boredom, they remembered their army experiences as a time of great freedom from responsibility, of camaraderie and fun. As I listened to them, I realized that except for the danger, I could have said the same.

FAMILY EVOLUTION

Mother's Death and Family Tailspin

Four years after my father's death, after law school and the army, I was back in Cambridge in the doctoral program at the Harvard Business School. One day I received a call from my "uncle" Dit Fenton, my father's best friend and now General Director of the LAM. He didn't have much in the way of details, but he needed to let me know that he had received news from Costa Rica that my mother had drowned. Her body was discovered near Puntarenas, where she had gone for a weekend at the beach. She was fifty-two years old.

Though an autopsy later suggested it was a result of a massive stroke that occurred while she was swimming, we didn't know that at the time. My journal describes my reaction to the news.

> My first thought was to wonder whether it was suicide. It all seemed to fit. Mother rarely went swimming and was

hardly likely to go alone. Her conversation with Johnny the Wednesday before had ended in tears, her saying she was a failure of a mother. She was no longer needed, her loneliness without Daddy great.

I later describe my feelings in the plane on the way to Costa Rica for her funeral.

> Thinking about Mother's life, I felt a great sense of distance from it all, that I was in a Greek tragedy which had followed its inevitable course across a great panorama covering generations. But then the movie moved from the vast sky and sea and slowly zeroed in with Panavision color and detail on one body floating in the dark water. At this point there was no sense of distance and I wept. I was struck by the juxtaposition of the calm resignation while looking at the vast panorama and the sharp grief I felt looking at a unique floating body in the water.
>
> We had grown up thinking we were a privileged family. Then Dad's death and the forces it set in motion shattered that illusion and the family began to disintegrate. By 1969 five of the six children appeared to be losing our faith in a way that distressed Mother. While I felt strongly the story wasn't yet over, the truth was our style of rebellion had soured Mother's last years.
>
> And I did regret what, in retrospect, seemed like a cruel selfishness on our part which I discussed with Clare when we joined in Miami for the rest of the trip. We felt we could not be Mother's ideal but we turned around and demanded that she be our ideal. Our letters to her had to be "true and authentic," "brutally honest." But Mother couldn't be brutally honest with us. Much better, I thought, to have written regular newsy affectionate letters.

I have no memory of the funeral in Costa Rica or the following week in which we processed her estate. My next family letter is dated June 24th after I'd returned to Boston and reflects my attempt to be an encouraging older brother.

I have been thinking of each of you often since we got back to Cambridge. I wonder what you are feeling and thinking. I wonder at times what I am feeling. There is a phrase in the Bible about how "curiously wrought" we are. Most of the time, I am busy with my life here as if San Jose and the funeral was long ago and far away. At other times I sense that right around the corner I will be feeling a gigantic hole in my life. Anything I try to say or write about my reactions to Mother's sudden death has a false ring to it.

Perhaps that's why a poem in the New Yorker late last night struck me hard. The poet's metaphor may have been Mother's literal experience

> Sailing the long hot gulf
> of her last sickness,
> out past the whispering beach,
> she saw the town lights dim.
> What were those voices shouting in her head?
>   . . .
> Now riding the slow tide
> she's dumb as driftwood, sheds
> her last light skins of thought
> easily as October.
> Mouthing the great salt flow,
> black with it, white with its foam,
> she's picturesque—no more than a design
> on the packed sand, a hieroglyph
> from another land.
>   Her Last Sickness, Sandra M. Gilbert

The letter ends with words meant to be encouraging, but which sound weak.

I came away from San Jose with a greatly increased admiration for each of you and a sense that things would be working out for all of us.

Love, Harry.
P.S. Phone at any time, even collect!

Things didn't work out quite as I expected—at least not in the short run. My brother Johnny missed the funeral because he was traveling in Europe, having dropped out of college. Several months later, I received a call from Aunt Grace informing me that Johnny and our cousin Buddy had been caught with hashish in the spare tire of their Volkswagen and had been put in jail in Barcelona. I flew to Spain to organize a legal defense for them. Three months later the charges were dropped, and they returned to the United States.

Johnny would continue to "wander in the wilderness" as my mother would have described it, first in southwestern U.S. and then in Costa Rica before his life began to take on direction. Later married and with two children, he returned to college, graduated, then got admitted with a scholarship to do graduate work in physics at Cal Poly. Ultimately he went on to a career as a scientist at Sandia National Laboratories in Albuquerque.

My other brothers and sisters rebelled, or didn't, in less dramatic ways, each of us making our way through school, marrying relatively late. Our lives took us to different geographies, I to Boston and Central America; Cathy to Ohio and then Latin America with the World Health Organization, then Washington State; Robert to Salt Lake City where he got his doctorate in psychology and became a child therapist; Clare to Boston then Brazil as a missionary working with the handicapped; and Marie to California where she became a nurse and married a minister. We stayed in touch by phone and occasional letters, often visited each other, and helped each other financially when we could.

With both Mother and Dad dead, though, the heart had been cut out of the family and we were each on our own. It felt beyond my powers to keep the family together. In any case, I was already at work with my new wife building our own family. Only later, when we were more secure in our work and lives, each with our own kids, did we begin to recover the sense of fun, mutual pride, and closeness we had known as children. It is probably only in the last fifteen years that I have felt I had the energy to be a good brother and uncle.

Launching a Family

Two years after the army and back in Boston, Deirdre completed her master's degree in social work. I had finished most of my doctoral course work and, ready to move to Nicaragua for my first teaching job, we decided to start a family.

At this time Deirdre saw a notice in the Harvard Crimson from the Harvard Medical School asking for couples who wanted to determine the sex of their child. We responded, and with about twenty-five other couples, we filled out forms asking for a lot of data. Subsequently, we were briefed on the theory and given the necessary paraphernalia.

The theory was that male sperm travel faster but die quicker; hence if you time intercourse relative to ovulation, it's possible to improve the odds of determining the child's sex by up to 80 percent. The key was recognizing ovulation and timing the intercourse.

I liked the idea. I wanted my firstborn to be a son and the second a girl. I thought I had good reasons, though later I came to realize how chauvinistic they were. I'd read about and personally experienced the impact of birth order. Firstborns tended to be more aggressive and achievement-oriented. Children born second were more socially adept. I found the first set of attributes more adaptive for a boy and the second for a girl. Deirdre, a first-born herself, strong-willed and achievement-oriented, appeared to agree.

Deirdre measured her temperature and kept a chart that signaled the right moment. Early one afternoon, I got the call and rushed home to implement our plan. Shortly thereafter, Deirdre was pregnant.

When we arrived in Nicaragua, we found a young gynecologist, Dr. Cabrera, recommended by our friend Dr. Gus Parajon. He had studied in Mexico and was open to father-assisted delivery. He was also fascinated when we told him we were part of an experiment. He described the experiment to the anesthesiologist who'd be in the room with us. The anesthesiologist considered himself a "Yale man," having taken a two-week course in New Haven earlier in his career.

Deirdre went into labor in January of 1971 in the middle of the night. We rushed to the Baptist Hospital and the large delivery room. There were six nurses in attendance, a number that struck me as a form of disguised unemployment. Gus Parajon joined us as the photographer. With the two other doctors, we scrubbed our hands and put on surgical gloves, gowns, and masks.

In the delivery room the anesthesiologist began proceedings by announcing to the nurses, "We are not here to find out what happens. We are here to deliver a baby boy certified by Harvard! Tell them, Dr. Cabrera."

Dr. Cabrera began, "When the moon is full, if you go out and find a *guayaba* tree in fruit and if you lie down under it for intercourse, the magnetism of the *guayaba* causes the male sperm . . . ." He spun out his tale, mixing in what I'd told him with the folklore of Nicaragua and plenty of his own invention. The nurses giggled. The mood in the delivery room had been set. The banter continued through the long hours of labor.

Sometime in the late afternoon, out popped Sarah! The nurses clapped at the successful delivery and the sight of a whole and beautiful baby, and then shrieked with laughter as it became clear she was a girl. The anesthesiologist melodramatically sighed, "That's Harvard for you; they can't get anything right!"

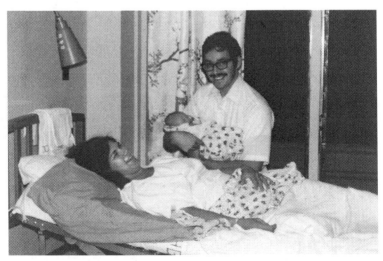

Happy parents celebrating Sarah's birth

I was thrilled. It surprised me that I was not in any way disappointed. Sarah looked exceptionally wonderful to me, even as she cried while being cleaned off. Later in Deirdre's room, we partied. While Sarah snuggled up to Deirdre's breast and got her first meal, the rest of us ate Chinese food brought in by Jim and Cathy Austin, a fellow faculty couple.

As I left the hospital late that night and walked into the dark night, I felt lightheaded from having gone thirty-six hours without sleep. A mist swept in over the hospital, turning the lights of the parking lot into white cones that looked like giant space ships pointing heavenward. It dawned on me that when Sarah reached my age, almost thirty, we would be in the twenty-first century in a world of things I could not even imagine, and I suddenly realized that I cared deeply about the future. I felt fiercely protective of Sarah and at the same time realized how powerless I was to guard her from the dangerous and painful things that would come her way. It scared me to realize how much suffering it would cause me when bad things happened to her. I'd given fate a hostage.

Kenny's Arrival

Two years later in 1972, we were still in Nicaragua at INCAE where I was academic director. We now lived in the Austin's old house near Km 11.5 on the Carretera Sur (South Highway). Christmas was approaching and Deirdre was pregnant, with our second child due in a week or so.

We were awakened at midnight by the violent rocketing of our bed back and forth across the room. There was a roar of noise that sounded like a tidal wave rolling through the house. I jumped out of bed and was thrown to the floor. On hands and knees, I crawled back into bed. I covered Deirdre's head with my pillow, certain the roof was about to fall on top of us.

As soon as the shaking stopped, I raced into Sarah's room. She was sound asleep. As I picked her up from the crib, I heard flowing water in the bathroom next to her room. Looking in by moonlight, I could see a dark hole where the toilet had been—the wash basin had been ripped from the wall, and water was spurting from the broken pipes.

We ran out of the house and into the front yard, and Deirdre and Sarah sat in the Toyota to stay warm, as the second earthquake hit. The trees bounced, as a wave about two feet high rolled through the ground. The car jumped and swayed, and I feared it would roll down the hill.

Down below, we could see fiery eruptions that later proved to be gas stations exploding, and other fires sprang up across the city. We decided to drive down to check on the Parajons, but a giant fissure in the road blocked our way. As the extent of the damage became clear, we realized we should be ready to deliver the baby on our own.

In the morning I borrowed a motorcycle and toured the city. The Baptist Hospital had been leveled, and Managua's other main hospital had collapsed like an accordion. Gus Parajon's advice was to get Deirdre out of the country. "Delivery won't be a problem if we have hot water and some drugs, but it's likely that there will be disease in the aftermath and a shortage of medicines. It's not going to be a great environment for a new baby."

Mike and Judy Dean, friends from the faculty, came by to check on us. I asked Mike if he would go to the airport and try to get us tickets out of Nicaragua. Deirdre was calm and organized. She had already packed a suitcase and put Sarah in a cute dress as if ready for a party.

Still covered with dust that I'd picked up on my motorcycle ride, I drove them to the airport by back roads, arriving in late afternoon. The top floor of the terminal was twisted, dark, and empty. Planes were just beginning to arrive with relief aid, and I found Mike on the runway, impeccably dressed as usual, directing the discharge of cargo. He'd gotten us onto a LACSA Medivac plane that had been emptied of seats to make room for litters. The plane was nearly empty because so few injured had been able to get to the airport.

The plane took off at sunset with a few patients and the three of us sitting in back with the nurses. When we arrived in San Jose, an ambulance took us straight to the *Clínica Bíblica* since Deirdre was already in labor. Reporters interviewed me in the anteroom about the damage in Nicaragua until Deirdre insisted I either help her with her breathing or go with them into the corridor. Charles Kenneth was born about six hours later in the early morning hours.

I was thrilled to have a son in addition to my daughter and relieved that the delivery had gone smoothly. It felt special that he had been born in the same hospital in which I had been born, founded by his great grandparents and directed by his grandfather. When he grew up, he could also be a *tico* (nickname for Costa Ricans).

With Ken's arrival a complete family enjoys visit of
Master Charles Dunn of Quincy House

WORK

FINDING MY VOCATION

A Moving Boat

In recent years, Tom Tierney, the former managing director of Bain, and I have taught a module in Bain's New Partner Training called "Success in Your Career and Life." We discuss, among other things, what distinguishes Bain partners who continue to grow and achieve great success from those that don't.

We agree that one of the critical success factors is a "purposeful life." We urge new partners to develop a life plan if they haven't already done so, and to regularly review it to evaluate their objectives and what is happening. I even distribute a set of planning exercises that have been useful to me. Though Tom and I plan in very different ways, we each believe being purposive about our lives has been an important determinant to whatever success we've achieved.

My message in these sessions is that it's important to take your own life seriously. Each of us is born with a unique set of talents and capabilities, not necessarily better than that of others, but nevertheless unique. Each of us also inhabits a unique moment of history. This gives us the opportunity to make a special contribution, and gives us a particular "mission." If you find and fulfill your mission, you'll have a happy life. If you don't, no matter how much money or fame you achieve, you won't.

I consciously use words that resonate with moral seriousness, perhaps even a certain pretentiousness, because I believe that moving into the future with intention pays huge dividends. To a person who has not experienced what I'm describing, however, phrases like "life planning" and "finding your life's work" might create unrealistic expectations similar to those I had in high school and college.

The religious world into which I came of age described this reality as "finding God's will for your life." This led many of us to expect some sort of divine blueprint to arrive in our mailbox. But my actual experience was more complicated and less magical, and it may be helpful in clarifying how life planning worked for me.

There were three practices that helped get me started in the right direction in high school and college.

First, my father emphasized that "if a thing is worth doing, it's worth doing well." This was good advice because most attractive options for the future are based on achievements of the past. Doing every activity, however insignificant, to the best of one's ability, is one of the best ways of opening doors of future opportunity.

The second idea came from David Howard, a missionary "uncle" that I greatly admired. In college he told a group of us, "The Lord's will is like a rudder; it only works on a boat that is moving. In absence of clarity about what you should be doing, don't wait dead in the water. Take the option in front of you that makes the most sense and get going." Therefore in college, law school, and the army, even when I didn't know how my life would end, I tried to keep my little boat moving.

Finally, my parents believed that everything learned would one day turn out to be useful, perhaps in unexpected ways. They encouraged me to try new things, experiment, and get involved. There was no class that didn't teach something valuable. Every job, however menial developed a skill that would be useful. Able to do my schoolwork quickly in high school, I persuaded the headmistress to let me take typing and then mechanical drawing during study hall. These skills led to higher paying jobs in college. My decision to go to law school wasn't as much for a career path as it was to continue my education and to explore areas I knew nothing about. I wanted additional skills as well as credentials. In the army, I took a job teaching law at the University of Maryland Extension campus, in part to gain experience teaching and in part for the extra money.

I nevertheless envied friends who knew exactly what they wanted. I sometimes wondered if, because I didn't know what I wanted, there was something wrong with me. Some had superior talents that made their careers obvious. John Nelson was such a musical prodigy and so passionate about classical music that it was a foregone conclusion he'd go to Julliard and into a life dedicated to music. Another law school acquaintance was distinguished, not by some blinding talent, but by his clear desires. Though he'd lived only in New York City, he arrived in Cambridge with a single objective in mind—he wanted to be a tax lawyer in Hawaii. He'd never even been to Hawaii, but he was certain that is where he wanted to go, and this made his course decisions and job search very simple.

Berchtesgaden Options

At the end of my tour in the army, I was twenty-seven years old and married, with nineteen years of education under my belt. I felt I could no longer duck the question of a career, and I agonized over the decision. When I looked for my inner passion, there was nothing I could envision doing for the rest of my life. Nor did I have a stellar set of talents that pointed me in a clear direction.

I therefore began a planning process by first trying to visualize options that appealed to me and might be realistic. I identified and fleshed out three possible careers:

I could return to New York and work my way up one of the good Wall Street law firms. After law school, I'd spent the summer in New York City, and I'd passed the bar exam while working there. I had several attractive offers from prestigious firms. The pay was good; I could try to make it to partner. If successful, I could move over into a management position with one of my corporate clients or take on public assignments.

Another option was to move to a community in Oregon, join a small law firm or put out my solo shingle. I'd make investments to achieve some degree of financial independence. Later I'd get involved in local politics and who knows where that might lead. A college hero of mine had been Senator Mark Hatfield, a liberal Republican senator from Oregon, and though I'd never been to Oregon, its vibrant, liberal reputation had caught my attention. The idea of sinking roots deeply in a place was very attractive.

My third option was to return for more education. I envisioned a doctorate that would permit me to learn more about economics, business, and politics. I could develop teaching skills or work in a development entity like the World Bank. It wasn't that I had a great passion to be a professor, so much as having a desire for options for international work. Among the programs I investigated, the doctorate at the Harvard Business School seemed the most flexible. Being in Boston would also permit Deirdre to get her masters in social work.

Once I had several realistic options, the next step was to evaluate them. I took advantage of an army religious retreat in Berchtesgaden, one of Hitler's vacation hideaways in the Alps, and slipped out of the meetings to a cave on the side of the mountain that had been a bunker. Looking out over the valley, I listed the criteria I should use in the decision and gave each factor a relative weight, one to five. My plan was to calculate a single number that reflected the relative attractiveness of an option by multiplying the score of each criteria times its weight and adding up all the factors.

Long before I had tabulated the results, I knew that the doctorate was my first choice. Though I enjoyed my summer in the law firm, I felt that as a lawyer, I'd be helping grease the wheels for others rather than being the active decision-maker I wanted to be. Oregon felt like too great a break with my past. Before abandoning work in Latin America and my family legacy, I should at least try to work abroad. I therefore chose more education and a chance for overseas work. Fortunately, Boston was also Deirdre's first choice.

First Life Plan

My doctorate at Harvard Business School and my paying job with the Harvard Development Advisory Service generated options for starting my career after completing the course work. We decided to accept INCAE's offer, largely because of INCAE's vision as a change-agent in Central America. I would be able to teach finance and work on my thesis on the role of business groups in economic development.

A good friend, Rodolfo (Fito) Paiz, returned to INCAE from Harvard during my second year on staff. He persuaded several of us to join him in a life-planning exercise that he'd discovered in

Cambridge. It involved writing a life plan using the same methodology as for a company's strategy. We each did the suggested homework, and subsequently we drove to the beach with our documents, a bottle of rum, and a cooler of Coke, to critique each other's plans.

As I tried to envision my options, I realized that while there were many things I wanted to do, there was nothing I wanted to do for the rest of my life. I therefore wrote up a life plan that called for ten years in academia, ten years in business, and ten years in public service. I figured I'd die young like my dad, so I didn't plan past sixty.

The exercise required setting specific goals, and I assumed I had done this when I made my academic goals to publish a book and learn to be a good teacher. Fito insisted that those goals were too vague. Exasperated at his prodding, I finally said, "Okay, tenure at Harvard Business School." We all laughed at what seemed like a preposterous goal.

I also had two objectives for the ten years in business: to learn to be a good manager and to achieve financial independence. When Fito again pushed for specifics I shared my formula for measuring financial independence.

"Not specific enough, Harry," he replied. "Give me a number. How much do you need to have enough?" I thought a minute, did some mental calculations that allowed me to significantly increase my current budget, and said, "two million in 1970 U.S. dollars." Again we laughed at what seemed wildly audacious, given that our current yearly salaries were under $20,000.

The last ten years of public service were the vaguest in my mind, but again pressured by the others, I said, "Undersecretary of the Treasury for Latin America Affairs." I figured that was the position from which I could most directly affect U.S. assistance for development in Latin America. Again, with all of us feeling the effects of the rum, my answer generated much laughter.

I left the beach in no way feeling I had committed myself to a course of action. But what happened was that I got in touch with some inner desires and visualized a path into the future. Looking back, it's amazing to me how closely that 1970 plan foreshadowed my life. I spent nine years as an academic at INCAE and Harvard, and then returned for a year as Rector. I was a businessman with Bain & Co. for twelve years before returning to Central America for public service. Thanks to Bain

Capital, I became financially independent. My experience working with the U.S. government on trade policy during the mid-1980s convinced me that Washington was not where I wanted to do my public service. Instead I began to think of Central America, which is where I've been since 1993 in what I consider my "social service" period.

In the years that followed, Fito and I would get together to discuss what was happening in our lives and consult each other on important decisions. As a result, I got into the habit of writing an annual plan.

During the last week of August, Deirdre, I, and the kids would take a family vacation. I'd use the mornings to reread the previous year's plan and to do some exercises to help me evaluate my current situation and explore the issues I was facing. Then I'd update my long-term goals and ask the question, "To have a chance of reaching those goals, what must I do this next year?" Some of my objectives and plans had to do with work and finances. Others concerned family relationships, travel, vacations, hobbies, or personal learning. At the end of the vacation week, I'd pull my work together and write up the plan for the coming year.

The Job as Platform

From my first job onward, I regularly experienced an existential crisis. "Is my job really the right one? Is the wear and tear of long hours and travel worth it? Should I be putting my energy somewhere else?" These questions plagued me at INCAE, Harvard, and Bain.

My way of dealing with this inner restlessness was to spend hours imagining other careers or jobs, writing long journal entries, articulating the pros and cons of different options. Prior to my return to teach at Harvard, I explored a variety of jobs in investment banking, academic think tanks, and the World Bank, visiting a number of different cities. I even wondered whether I should return to a career in law. Many of the positions I was offered were attractive, but none felt perfect.

Somewhere in the early 1980s, I had an epiphany which, while not totally eliminating these periods, did dramatically change my experience of job satisfaction. I realized that searching for "the perfect job" was futile. There was no job out there that was perfectly aligned with my talents and ambitions. This was not surprising because my objectives were many and varied: making money, getting promoted, having impact, making friends, ending poverty, adding to the world's knowledge, etc. Most organizations require more focus.

Instead of asking, "What job?" I needed to ask myself, "What is it that I should be doing? What is worth my time, energy, and talent?" I gave myself the speech that I now give others, "Imagine, Harry, without falling into the trap of grandiose self-inflation, that you have a unique set of talents. Imagine that you're on this earth to do something. What is your mission, and what type of person do you have to become to achieve it?"

Approaching the problem this way, the focus shifted away from which "job" to which activities, roles, and contributions. These weren't always easy to identify, but it was easier than finding a perfect job.

The next question was, "What organization is the best platform for me to be doing these things?" The schools where I'd taught, INCAE and the Harvard Business School, had been great platforms in an earlier period of my life, but they were not what I needed in the 1980s. When I had the right goals, I was surprised to find how many could be achieved from the platform on which I was standing. Bain had obvious advantages—namely, learning, self direction, encouragement for community contributions, financial income, and investment opportunities.

So I discovered my job wasn't the cause of my restlessness. It didn't put significant constraints on me. It wasn't unbalancing my life. I was doing that to myself. I could do many of the things I wanted to do, like staying in touch with Central America and contributing to the region by being on the board of INCAE or linked to Harvard. This was actually complementary to my work at Bain.

If this insight was relevant for me, it was also relevant for everyone on my team. About that time, I told my direct reports and teams, "None of us were born to make Bain a big success. Bain & Company exists to help each of us, individually and collectively, achieve our goals in life. What are they? How can we organize our work to help you advance your life plan?"

Implicit in this was the recognition that for some, Bain would be a two-year stint before another platform presented itself. For others, it might be eight or ten years, and for still others, Bain would be the best vehicle for their entire career.

In a weekend retreat at Nantucket with my direct reports, we began the session by going around the circle of eight and having each person share his or her long-term aspirations. One admitted that he hoped to be Secretary of Navy, and once he was financially independent, he wanted to be a professor. Another had his heart set on becoming CEO of a Fortune 500 company and had had this ambition since before college. A third, with a strong tech talent and a fascination with PC products, wanted to head the product development division of a major software company and then become a film maker. A fourth was drawn to private equity. Several visualized themselves with Bain for their entire career, but even these had different aspirations. One felt the role of office head would fit her life. Another was more interested in writing books and becoming a recognized expert.

When we later focused on the main agenda of our retreat—full potential for clients, account plans, our marketing and sales effort—we were surprised to find the number of creative ways these activities could be organized and allocated so they also advanced personal plans. In the year that followed, we not only continued to tailor assignments to long-term objectives, but found that, now that we knew what each one wanted, we could help in other ways, like with introductions, books, articles, etc. We became invested in each person's larger mission and became closer friends. It even gave our Bain work an added sense of importance.

If You Can See It Clearly

I've mulled over the question of why planning, or more precisely, visualizing the future, has been so powerful for me. Several answers come to mind.

Planning put me in touch with my inner desires. Visualization helped me see things in time and space, so that I could recognize opportunities as they presented themselves. I could also spot traps likely to lead me astray.

The process taught me that thinking about *whom* I wanted to become was as important as what I wanted to do. Success in both doing and being were deeply linked. One quote says, "You tend to become what you do," and another suggests, "Be careful what you ask for, for you shall surely get it." Who I am and what I do are inextricably bound together.

Finally, however flaky it might sound, I've become convinced there is truth to the quote attributed to Ralph Waldo Emerson, "Once you make a decision, the universe conspires to make it happen." If you can see something clearly and wish for it with all your heart, the powers of the universe mobilize themselves to help you get it.

During an August vacation/planning session around 1985, I decided that even if my Bain workload was heavy, it was important to get politically active if I expected to have opportunities for public service in my third decade. So in my plan, I wrote. "I'd like to do some pro bono work this year that will get me closer to government." I had no idea of what to do to make this happen.

A week after returning from the vacation, Bill Bain called me into his office. He had received a request from John Young, the president of Hewlett Packard who was heading up a Presidential commission on industrial competiveness. The sub-group entrusted with the task of U.S. trade policy was in disarray, and he was asking Bain for a pro bono team to help lead them to a coherent set of recommendations for reconciling tensions between the "free trade" and "fair trade" factions. Bill felt that, given my experience teaching at Harvard, I was the best qualified for this job. Fearing I'd be resistant, he made it clear that the firm would reward my efforts if I were willing to undertake the assignment.

I immediately recognized this as the very opportunity I had wished for in the previous week. I wasn't sure that a small Bain team made up primarily of young MBAs would be able to contribute much in an area where the government had hundreds of PhD economists working, but it was worth a try. We did a huge amount of theoretical and practical reading on the nature of trade economics. We met with the economists in the U.S. Trade Office and talked with people from many different sectors who were competing in the international arena. We also found a way to pull together a presentation for a national strategy based on good data. It advocated a more open world trade system, but one that took measures to ensure a level playing field.

There were about fifty businessmen in the large sub-committee, and they found the presentation persuasive and endorsed it. The government economists also liked it, and a large number of senators supported our suggestions. It was fun flying to meetings in the private jet of our subgroup chairman. He became a friend and offered to connect me with leading politicians in his party. It would have been a wonderful doorway to a position in Washington, but ironically, what I saw during this project convinced me that D.C. was not the place I wanted to live. Instead, it got me thinking of returning to Central America for my third career.

The Work I Did

So what then became my mission? The sectors in which I played were academia, business, and the social sector. Four organizations paid my salaries: INCAE, the Harvard Business School, Bain & Co, and Mesoamerica. My job titles over the years were instructor, associate professor, academic director, rector, consultant, manager, partner, Group VP, and managing director.

But though titles and organizations changed, what filled my days tended to be the same sort of activities, though perhaps in different proportions. What I did was case method teaching, strategy consulting, management chores, investing and mentoring. The consistent thread has been training leaders, helping them find good strategies for their organizations, and encouraging them to make contributions to the larger society.

There is not room in this book for all my work stories. Some have been collected in the INCAE and Bain books mentioned earlier; others I hope to collect in a sequel on the Mesoamerica years. The examples that follow are designed to give a taste of what I did and why it was so meaningful to me.

TEACHING AND LEARNING

Wowing Them in the Doctoral Program.

The first year in the doctoral program I was surprised at how much pleasure I got from my demanding academic workload and particularly from the study of business by the case method. Those of us who didn't have our MBAs from HBS were required to take the DIGs (Doctoral Instructional Group courses), a mini-MBA. The DIGs were my first exposure to marketing, production, organizational behavior, strategy, and finance, as well as the HBS case method.

A typical case began with a paragraph presenting a situation, usually one involving a real executive confronting a unique business situation, such as:

> At 8 a.m. John Smith, the CFO of Big Business, Inc., sat at his desk cursing the bank's decision to cut back on his line of credit and wondering how he should explain the disappointing second quarter financial results.

The following pages generally described the industry, provided a history of the company, and data on its financial problems. This information was both explicit and buried in the financial statements and statistics in the appendices. Harvard proudly claimed that three cases a day during a two-year MBA program gave the typical MBA a wider set of business experiences than a typical executive faces in a lifetime, and that these vicarious experiences were the foundation of good judgment.

As in law school, the professor generally called on someone to "present the case," that is, describe the decisions or issues faced. Unlike the law school, the professors did not grill one student or raise hypothetical cases. Rather they jotted down the main points on the blackboard and pushed the discussion forward, sometimes with questions, sometimes asking for supporting evidence. It was not uncommon for thirty or more students to participate in a class. When differences arose, the professor might simply direct the back and forth traffic.

A good case method teacher did not take a position. He or she forced the student to make a decision, defend a position, and explain how to implement the decision. One of the school's guiding principles was that each business situation was unique. Rarely was there one right answer, although there might be many wrong ones. The student's objective was to develop skill in identifying the core issues, processing data, and making sound, implementable decisions.

Coming from the Harvard Law School, which also used the case method and many of the same words (like "key issues," "sound analysis," and "good judgment"), I assumed I knew what was required to make a positive impression. My strategy was to read the case carefully, do the required analysis, understand the options, and prepare my solution.

I figured that being brilliant meant understanding the obvious, but seeking out the hidden, subtle problems. What differentiates top law students from the run-of-the-mill is the ability to anticipate bizarre situations that are unlikely but possible. Anyone can make up an inheritance will for the typical situation of grandchildren, but it takes a great lawyer to anticipate the marriages and divorces or adoptions and disinheritances that might occur and write a will that reflects what grandparents would want should such situations materialize after they die.

Prepared with my subtle analysis, my strategy was to wait to make my intervention until the second half of class, letting others make the obvious points. At an opportune moment I would raise my hand and raise the unexpected angles of the case, expecting to wow both the professor and my classmates.

Sure enough the class would come to a halt. No one quite knew what to do with the point I had made. No one had thought of it, mainly because it was so highly unlikely as to be irrelevant. The professor would roll his eyes at the comments that had momentarily derailed the discussion, then quickly call on someone else to get the class going again.

After a few of these "lead balloon" interventions, I realized that "good judgment" meant something different in business than it did in law. The good lawyer was paid to anticipate and guard against low-probability events. The business executive was paid to be practical and focus on what was most likely to occur.

It's Unfair

In my second year of teaching at INCAE, I was asked to develop a new course called Management of Financial Institutions. Harvard had a solid course on money and banking, but it contained virtually nothing on the nuts and bolts of running a bank. Stanford, though, had a wonderful course with just the materials I needed, and they gave me permission to translate them into Spanish.

Shortly before the semester was to begin, I gave about fifteen cases, each with twenty-five pages of text and fifteen pages of dense tables and charts to Veronica Gurdian, the efficient manager of the translation department. She told me that a complete translation by the deadline was impossible. So we negotiated a deal where they would translate the text, and I would provide an English-Spanish key for the labels and words in the tables and charts.

The time frame was so tight that students got their cases damp off the press in the late afternoon of the day before class. The cases had not been proofed to ensure that the technical terms were accurately translated. Students would read the too-long cases late into the night, struggling to make sense of the tables and charts. The next day, I would push them mercilessly in my poor Spanish, not only to unravel complex business models, but also to discover the subtle aspects of each case.

About halfway through the course, thoroughly frustrated, the class persuaded one of the best students to voice a request for a significant lightening of the load and the elimination of the half-translated cases. He was eloquent. He was also right—the cases were confusing, the class was being overloaded with reading, and this was negatively affecting their ability to prepare for other classes.

His only mistake was using the argument that it was "unfair" to expect INCAE students to be able to solve these cases, since their university preparation was not at Stanford's level. This touched a hot button in me.

Inappropriately in hindsight, without collecting more information from the class, or listening well, I soared off on a passionate speech that went something like this:

> You're right—it is unfair! It's unfair to ask you to work harder than MBA students in the U.S. It's unfair that you

haven't had access to the university training they have had. It's unfair that most of the business literature is in English and not Spanish. You are absolutely right. And it's only going to get more unfair when you interview for jobs or make sales calls and find that you are discriminated against because of your poor English and perhaps the color of your skin or the way you dress. That's why for you to succeed and for Central America to have any chance of closing the wealth gap with rich countries, you must demand more of yourselves, not less. You have to work harder! Read more! Analyze better! Put in longer hours! INCAE is not here to make it "fairer" for you. We are here to help you overcome the unfairness by demanding levels of effort, skills, work habits you now consider impossible. Now let's get back to the case and start building the muscles you're going to need for the unfair journey ahead!

As I look back on this incident, I'm embarrassed by my insensitivity. Having coached other young professors, I should have asked questions and understood the situation before responding.

But in my visceral, unreasonable response, there was an element that was profoundly correct. It reflected an attitude that made INCAE special in those early years for everyone associated with it. We all held ourselves up to standards of excellence measured by comparing ourselves to the Harvards and Stanfords of the world. We knew we had to work harder, actualize more of our talent, and help each other, but we believed we could compete at the highest level. And we felt it was critical to the region's development that we do this.

And the careers of many of the students, who continued to work these difficult cases, proved the value of those aspirations.

Ayagualo and Political Polarization

We developed a number of new cases during my time at INCAE while Director of the Development Banking Program. One was on the *Banco de Fomento Agropecuario* (Bank for Agricultural Development) of El Salvador. Once the case was written, this state-owned bank asked us to lead a weekend strategy workshop for its board of directors and top management team. The three-day seminar included cases on strategy, team building exercises, and a simple financial model to test the financial implications of the various options. The seminar was a big success.

Harry in academic splendor at the INCAE Campus in Nicaragua

The bank's president, don Roberto Castillo, was a courtly gentleman who was also president of a relatively new housing foundation. He and the leadership of the foundation, Padre Ibañez and Alberto Harth, asked us to lead a similar seminar to help them develop an ambitious growth strategy that might tap into World Bank funding.

Fundación de Vivienda Mínima's (Foundation for Low-income Housing's) first project had been building housing for fifty families who lost their homes in a flood. It was an unusual organization in many ways. It conceived its mission to be more than building houses: the most important "product" was the community that emerged from people building their houses together and their increased capability for solving their problems.

The staff and board spanned a broad spectrum of conflicting political ideologies. Padre Ibañez was a Jesuit priest whose philosophy was greatly influenced by the theology of liberation. Many of the community organizers were self-declared "communists." Alberto Harth had his doctorate in architecture from MIT, and his management team tended to be professional engineers. The blue chip board had recruited many scions of the wealthiest families of the country who had just returned from their U.S. MBAs full of idealism. These included Bobby Murray, Ricardo Poma, and Francisco de Sola, Jr.

The strategy workshop was held in the mountains outside San Salvador in a monastic retreat center called Ayagualo. The deputy director, Mauricio Silva, who met me at the airport, explained they had a "slight problem." The community developers had decided to boycott the seminar because I was from Harvard and a "capitalist." Alberto Harth was negotiating with them to at least come to the first evening session before walking out.

We arrived at Ayagualo mid-afternoon. I checked on the classroom and was dismayed to find that the sessions were to be held in the chapel, as the columns cut off the view of the front, the dim lighting made reading the old blackboards difficult, and I feared the reverberating echoes would make any case method dialogue hard to understand.

Totally demoralized, I went to my bedroom, a monk's cell, and lay on a cot so narrow my arms fell off the sides. As I stared up at a crucifix on the white wall, I wondered if I was in for similar treatment. *What in the world*, I asked myself, *leads me to take on these quixotic assignments?* Though I tried to figure out how to handle the challenge of that evening's case (Alberto's negotiations had been successful), I was still bereft of ideas when the session started.

The first case was on a development bank in the Dominican Republic. It had nothing to do with politics or ideology, so far as I could see. Nevertheless, ten minutes into the class, after we had managed to get the major strategic issues of the bank identified, a young man raised his hand. "I don't think this case can be resolved until the philosophical issues have been addressed," he said.

I thought *Shit, here comes the challenge.* Stalling for time, I asked, "What do you mean, Carlos?"

"Well, until the bank realizes the underlying class conflict . . ." and he went on to make a rambling Marxist statement.

On impulse I said, "If I understand what you're saying, Carlos . . ." and I let loose an eloquent Marxist speech on exploitation of the proletariat, the inevitability of class conflict with the bourgeoisie, and how this cannot be resolved except by total domination of the proletariat. (At the same time, I said a thankful prayer that at one time I'd tried to understand Marx and the Communist Manifesto.) Then I wrote up a quick summary on the board. Somewhat taken aback, Carlos stammered that, yes, more or less, that is what he meant.

Among the shocked gasps, I turned and walked across the room to stand in front of don Roberto, who happened to be married to one of the largest landowners in El Salvador. "I think he is talking about you, don Roberto. What do you think?"

Don Roberto, caught off guard, started to stammer some conciliatory words, but I stepped in and said, "Don Roberto is far too much of a gentleman to say it, but I suspect he is thinking . . ." and I gave my most eloquent defense of individual freedom, market efficiency, and capitalism, and wrote the key points on the right side of the board across from my summary of Carlos' position.

By now there was total silence in the room and a palpable tension. I walked back over to Carlos' side and said, "Assuming, Carlos, you could persuade everyone in this room of your position—everyone that is except don Roberto—what would you have the Foundation do next year?"

I went to the board while he began, "Well, I'd make a plan to build a thousand houses, get funding from the World Bank, ..." I wrote each idea on the left side of the board under the Marxist ideology.

Turning to don Roberto, I said, "Don Roberto, assuming for the minute you could persuade everyone here to your point of view—everyone that is except Carlos—what would you have the Foundation do next year?"

He began, "Well, I'd make a plan to build a thousand houses, get funding from the World Bank, ..." Before he could finish or I could write up his answer, the room burst into laughter.

I said, "We can use the three days to discuss our political philosophies or we can work on a strategy for the Foundation. What do you want to do?" The vote was unanimous to work on the strategy.

The workshop was a great success. The results got them World Bank money and they built one thousand homes. The Foundation became a much admired and replicated model of low-income housing in Latin America.

Ayagualo ended up paying huge dividends. I learned a lot about pragmatism and dialogue. I made friends across the political divide, some of whom ultimately became my closest friends in the region. It led to many more opportunities for workshops, including several with government cabinets that in turn, pushed me to learn more about political processes and political solvency during the change process.

CONSULTING

Hospitals and Strategy

One day in the period after I had been made a Bain partner, Bill Bain asked me to leave a New York client I was working with. This company had recently had a major breakthrough, and the future looked promising, but Bill wanted me to become the head for a major client whose prospects did not look good. The company in question was in the health care industry, and Bain's work with them had started when changes in health care reimbursement began to significantly impact their profitability. Bain had helped them implement a program of capacity rationalization and cost cutting, but in spite of their efforts, margins continued to shrink. The solution that the investment bankers had proposed and our client had accepted was to acquire another health sector company roughly its same size, a solution Bain had advised against.

As a result, the client's CEO had decided to wind down Bain's role and bring in a fresh group of consultants. He had great respect for Bain and was quick to enumerate the many areas in which they had helped transform his company. He respected the fact that the Bain team had stuck by its analysis and advised against the merger. But since he and the board had instead chosen to make the acquisition, he felt he should get another consultant. When you're in port deciding whether or not to sail, you want a navigator who will give you dispassionate advice and assessment of the odds. If you're out on the high seas in a storm, you want a navigator committed to making the voyage a success, determined to find some way out of the problem, not thinking, "I told you so."

Both Bill Bain and John Halpern, the project director, thought Bain could still play the role of the navigator, but decided they needed to put a fresh face as client head, without losing the accumulated experience of the Bain team. They persuaded the CEO to give them a chance to develop a strategy to make the acquisition pay off, and I was asked to come over as head of the one Bain team that was still working at the company.

I was flattered to be chosen for an assignment that required "fresh, creative strategizing." I was much less excited when I realized they expected me to leave my New York client and nearly three times the monthly billings. I tried to persuade them to let me work on both, fearful that my compensation would be negatively affected and that the odds were against turning things around for the new client. But John patiently convinced me that the job required focused effort and that this was how I could best help the firm. He assured me I could trust the Bain compensation system.

I began to fly to the job on Mondays, staying through to Friday. I tried to absorb all the work Bain had done in the various divisions. John introduced me to other members of the client management team and let me sit in on his meetings with the CEO. I debriefed him on my meetings and shared impressions, hypotheses, plans, and drafts of any presentations.

I also began to walk the halls of headquarters to get to know the staff and top management. Immediately after the acquisition, in an attempt to ensure that the human resources of both firms were not lost, the two management teams were merged. Instead of one CEO and six vice presidents, there were now two co-CEOs and twelve vice presidents. There had been little reallocation of responsibilities. Everyone knew that the current organization was untenable long-term, but until the strategic direction for the combined organizations was clear, this was regarded as the best way to maintain momentum and assure people of a legitimate chance to prove themselves in the new entity.

I was initially reluctant to ask for a vice president's time unless I had a specific topic for the meeting or some interesting analysis to share. Soon, though, I found that my best interviews occurred when I came in with no fixed agenda but curious to get to know the VP, his business, what he thought needed changing, and what he would do if in the CEO's shoes.

At first, the conversations were guarded since the atmosphere was highly political. I took copious notes and promised confidentiality of anything that might be interpreted as critical. I took the promise seriously, and as a result, the tone of the meetings changed, and we punched down to a more authentic level of communication.

Soon I was hearing a lot of anxiety, frustration, and resentment, some of which included resentments against Bain. Many executives in our original client and virtually all in the newly acquired company believed "real managers don't use consultants." There were negative feelings about all the changes introduced by the merger, as well as the normal rivalries of a large corporation.

Though it wasn't comfortable to bear the brunt of these negative feelings, anytime I heard of someone bent out of shape, I'd follow the advice of "bearding the lion in his den," go directly to the unhappy persons, and try to understand the source of their criticisms. As a new face, I didn't have to pretend to know a lot about the business, nor was I forced to judge or defend any particular position. I could be loyal to everyone and presume good intentions.

I did, however, try very hard to distinguish the source of concerns about strategy, and whether they were based on data or solely on tradition. I assumed that buried in the idea that "this is how we did it" were two important elements. First, we needed to preserve and build upon the things that had made them great, what in business jargon are called "core competencies." Second, we had to identify those things that were no longer adaptive in the new regulatory and competitive environment and had to be changed. Many times they were hard to separate.

I also spent a lot of time with the Bain consultants and managers who had been working before I arrived. They were a brilliant group. At times it felt we were looking for a pony in all the horse manure. But gradually a strategy emerged that integrated ideas from a number of different sources. The strategy felt brilliant to me, though I've forgotten some of the elements.

I know we started with the hospitals' needs. Our client sold supplies and services to hospitals. Some of Bain's work showed that hospitals spent on average about a dollar managing supplies (selecting, negotiating, storing, and moving them) for each dollar they spent on the actual supplies. Virtually no one in the hospital was happy with the time this took or the "fill rate" of supplies at the point where they were needed.

From work with other clients, we appropriated the idea of "Value Managed Relations" (VMRs), a concept based heavily on the Japanese model of vendor relations. The idea was that in purchasing supplies, it makes sense to substitute the traditional annual auction between vendor and buyer with a long-term agreement in which both parties commit to sharing information about the value chain, where mechanisms are set up to share the savings, and where the buyer is ensured that his costs will come down the experience curve. In the auto industry, the savings in time and capital made possible by this approach represented most of the competitive advantage achieved by the Japanese over their U.S. competitors in the 1980s.

Under the severe cost pressures of the environment, the new strategy would be to expand services for hospitals, help them with inventory management and logistics. The merger had given the client the largest line of products and services, and they were now in a unique position to help hospitals solve supply chain problems, to buy better, and to deliver products in a more timely fashion. The hospitals would receive guarantees of cost containment and a share of the savings that resulted from rationalizing supply management and from the cost savings in logistics and selling. Growth could come from new products and services that could be added to our client's system.

The amount of change involved to implement the strategy was huge. It required a new relation of trust with clients. It involved consolidating the sales forces and a new way of selling based more heavily on economics and hard analysis. It entailed developing skills and systems for delivery of new services to hospitals. It required new pricing and long-term contracts in an environment where inflation was significant. It involved consolidating plants and distribution centers across the United States. And it called for, above all, a redoubling of efforts to get all unnecessary costs out of the system.

My memory is that it took about three months of walking the halls and reviewing the data for the elements of the strategy to start to come together, but when they did, things moved quickly. One afternoon, we shared the strategic vision with the CEO in the form of a draft presentation. It wasn't highly polished. He listened intently, asked a few questions, didn't signal whether he agreed or disagreed, but immediately called a meeting of his top management team and staff for the next afternoon in the largest board room. We had to work most of the night to produce a final presentation on acetate slides.

We expected to deliver the presentation to fourteen people, so we were shocked to walk in and find almost sixty—the two co-CEOs, the twelve VPs, and about forty more managers sitting or standing around the board room. The slide presentation began with industry trends. We argued that these would continue as in the past, and if anything, would put even more severe pressure on prices and profits. We then covered the needs and economics of hospitals with the data we'd collected on the costs of managing supplies. There followed a section introducing the logic of VMRs and marshalling the evidence from the automobile industry and several other companies that showed that it worked and, more importantly, that it had significant economic impact. Finally, we pulled all these ideas together in a coherent strategy for the client and made clear the major areas of change that would be required, if not exactly how those changes would be accomplished.

We went out of our way in the presentation to use client language and to give credit for all of their ideas. We tried to show how this strategy built on their input and on the traditions of both companies, but also fit the demands of the new industry environment.

I thought the team had done a great job on the presentation. My fervor for it showed. So it was quite a letdown to sense the chill in the room when we finished. There were some technical questions and a request to clarify certain of the economics, but the skepticism was palpable. The CEO remained a silent master of ceremonies and let the criticisms and skepticism mount. They reached a new level of hostility when one of the VPs who headed up a sales group that was likely to be changed, called the strategy idiotic, unfeasible, and one that could only be hatched by consultants who didn't understand the industry. The room went silent.

I would normally have turned to John Halpern to handle things, but because of the late notice, he had not been able to make the meeting. It was clear that everyone was waiting for my reply. When I was a professor facing an attack, I had often used a jujitsu approach: ignore or deflect with humor any personal insult, restate the substantive objection so it was clearly understood, then throw the onus on the group to address it with a question like, "What do the rest of you think?"

This time, though, I felt that we needed to defend our analysis and that the client needed to realize that the choice wasn't between maintaining a safe status quo and launching an audacious strategy. Rather, it was choosing between a status quo bound to fail and a strategy that at least had a chance of succeeding.

"You may be right," I replied addressing the VP. "We recognize that it's an audacious strategy and that it requires major changes from both companies. We can't prove it will work. But everyone knows that the current strategy is doomed to fail. Virtually all of you in private have made it clear that the current strategy and structure are not working and cannot be made to work. The ideas we have pulled together draw on the deep historic strengths of both companies. The strategy incorporates the best creative ideas we've been able to find talking to all of you and the people in your organizations. We've also scoured the experience of Bain's other clients for ideas and strategies that have worked in situations with some of the same characteristics. The strategy is audacious, but it is coherent. Yes, it will take a lot of work to refine it. Yes, it will require organizational changes. But it's the best all of us together have been able to produce. You really have only two choices: stay on the course you know in your heart won't work, though it may be comfortable in the short term, or begin to implement a new strategy that's risky, but promises both growth and profitability. All of us on the Bain team recommend this strategy strongly, but you are the ones that have to make the choice."

This speech was delivered with a heat that probably reflected my having been stung by the attack of individuals that I felt I had befriended. As I finished, I wondered if I had crossed the line of respect. It turned out, however, that showing both passion and conviction was the right move. Many heads were nodding in the audience, and I sensed the majority were with us. Following the silence, the CEO took a position. In a forceful way, he indicated that he believed this was the strategy the company needed to follow. He asked the group for its support and indicated he was going to take it to the board.

He then took me into his office afterwards and asked me to clear my calendar for the next two weeks. He wanted us to visit each of the members of the board of directors and share the analysis and recommendations with them in private, prior to the special meeting he was calling to approve the new strategy. He also asked us to prepare the "full potential program" of assistance, recognizing that he needed all the help he could get in turning this large ship around. Within a week, we had formulated a three-year program of multiple consulting teams. It turned out to be the largest program up to that point in Bain's history.

This case was rich in lessons for all of us on the team. Besides learning that sometimes it's important to passionately defend your position, it ratified the wisdom of many of the values inherent in Bain consulting: the importance of listening and walking the halls; the value of teamwork; the idea that structure follows strategy, not the other way around; the importance of coherence in a strategy and how powerful a lever such a strategy can be for leadership.

At work on a strategy presentation

I also took away a major insight regarding successful strategies. I realized that we had not really been the "authors" of the strategy that captured the allegiance of our client. We had been its "discoverers and articulators." When a new strategy clicks for an organization, it is because it has emerged from *their* experiences and insights. The desired inner reaction of the executives should not be, *Wow, that's a fascinating new strategy*, but more along the lines of, *that's a great way of putting what I intuitively know. It makes sense to me.* The corollary of this insight is that consultants don't earn the right to articulate the new strategy until they have really tapped the full wisdom of the organization, understood its culture, and learned to use its language.

A strategy is only likely to work when it answers four questions. First, does it explain what made the organization great and successful in the past? Any corporation of significant size has to have done a lot of things right to survive the Darwinian winnowing process. Second, does it explain why, given the current environment, continuing to do what was done in the past will no longer succeed? Does it clarify why change is absolutely necessary? Third, does it lay out a path into the future that can be competitively successful and answer the challenges of the situation? And finally, does it resonate with their values? Does it motivate them? Is it articulated in language that they understand and that reflects their aspirations?

MANAGEMENT AND LEADERSHIP

The Earthquake Crisis

In 1972, four months after I was named academic director of INCAE, a major earthquake destroyed Managua. As mentioned previously, the next day the family went by Medivac to San Jose, and Ken was born that evening.

As soon as it was clear that Deirdre, Sarah, and Ken were safe and healthy, I made plans to return immediately to Nicaragua, leaving them in the care of my aunt and uncle and cousins. I borrowed a jeep and accompanied by my cousin Bary, we left for Nicaragua carrying a barrel of gasoline in the back. He insisted that we go armed, given the rumors of looting, so we had a long-barreled "Dirty Harry" type of revolver on the dashboard.

As we drove through Guanacaste toward the border, my head was full of gloomy thoughts. Two of the INCAE faculty had already told me they were convinced the school was finished. They said it would be months before students from other countries (about 80 percent of the student body) could return, and rather than wait, many of them would probably make alternative plans. The school's cash flow, already tight, would dry up. With no classes, the faculty would not stay in Managua exposing their families to plagues and hardships and would begin to seek jobs elsewhere. In fact, some who were in the U.S. for Christmas vacation were already exploring alternatives.

The day was so bright and sunny, the countryside so beautiful and fertile, that it was hard to stay gloomy. Suddenly, a solution began to take shape in my mind, and the ideas and suggestions I had been collecting fell into a plan that filled me with a great sense of excitement. Managed correctly, this earthquake could be a motor for development in Nicaragua and a vehicle for INCAE's entry into public management. Nicaragua's main productive capacity was agricultural, and that had been unaffected by the earthquake. The reconstruction of the city was a labor-intensive activity that could absorb a lot of the unemployment. Foreign assistance and hard currency loans, motivated by an earthquake, would provide the dollars needed for rebuilding. And if we were creative in our planning, we might introduce a number of reforms to improve the efficiency of the reconstruction and perhaps lead ultimately to greater democracy.

INCAE could become the hub of reconstruction planning, and in the process save itself. Most of the government buildings had been destroyed, but our campus, fifteen kilometers outside of town, was largely intact. We could offer to house the government planning ministry. We could divide the faculty into three teams: one to take care of our INCAE families, one to work with the government, and one to re-open the MBA program as soon as possible.

We crossed the border in the afternoon and arrived in Managua at dusk. Our first stop was at the house of a faculty member on the south highway. They had just received a phone call warning them that a band of fifty men with machetes was marching up the highway, and our friends were preparing to flee the house to avoid being slaughtered. Doubting that the story was true and angry at those who were spreading such fears, Bary and I decided to drive the jeep down the highway to disprove the rumor.

Though certain it was nothing, I still thought about what to do if the rumor proved to be true. Should I put the jeep in reverse and try to back up faster than they could chase me, or gun the motor and charge through them? Fortunately, we didn't have to make the choice. The only two things we saw in the next five kilometers of empty highway was one *campesino* trudging home with his machete, and further down the road, a military truck unloading supplies into a garage.

That night and the next day, we visited faculty members still in Managua. Everyone agreed to wait on their personal plans until we had a faculty meeting, which we did the following afternoon. There we discussed the plan and organized ourselves into the three groups.

One team was responsible for making sure every family had the basic needs of food and water. Any family that felt unsafe would come to stay on the campus in the now empty student housing. A second group would keep the MBA program alive. They would get in touch with every student to assure them of the program's continuation and then figure out how to get back on schedule so as to restart at the earliest time possible. The third team would offer our campus and services to Somoza's government to help assess the damage, identify the needs for foreign aid, and plan the reconstruction.

That night the rector, Ernesto Cruz, and I visited President Somoza's farm on the outskirts of Managua, which was serving as headquarters for earthquake relief. Walking up the tree-lined drive, we could see military tents on both sides and soldiers in fatigues coming and going. In the main house, we found Somoza busy with the distribution of medicines, water, and food. As best we could tell, no one was preparing for the mission of World Bank and AID officials due to arrive on January 2, only five days away. After we assuaged his initial suspicions, Somoza accepted INCAE's offer to house his reconstruction planning team, assembled from the Central Bank and the Ministry of Economic Planning. INCAE would aid them in preparing a briefing for the visitors on the 2nd. Somoza, though, made it clear that care for the wounded and hungry was his top priority.

The next four days were spent meeting with a team of about twenty government officials and faculty. We worked around the clock to get ready. A student who was a rice farmer offered his plane to fly over the city to take pictures. Then a group put together an aerial map from the photos and used it to estimate the extent of damage. Another group used the school's small computer to prepare a macro-economic model to estimate the foreign aid needed and to project economic growth with and without foreign aid. Other teams prepared simple plans to stimulate agriculture, re-activate industry, and eliminate the bottlenecks in construction. It was my job to bring all the pieces into a twenty-four-page document titled *Assessment of Earthquake Damages and Plan for Reconstruction*.

At twilight on January 1, Ernesto and I once again walked into Somoza's headquarters. We had copies of the document and some flip charts to present the major findings. We were taken into the main living room. Ernesto made an introduction and asked me to make the presentation. Somoza and the assembled group of ministers and generals listened intently. It was hard to read their reactions, and I feared they didn't understand what we were proposing. When we finished, however, Somoza expressed his amazement at all we'd been able to do in four days. Our recommendations had his total support, and he asked us to make the same presentation the next day to all the foreign visitors.

The following day the presentation had a similar impact on the international experts. Both our assessment of damages and recommendations were incorporated almost verbatim into their reports. Within a week, INCAE had received a special grant of $1 million in additional support from USAID to set up a center to help the Nicaraguan government in its reconstruction planning. We called it the Centro de Asesoramiento (the Center for Consultation). To help us in the effort, we also had a mandate to bring down a team from the Harvard Development Advisory Service, where I had worked as a doctoral student.

Recovery from the earthquake was quicker than we expected, and two months later we resumed the MBA program without losing any students or faculty. Instead, we had plans to expand the faculty offices and library to accommodate the enlarged faculty needed to staff the new center.

INCAE's post-earthquake experience taught me two great lessons. In a crisis, while you take care of yourself and your family, make sure your main focus is on the larger whole. INCAE survived the earthquake because it paid more attention to Nicaragua's needs than its own. It became so valuable to the larger society that the larger society made sure INCAE got the financial resources it needed.

Second, as first director of the Centro de Asesoramiento, I also learned that if we wanted to have impact as consultants, we had to adjust our work to the calendar of the decision-makers, not our own desires to have a perfect analysis. If a government official has to make a decision in three weeks, a study that takes two months is useless. Government executives have less freedom than we think. Most of their decisions are opportunistic in that they must accommodate the flow of events. Analysis that effectively supports these decisions must be anticipated in advance and prepared so as to hit the policy-makers' desks in timely fashion.

The Sandinista Crisis

In 1980, eight years after the earthquake and coinciding with the Sandinista's consolidation of power after the revolution, INCAE's survival was once again in doubt due to financial problems and internal conflicts.

It was not only the political and revolutionary turmoil that caused some older faculty to leave Nicaragua, but also the country's massive economic depression, greater than that of the U.S. in the 1930s. The oil crisis, plus misconceived government policies, led to mounting public debt and the destruction of the agricultural sector, with resulting impoverishment and unemployment all around. There was hyper-inflation and huge devaluations in the region, which, incidentally, made the repayment of student loans in dollars exceedingly difficult.

In this environment it was not hard to see why a school like INCAE, dependent on tuition and fees from executive programs and on gifts from the business community, saw its revenues shrink by more than half and its operating deficit balloon, in spite of all cost-saving efforts. There were moments when it became nearly impossible to meet the school's payroll and its obligations to suppliers.

The political polarization in the region spread to the faculty and reduced the school's capability to respond to the crisis. Some felt the Sandinistas represented the socialistic solution to poverty and inequality. Others saw it as the first step toward a communism that would destroy the region. Many felt the school needed to be moved to another country to survive. Others felt this was neither feasible nor desirable. Nicaragua was not lost and if INCAE was to fulfill its mission, it should do everything it could to help Nicaragua. At one point, the National Committee of INCAE in a neighboring country threatened to withhold any support for the school if it worked with the Nicaraguan government. On top of that, Reagan promised to terminate U.S. support for the new regime in Nicaragua.

In this deteriorating spiral, though now by this time working at Bain & Co, I was asked by don Chico de Sola, the chair of INCAE's board, to lead a committee to develop a strategy to save the school. With the help of many people, particularly Marc Lindenberg, my brother-in-law, who was teaching at the University of Washington, we made trips into the region and tried to understand the problems from the viewpoint of everyone involved. We collected ideas from faculty, national committees, and alumni on how the school might be saved. It was on a flight to Honduras that we had one of those moments where the pieces of the puzzle, collected from so many people, came together in a promising strategy.

The strategy had a number of components, the following being among the main ones:

> Rather than shrink the school, we would launch a regional expansion into the Dominican Republic and the Andean region.
>
> A new set of special programs would be developed to meet the particular needs of the region: one in public management, one in export promotion, and another to bring the conflictive parties together in constructive dialog and study.
>
> We would confront the political polarization in the region by preemptively indicating to everyone our willingness to work with all regimes and countries.
>
> We would open a second campus without closing the first, making it possible to serve students who would not come to Nicaragua and also ensuring that no government could take control of INCAE's curriculum.
>
> We would recruit the old faculty to come back and help save the school.
>
> We would extend our fund-raising in Europe, in part for the additional funds and in part to create a countervailing political pressure to those we anticipated would be coming with USAID money.
>
> We would try to make INCAE relevant, but not partisan. We would try to mobilize the entire larger INCAE family as a constructive pragmatic force to keep Central America from going under, both politically and economically.

And we would mobilize a group of influential Republicans who were friends of don Chico and Harvard (Governor Elmer Anderson and Louis Cabot, among others) to ensure that Reagan continued to support INCAE as a regional organization.

The strategy also called for a new rector, as Dr. Cruz had decided to turn over the job and move on in his career. I told them I was not a candidate for this position since I was now working with Bain and deeply believed the rector should be a Latin American. Nevertheless, after a year of fruitless searching and in spite of my trepidation, I agreed to take a two-year leave from Bain and accept the position. Marc accompanied me as academic director.

Our family arrived in Managua at the beginning of 1981, and shortly thereafter I presented my credentials as rector of an international institution to the Sandinista government. Sergio Ramirez Mercado, a noted Nicaraguan novelist and member of the revolutionary junta, received us. Roger Quant accompanied me to the meeting and told me that these were symbolic courtesy meetings where one drank coffee and made small talk. Under the guise of being naïve bumpkins, however, we'd planned one of our pre-emptive confrontations to ensure that INCAE could be both relevant yet avoid the political polarization dividing the region.

Shortly after coffee was served, I said, "I'm not sure whether I'm violating diplomatic protocol, but I'd like to talk to you "*de calzón quitado*"—a vulgar expression for "honestly, with my pants down." When he didn't object, I said, "I can imagine that with our Harvard Business School heritage, you see us as capitalistic and incompatible with what you're trying to do. If that's the case, we're more than willing to turn our campus over to you and leave.

"But first let me explain what we do. We are founded on the case method of study that says there is no single way to do things. The student has to figure out what to do by studying the problem. The professor doesn't have the answers, he has the questions. We think this methodology might be particularly suited to the management challenges facing the Sandinista revolution. For it to work, however, there are a number of conditions that must be met. We have prepared some slides of the principal ones: freedom to come and go for faculty and students, freedom from government regulation of the school (a law was already being discussed to impose state control on all the universities and schools), and adequate compensation, as we have no endowment."

I also mentioned that we were sharing the same slides with the president of Honduras the following day, and would be asking him the same question. (At the time, Nicaragua was in a virtual state of war with Honduras over their protection of the *contras*.) "We hope to work with all the governments and all the private sectors in the region. We're really here to find out if Nicaragua is for us or against us, whether it wants INCAE to stay or go."

His reply was quick and emphatic. "We don't want INCAE to leave. We agree with all the conditions." Later I found out that a number of Sandinistas assumed I was a CIA agent, but this open direct approach had made a positive impression in Sandinista circles. "*Navegando bajo bandera de pendejo*," loosely translated, "Flying under the flag of a fool," was my only hope. Assuming that my phone was tapped and every conversation reported. I'd decided on a direct approach with everyone.

INCAE's stance when faced with the political polarization around us was to be as constructive a force as possible without getting into the ideological debate. We did not pretend direct approval of the Sandinistas, nor of the military governments of the left or the right. We wanted to help all regimes. Before we were asked by a government if we were for or against their regime, we planned to frame the discussion around whether *they* were pro or con INCAE.

As rector of INCAE, there were many complicated decisions to be made quickly and under high stress. I often wished that I could meet my father for a weekend, perhaps at the beach, and get his advice on how to handle the situations I was facing.

One challenge was explaining and selling the new strategy to our staff of nearly two hundred people on the Nicaraguan campus. Many of them feared we would abandon Nicaragua or have to drastically reduce headcount. It was important to get to know them and reassure them without misleading them on the tough changes that were required. Instinctively, I decided to set up small meetings with each administrative department of the school, rather than follow the normal procedure of calling them to a big meeting in a classroom.

The administrative director and I visited each group in their place of work—the cleaning women in the dorms, the mechanics at the garage, the kitchen staff in the kitchen, and so forth. In each meeting, I would greet every person, shake hands, repeat his or her name, and perhaps ask a question about their work or family. Then as briefly and simply as possible, I'd explain our situation and its difficulties; our strategy, which involved some decisions that might be threatening; our commitment to each other; and how INCAE would help solve the problems in our region. I explained why their work was important to our success, and I tried to answer their questions honestly.

In the garage with the drivers and mechanics, I suddenly saw myself, as if from on high, shaking hands, tilting my head to hear better, asking a personal question in a humorous way, and I realized that I was copying my father's style, even down to some of his mannerisms. I discovered that when I was in a leadership situation, he was the model I unconsciously followed. He was not alive to give me advice, but his leadership style was serving me well.

The entire faculty mobilized in support of the five-year strategy. Our hope was to break even financially by year five. It worked out even better than we hoped, with all the elements succeeding and INCAE breaking-even one year earlier than planned. The special programs from that period helped persuade governments to change to export-oriented strategies. INCAE's campus became the choice spot for dialogue in the region, the place where presidents met and conducted the peace process that brought democratic regimes back to power. Graduates served as government ministers in each country's cabinet. They also led the process of transforming local companies into effective global competitors. To my knowledge, INCAE was the only organization in the region that worked every year with the governments and private sector of every Central American country.

The credit for INCAE's turnaround goes to the board under Walter Kissling and the faculty and staff, led by Marc Lindenberg. I returned to Bain in 1982 as planned, but joined INCAE's board of directors, where my role was to support the leaders in subsequent periods and to occasionally teach in an INCAE program.

People Management

I knew my consulting skills were better than my managing skills, but I had no idea how poor a manager I was until I got some serious feedback. It was the mid-1980s, and I seemed to be having great success. Bain was growing at nearly 50 percent a year, and we felt that we had a unique approach to creating value that seemed to appeal to both clients and recruits. Everyone was working hard, operating at one of the highest levels of utilization in our industry. This meant battlefield promotions, good bonuses, and intellectually exciting work. We therefore assumed we had high morale among the troops.

Suddenly, a rash of consultant and manager resignations woke us up to the fact that perhaps things weren't as much fun for our staff as we thought. With our high turnover rate, we weren't going to be able to continue to grow rapidly.

At first many of us believed the discontent was caused by the nature of the work, the long hours, and the extensive travel. Maybe some people weren't really cut out to be consultants. Exit interviews suggested, however, that it was less these factors than the frustration of being poorly managed.

We all gave lip service to good people management and teamwork, but the reality was that client satisfaction and demand for continued work counted for more in the promotion and compensation process than case team contentment. If your case team felt abused, your boss would call attention to your people management deficiencies, but so long as the client was happy and you were selling a lot of business, your team's unhappiness didn't affect either your bonus or your promotion.

In his typical deliberate way, Bill Bain did an analysis, and then called in some outsiders to help. One of their first actions was to do 360 degree feedback on each partner, using anonymous feedback forms that were detailed and comprehensive. The evaluations contained not only hard scores and comments, but a ranking on each aspect of management that compared us to the other partners.

When it came my turn to sit down with the outside consultant, he told me that I had been rated in the bottom 10 percent of my cohort group. I was shocked. My first reaction was to assume I had been given someone else's scores, but he quickly made it clear, "No, Harry, that really is the feedback on you. I've checked it out."

My next reaction was to wonder if I had unwittingly made enemies and was getting artificially low scores because of personal animus. "No, Harry, if anything, your direct reports have pulled their punches because they recognize your good intentions and like you."

Perhaps, I asked, the scores were distorted because some of my direct reports were among the weakest on our staff, and I had been trying to be honest with them on their performance. "No, Harry, I checked your scores and actually the highest performers in the firm are the ones who are giving you the lowest scores. They have learned to work with you, but you don't make their life easy or pleasant."

When I accepted the veracity of the ratings and focused on the feedback, there were more surprises. "Little things" that I had treated as unimportant were in fact quite important to the people on my team. For example,

> "Harry doesn't always remember to let us know in a timely fashion what he learned in a client meeting. Sometimes we learn something several days later in a case team meeting that would have saved us unnecessary work."

> "Harry may think it's easy to read his reaction to my work, but I often have a hard time knowing whether he's happy or not, agrees or disagrees, or even if he's aware of the weekend work I put in to get it done. He doesn't seem to realize how motivating a word of thanks can be."

> "Sometimes I wish after we've spent an all-nighter getting ready for a client meeting that went spectacularly well, that in the airport waiting for the plane that will take us back to Boston, Harry would 'celebrate' our success, that we'd all have a drink and savor what went on in the meeting. Instead, he's already talking about next steps."

These comments were hard to hear, but the heart of the feedback, the things that apparently put me in the bottom 10 percent were also perplexing because they seemed to be inseparable from the things that were making me successful with the clients.

> "Harry needs to make his suggestions a lot earlier. He is meddling with the presentation up to the last minute. Yes, his

contributions make it better, but they also add unnecessarily to the stress and late night work, sometimes all out of proportion to the value they add."

"Harry makes way too many changes to the work plan over the course of the project. Things he initially felt were critical to the answer, he downgrades once we collect some data, and he introduces other 'critical questions' late in the process."

"Harry over-promises and seems constitutionally incapable of saying no to the client. It's unhealthy the way he kills himself, but it's worse when he also kills us. He needs to learn to push back and educate the client on how long and how much work it will take to deliver the answer to certain questions."

"The reality is that Harry is not very organized, is always juggling too many things. He needs to learn to prioritize better, organize things in advance, manage his and our efforts better."

Faced with this feedback, I recognized that in order to give the team what it needed I had to get better organized. I consequently asked for and got the firm's support in taking a time-management course. I also went around to members of my cohort group who were famous for being well-organized and asked for their secrets. I was sufficiently stung by the feedback to make a determined effort to improve.

In the next round of 360 degree feedback, it was devastating to find out that, while people recognized my efforts to improve, they still considered me in the bottom 20 percent. The despair I felt on getting this feedback, had it not coincided with some major client successes, might have been enough to cause me to start looking for another job. Instead, I talked with Bill Bain about experimenting with a different way of dealing with my deficiencies.

"Bill," I said, "in spite of my best efforts, I don't think I'll ever be organized enough to be a good people manager. So I'm asking that you give me some of the best partners and managers and the freedom for us to redefine our responsibilities so that they cover for my weaknesses, and I focus on the things I do well." He agreed.

With my direct reports we did a one-day offsite retreat, which later became an annual custom. I openly shared the feedback I had received and acknowledged my deficiencies. I let them know how disappointed

I was that my effort to improve had only been marginally effective. To really solve the problem we needed a new *modus operandi* for defining roles. My suggestion went something like this:

"I want and need to be involved in the work. You think I'm a good salesman, but I know that any success I've had comes from being so deeply involved in the analysis that I can see the potential for wealth and make it come alive for the clients. So I need to be able to get involved in focusing the work at the beginning, and adding ideas and changing priorities as we go through the work. You have to give me permission to throw out ideas and make suggestions throughout the process.

"But so it doesn't kill you and the teams, I'm going to give you the responsibility for deciding which of the many ideas I float actually get worked on. You'll listen, sift through them, calculate the cost benefit analysis on them, and decide which ones you're going to set aside as not worth the effort of the team.

"The first time I make a suggestion, you don't even have to tell me if you've decided to ignore it. If I raise the idea a second time, however, and you still feel it's not a priority, then you need to tell me. At that point we'll discuss it and reach a decision with which we both feel comfortable. You can make me give up some other piece of analysis to make room for it if I feel it's critical. If you convince me I'm wrong, then I'll stop making the request or we'll find some easier way to get an answer that will satisfy us.

"I'll commit to turnaround times on presentations or decisions that affect the case team's work and to keep you informed of my meetings. It's your responsibility, though, to get on my schedule, so that I'm not seeing the work for the first time the night before a presentation."

Along with these policies, I began the practice of having at least one lunch a month, one on one, with each direct report. We'd each bring a list of the three most important objectives we had for the next two or three months. We'd be specific about the support needed from each other. I'd get my assignments for the next month from them. They'd get clarity on my expectations.

To an extent that surprised me, the monthly discussions spilled over into topics outside the scope of work. Relationships turned into friendships, many of which were maintained even after they left Bain. I decided that whatever the organization chart says, everyone needs a boss. Sometimes that boss is the supervisor on the organization chart, but often, parts of the boss's role can be played by other colleagues or direct reports. Whatever the situation, it is my responsibility to find and train the bosses I need.

My skill set never reflected a "balanced comb." I wasn't equally good at all aspects of the job, but the new *modus operandi* worked. Shortly after implementing these changes, my ratings jumped dramatically, often into the top decimal. The redefinition of roles didn't just help me be more successful, but greatly expanded the role of my direct reports and accelerated their development as managers and partners.

For many years I was embarrassed that I had solved my problem by abdicating my leadership functions, until one of my direct reports told me "Hell, Harry, you're not abdicating leadership! You're stealing the solution of the president of the United States. He gets his orders every day from his chief of staff."

INVESTING FOR PROFIT

Head and Shoulders Investing

In the doctoral program I had a long-running series of tennis games with a classmate who later became dean of one of Canada's leading business schools. At the beginning of each game he would tell me how much money he had made on the stock market that week. He was in and out of the market in what today would be called "day trades." He was a "technical" investor who worked mostly from charts of recent stock market prices and volumes, making his moves without knowing much about what the company did or its performance. I was intrigued, but did not understand how the different "formations" on which he based his decisions could possibly predict future stock prices. After observing his considerable success, though, I asked him to give me a tip for $500 of hard-earned savings. "When you have something sure, let me know."

The next time we played, he told me, "I have something—Diamond Shamrock. It's just completed a 'head and shoulders' formation and my guess is that within six months it will double."

"What's a head and shoulders?" I asked. His explanation, if I remember correctly, was that the past chart of prices looked like a head and shoulder. Though how this past movement of the stock price could predict future improvements made no sense to me, I went out and purchased the stock at something like $21 a share. Within several weeks the stock was selling at $13 a share. I held it for about ten years as it bounced between $5 and $13 a share and finally sold it for less than half of what I had invested.

So long as I had this stock in my portfolio, it was a powerful reminder of a lesson that was easily worth the money I lost: don't invest in businesses that make no sense to you. I promised myself I would not invest in "tips" if there weren't clear indicators for their appreciation. Years later during the dot.com bubble, friends urged me to invest in companies valued at multiples of their revenue even though they were losing money and were not projected to be profitable for years. I avoided these investments because no theory of valuation I understood suggested these stocks were worth what the market was paying. As a result when the dot.com bubble burst, I was saved significant losses.

Financial Independence

In my early years at Bain, a client asked us to help him figure out how to maintain the half billion dollars he'd received from his family in a split up. He was particularly interested in how wealthy families had done this in the past and what were the best vehicles for holding wealth. I was asked to oversee the project.

We decided on two somewhat different approaches. Part of the team went back to business magazines in the 1920s and 1930s to research articles on the wealthiest families of that time, and they compiled a list of about thirty-five families like the Rockefellers and Fords. Our work consisted of creating a record of what had happened to that wealth across time, how it had been invested, and the returns achieved. Since these fortunes had been split among heirs or placed in foundations, they weren't always easy to trace. The discouraging news from this first study was that less than one third of the families had managed to maintain or grow their wealth in real terms (after inflation). There was no single pattern among the more successful.

The other part of the team took historic data from 1920 to 1980 on the various assets in which wealth was invested and held: equity stocks, bonds, bank saving accounts, real estate, gold, art, etc. This team divided the data on each asset class into twelve five-year periods. For each period we calculated the "nominal return," dividends plus appreciation minus holding costs and fees. We then estimated taxes and calculated the "after tax returns," since certain asset classes paid higher taxes than others. Finally we deflated these net returns by the effect of inflation, calculating the after tax return in constant dollars.

The conclusions from this study were more interesting, but also discouraging. There were five-year periods in which every class of assets had generated attractive returns, but rarely did the best performing asset of one period do well in the subsequent period. It also appeared that intermediaries—the brokers and dealers—managed to take significant portions of any gains in the underlying assets. Real estate owners, for example, did significantly less well than real estate developers. And while real estate had favorable tax treatment, it also had high carrying costs and was a much less attractive long-term investment than conventional wisdom suggested.

The best performing asset class was equity stocks. But even for this class the returns averaged less than 2 percent per year in constant after-taxes dollars. No other class consistently earned over 1 percent per year. The average returns on art and gold were actually negative, in part because of high carrying costs.

The combination of taxes (always figured on nominal income) and inflation made it very difficult to earn real money on savings. A person was lucky if they earned enough to preserve the money's original value, and the average person with access only to public vehicles for savings had to save virtually 100 percent of what they hoped to spend in retirement.

One of my objectives on joining Bain was to become financially independent in ten years by building a net worth large enough to permit me to live on its income the rest of my life. I had calculated that if I kept my lifestyle at a professor's level and saved the rest, I could save half of what was needed to reach that goal. But my study for the wealthy client was telling me that if I put my own savings in the normal diversified portfolio of stocks, bonds, and real estate, I would only get halfway to my goal. Financial independence required investment vehicles that would give me a real return of over 7 percent, and achieving that meant taking more risk or investing more directly in private money-making companies.

Bain Capital

Other partners in Bain were thinking the same way. We believed our way of consulting created a 5:1 return for the companies that used us. Was there a way for us to buy profits rather than sell them? If we bought companies for what they were worth, perhaps leveraged with debt, improved their performance with our consulting magic, then sold the business for a higher price, we figured we could achieve superior returns on our investments. I hoped that if we did this we could earn the nominal 15 percent I needed to double my savings.

Mitt Romney was one of the promoters of this idea and put together a plan for Bain Capital I. Partners would invest half of the first fund, and we would open it up to friends and family for the remaining 50 percent. Our formula for creating superior value involved looking for situations where as many as possible of the following five factors could create shareholder value:

1) A superior management team
2) An industry cycle working in our favor
3) A superior strategy
4) Immediate cost savings and operating improvements
5) Financial leverage and good exit strategies.

I wrote several of my Central American friends and former clients about this opportunity, inviting them to Miami where Mitt and I were to present the new fund. My friends were impressed by Mitt and the team and signed up for 20% of the fund. Ricardo Poma, a close friend as well as a successful investor in his own right, was enthusiastic, and he so impressed Mitt that he was invited to join the Bain Capital Investment Committee, and became the de facto leader of our group.

I, myself, decided to put over half of my current and estimated future savings into Bain Capital. Mitt Romney told me that I was signing up for a higher amount than any other partner except the four founders and that I ought to reduce it. I explained why this was what I really wanted to do. I believed there was less risk and more upside to investing directly in companies we knew and could control than in the public markets. Liquidity was less important to me than higher returns. If I lost the savings, I'd have to continue working, something I'd have to do anyway if I wasn't able to double my savings. If, however, the investment strategy worked, I'd be financially independent, free to choose any work I wanted for my third period of life.

After a somewhat slow start, Bain Fund I was invested, but even before it was fully invested, it was already harvesting returns, so my cash flow estimates proved too conservative. Other funds followed, including one in Information Partners led by Steve Pagliuca, a former Bain VP, friend and mentee.

I made increasing commitments in subsequent funds, rolling over my savings so that two thirds of my portfolio was in private equity funds. I was very lucky. The first fund achieved a net return after fees of 70 percent. Net returns on Fund 2-4 while lower than the first, were still in the 20-50 percent range. This made it possible to grow my net worth as I had hoped.

I used a simple index to measure my progress toward financial independence. The numerator consisted of two variables: my net worth and the sustainable long-term return after adjustment for inflation. The other and most important variable was what I actually spent during the year, the denominator of my index. When my index exceeded 1.0, i.e. when what I earned on my net worth was greater than my annual expenditures, I became financially independent, free to take a job for $1 a year without reducing my standard of living.

INVESTING FOR IMPACT

I have always envied compassionate people, like my Aunt Grace and my sisters, who instinctively give to others in need—the greater the need, the greater their compassion. Unfortunately I'm more an investor than a philanthropist—I want to see a positive return on my charity.

But like my sisters or my good friend, Tom Tierney, I strongly believe that all of us, particularly if fortunate, should make a habit of giving part of our time and money to others. I concur that there are no successful companies in failed societies and that building a good society requires effort from all of us. I can also attest to the high personal dividends that come from "social investing" and of the learning and special relationships these activities generate.

Gasoline Board of Director

During our time in Nicaragua, both Deirdre and I were directly involved in development work. Deirdre and a number of other wives helped in Dr. Gus Parajon's health clinics in remote rural villages. They'd return from their trips covered with dust and exhausted, but also exhilarated with the contribution they had made. I tried to set aside at least one week a year to go out in the field with development projects.

One evening Gus came by and asked if I'd be willing to serve on the board of directors of a gas station. He explained that a number of high school and university students in the Baptist church could stay in school only if they earned enough money to support themselves. A member of the church who was an executive at Chevron had a gas station that had been returned to the company because it had gone bankrupt for the third time. He persuaded his boss to let Gus's group of students take charge of it. The station would be open twenty-four hours so students who had no home could sleep in the back. Sixteen young men would work the shifts and thus finance their studies. Gus wanted me to help them set up the accounting system and find a strategy to stay out of a fourth bankruptcy.

I had some qualms, but accepted the challenge and attended the first board meeting. The young people had been trained in Robert's Rules of Order and used the majority of the time for formal preliminaries that nearly drove me crazy. When I did my tutorial on basic accounting I discovered how difficult it was to explain accounting in a way they understood. Finally we got a set of books they could keep and their gas station got under way.

The big challenge was to increase traffic despite the station's poor location. We added car washing, sent out flyers to the neighborhood, and tried a variety of things. Slowly sales built up. The third month, to my relief, we inched past the break-even point. The following month sales were up even further, but then to my horror I saw that we were once again in the red—as soon as the boys realized we had a small profit, they had added two more of their group to the payroll!

Given the precarious finances of the business, I began to dread hearing about the latest crisis that had plunged us into the red. No matter what the problem, though, the boys were always optimistic and sure that things would work out.

The business came to an end when the Managua earthquake destroyed the gas station and closed off that part of town. Fortunately, relief efforts soon provided the boys with employment, and they were able to continue their studies.

Twenty-five years later I returned to Nicaragua on a visit. Gus told me that the gas station boys wanted to invite me to a reunion dinner. About a dozen of the original group showed up, and each described what had happened in his life. Several had become pastors; two had been elected to the National Assembly as congressmen. Several ran profit or non-profit organizations. All had completed their studies. Each felt the gas station had played a pivotal role in his life. It had not only helped them finance their studies, but taught them problem-solving and business skills.

I was deeply moved by their warm *abrazos* (hugs) and thanks. I was also a bit ashamed that I had worried so much about the profitability of the gas station and not seen what was truly important, namely, their personal development. Seeing their success was priceless.

Hospital Clinica Biblica and the Wheel of Life

When I returned to Central America in the early 1990s, the board of the *Hospital Clinica Biblica* asked if I'd head up a strategy consulting project. They even offered to pay, but I refused.

The hospital had begun as a clinic for women in my grandmother's house and developed under the LAM into the leading private hospital of the country. After my father's death and the dividing of the mission into autonomous entities, it became a stand-alone nonprofit ministry led by a board of local pastors and Christian businessmen.

In 1993, the *Clínica* was struggling under a large debt. It had bought some modern medical equipment that had not generated the promised payback. Financial problems caused in part by the debt, had forced the hospital to suspend many of its social-action programs. There were divisions within the board that seemed to paralyze decision-making, and mutual recriminations made solutions more difficult to find.

The consulting group was comprised of myself, a group of *Clínica* executives several board members, as well as some outside consultants including, INCAE professor Esteban Brenes and my nephew Neill Goslin, who was in Costa Rica from Tulane University for the summer. When we completed the analysis and strategy, they asked me to lead a workshop to bring together the conflictive parties to approve it. The strategy called for a three-year program of "consolidation." It required significant cost reductions. The limited capital expenditure budget focused on fewer initiatives to be chosen after analysis, as we recommended investment in only four of the hospital's twelve specialties, one of which was cardiology.

Implementing the strategy meant making major changes in the organization and management team and bringing in a more professional CEO and CFO. The large board, primarily composed of older religious leaders, met each Saturday and meddled in small administrative decisions. We recommended they should meet once a month and should delegate management issues to an executive committee. These changes were not easy or popular.

The workshop to approve the strategy met in a hotel with thirty in attendance, a mixture of the old and new guard. Having come on the scene late, I suspected that one of the reasons I was chosen as moderator was my independence and perhaps because I'd been a business school professor. I figured I'd probably get a respectful hearing for at least the first fifteen minutes since I carried the name of the founder of the hospital, and we decided to use our political capital to ratchet up the pressure to make the tough changes.

After the customary reading of a passage of scripture and a prayer, I described the agenda and said that before the strategy was presented, we wanted to remind them of a familiar parable in the Bible:

A master leaving for a far country called his three servants and gave one five talents, another two, and the third only one. When he returned, he asked each for an accounting. The one with five and the one with two both doubled what they had been given and were rewarded as good stewards. The one receiving only one talent knew his master was tough and demanding, and he had cautiously buried his talent so as not to lose it. When he returned only the original, the furious master punished him severely.

I concluded, "So far as the hospital is concerned, we're flunking as stewards. We've not met the Master's expectations. We think this strategy, developed by a large team, can save the hospital from bankruptcy. But it's not clear that the political will and capability exist to implement the strategy.

"I want to propose, therefore, that if within two years we haven't restored the hospital's profitability, you allow me to sell it to someone who can manage it well. I'm certain Mesoamerica and Bain can get you a price that will provide an endowment that will enable you to resume the level of social services you've had to suspend."

The strategy was approved. The management selected Jaime Cabezas as chair of the board, Bernal Aragon as CEO, and Gerardo Sanchez as CFO. They led a successful turnaround, and the hospital resumed making its social donations as well as paying down its debt. That first strategy was followed by another three-year strategy, which involved investing in additional specialties. In the third period's strategy, a major physical expansion was done that more than doubled the facilities, and the *Clínica* took over the management of several government clinics in poor parts of the country. In the fourth period, the hospital became the first in Central America to be accredited in the U.S. and was rated one of the top five hospitals in Latin America.

My advisory role widened my network of friendships and helped reconnect me to my evangelical past. It also paid a dividend I never expected. In early 1998, I had a heart attack and was rushed to the hospital. Waiting for me at the entrance was a team from the cardiac unit that had been developed as part of that first turnaround strategy. Tests showed that 50 percent of my heart was not getting the blood it needed, a situation that could quickly kill me or leave me crippled. The excellent doctors and nurses, however, using the new equipment and skilled in the latest medicines, kept my heart from further damage. The social investments made by my grandparents, parents, and myself in the *Clínica*, I'm convinced, saved my life. What you put into the wheel of life has a way of coming back.

MENTORS AND MENTORING

Professors Vernon and Skinner

Early in my academic career, I was lucky to find among the many excellent teachers and scholars at Harvard Business School (HBS), two professors who went the extra mile to invest in my development. They became my mentors and role models.

Raymond Vernon was the reigning guru in the area of international business. He was to the business school what Professor Casner had been to the law school. With Professor Lou Wells, he taught the Reading Seminar in International Business, and he assigned mountains of material that we were expected to read and critique.

During our weekly seminar, Professor Vernon was ruthlessly cruel when presented with sloppy thinking or lack of preparation. He was very direct in his criticism and suggestions. He didn't waste time, and he didn't suffer fools. What made this all tolerable was that it was clear he was investing a huge amount of his time and energy in trying to help us realize our full potential. We didn't feel he was just going through the motions of teaching in order to get back to his research. Nor did he appear to have a need to show off his brilliance or gain our approval.

Many in the field of international business avoided having him on their thesis committee as it was said that his students took at least an extra year to complete their dissertation. Nevertheless, in mortal fear of his sharp tongue, I asked him to be my thesis chairman because I felt he'd help me do a better job and his reputation would give my degree more credibility among professional economists. He was a role model for rigorous research, clear organization of data, and lucid writing.

Sure enough, my thesis took me a year longer than most. He forced me to tighten up the 600-page first draft of my *Family Business Groups of Nicaragua and Their Role in Economic Development*, reducing it to 250 pages. At times he was so critical of my writing that I feared he might simply give up on me.

Professor Wickham Skinner was another of Harvard's star teachers. He was also very involved in helping INCAE get the support it needed. Early in my tenure at INCAE, he came to some of my classes and sat in the back row charting how I managed the discussion, much the way scouts at a basketball game note the exact spot on the floor from which shots are taken.

He wrote down where and on whom I called. He watched the sequence of my questions and how they were worded. Afterward, we had a debriefing session. He always began with enthusiastic praise that seemed genuine. Then in a shrewd Socratic manner, he'd go through his notes, reminding me of what I had done and asking me why I'd done it and if I'd considered doing something different.

His questions opened up options I had not thought of, and we'd discuss the pros and cons of those options. I don't recall his making any critical remarks; rather, he let me criticize myself. At the end of a session, he would return to the positives and reinforce ideas I'd come up with for future experimentation.

Although I should have been depressed by the opportunities I had missed and how far I was from being a good teacher, I always left a coaching session with him feeling exhilarated. Somehow, in all his feedback, he made me feel that I had great potential, was in fact, already a hell of a teacher and could become even better. When I was promoted to Academic Director, he became my mentor in issues of academic administration.

These two men had completely different styles, but in my case, both were effective. My natural propensity was probably to be more like Professor Vernon, but I noticed in the years after Harvard that Wick was the mentor I most frequently called on for advice. When faced with a tough decision, Deirdre and I would call him and his wife Alice in their Maine home. They'd invite us to come up for a weekend and give us counseling sessions, as well as great meals.

From Professor Vernon, I learned the importance of analytic clarity, knowing what excellence is, and demanding it. From Wick I learned that mentoring is mainly about "cheerleading." He was discerning. He was not fooled about mistakes or weakness. But you felt he saw gold in you that you were unaware of. He saw potential you didn't know you had. When asked to be a mentor, I try to be as rigorous and concrete as Professor Vernon and as encouraging as Professor Skinner. I try to listen carefully, ask good questions, avoid giving advice, and give lots of positive feedback. And I try to be as generous with time and effort as both of them were with me.

CALI Mentor

Around 2000, I joined others in helping INCAE and the Aspen Institute to establish the Central America Leadership Initiative (CALI). CALI is a program which each year gives a fellowship to twenty-four successful young leaders, four from each country. Half are women, half men. Half come from the private sector and half from non-profits and the government. Each fellow commits to attend four weeklong seminars over a two-year period and undertake a project to benefit the region. Fellows range from thirty to forty-five in age, but they are already recognized as successful leaders. In the seminars they "join the two thousand year old conversation" on how to build a good society. They think about how to move in their lives "from success to significance."

In addition to providing financial support and serving on the CALI board, I have become a moderator in the seminars and a mentor to those who request my help. As usual, I've discovered I still have much to learn.

Two years ago a participant approached me asking for time to discuss some important decisions in his life. He worked in government leading a major urban renewal project that involved attracting hotels to the area, putting gang members to work, restoring some grand old houses, helping poor women learn job skills and set up their own businesses. He wanted to do this on a larger scale, but felt it was important to convert the effort into a public-private venture, so as to become more insulated from the vicissitudes of rotating governments.

He arrived for our first session at 7:15 a.m., and we had forty-five minutes together. From the materials he had sent me in advance, I assumed he wanted my help in finding willing investors for his new venture, so I listened somewhat impatiently, feeling I already understood his project and what he needed. When he asked for advice, I pulled out my notes on the questions potential investors would need to see answered before they invested in the venture. I even suggested an outline for the prospectus he should prepare.

I was proud of my feedback, but, as we walked over to class, he said, "We're not through yet, are we?" So we scheduled a second session.

In the second session, we sat out behind my little apartment watching the setting sun. This time he talked about his ambivalent feelings on leaving the government and giving up his ability to direct the project he had birthed. I sensed he wanted to retain a base of power in the new project, but still be able to return to private practice as an architect. I felt he was asking me to help him visualize a public-private structure that would permit him to exercise CEO power in the new project, yet get paid private sector rates. As I listened carefully, I could sense underlying frustrations, but couldn't think of a solution that would give him everything he wanted.

When he stopped and asked for ideas, I was honest with him. Referring to a remark in a CALI session about the obvious lack of credibility of a Minister of Security who gave security service contracts to his own company, I said, "I don't know of any way you can be the one ultimately deciding on public contracts, yet also receiving them"—a point he readily admitted. I then talked about some alternative models of public-private agencies or foundations that might permit him to earn more yet stay involved. I cautioned that it was not likely he could get everything he wanted.

I ended this session feeling much less brilliant. He thanked me, but I sensed that my answers hadn't helped him that much. After one of the CALI sessions he returned saying, "Can we have another session?"

This third time I listened even more carefully. I heard his sadness at having to give up his government position in part for financial reasons. He talked about his wife's feelings about earning the bulk of their income as a psychologist while he earned only $3,500 of the $10,000 they needed each month. I gently asked questions about the state of their marriage. He told me his wife wanted to work less, a desire that conflicted with the priority they had for sending their kids to college in the U.S., and of her concern over his long hours and the demands his work put on the family. I asked other questions designed to get at the fears he had expressed about turning over control of his project to others.

As he talked, I asked myself, "What's underneath all these feelings?" Having failed to coach him in a way that addressed his deepest needs, perhaps even needs of which he was unaware, my self-confidence as an advisor was low. When he asked for my thoughts, I began with the following disclaimer, "I don't know the answer for you. Three ideas, however, did occur to me as you talked. Take any of them if they feel helpful to you.

"Like it or not you're in a major transition: a transition from government to your private work and a transition in your family as your son goes off to college. What we know of transitions," I said, summarizing what I had learned from William Bridges, "is that successful ones have three phases: 1) saying goodbye and mourning the loss, 2) a period in a neutral zone with some confusion and distress, and 3) eventually arriving at a new beginning. Before you can get to new beginnings, you have to have the endings.

"Part of your sadness is necessary as you say goodbye to your earlier role, and it is important to mourn it. Your muddled feelings are also a necessary part of the process, but you have to have faith that if you push ahead, things will become clear in their own good time."

"Secondly, as you talked about your marriage, I remembered a time in my previous marriage where each of us resented the other's work." I then described the way that I gave Deirdre the job of choosing my "work plan" for the year and undertook to do the same for her. In the process of considering all the tradeoffs, we both ended up choosing for the other what each wanted and in the process, lost our resentments. I continued, "You might want to consider truly sharing this decision with your wife and having her step into your shoes, just as you step into hers.

"Finally, as you talked, I remembered a seminar on the Sedona method of releasing negative feelings that helped me greatly. This method asserts that negative feelings ultimately trace back to either a need for approval or a need for control. The paradoxical truth is that the only way to really secure control and approval is to let go of the need for them."

Before I had finished talking, he admitted to both the need for approval and control and was shaking his head in recognition of the need to release. He seemed pleased as we finished up this third coaching session. Somehow it finally had addressed his felt needs. He had seen his problems in a new light that filled him with hope. He thanked me profusely, promised to continue working on his decisions, and expressed the hope we'd have another chance to talk at the next CALI session.

I left this last session feeling good, but also chastened. In helping others, listening is critical, but it must be an active listening that pushes down through layers. My inclination is to assume I have come upon the true questions, when, in fact, they are often only surface concerns. I promised myself that next time I would listen well, and then listen some more. I would remind myself that I don't know what I don't know. Then with real humility, I'll offer ideas.

PICKING THE RIGHT TEAM

One of the planning exercises that I distribute following the New Partner Training module concerns the organizations you choose as your platform—the ones that will determine your work, your friends, your status in society, your salary, and to a great degree your personal growth. Taking a job or switching jobs has huge ripple effects on the rest of life. It is important not just to join the right team, but to have a strategy for managing relationships to both the organization and your colleagues. Organizational relationships should be thought of as assets built over time that are not casually thrown away when it comes time to move on. Let me share some of the guidelines I developed for myself over the years:

My "mission" is my responsibility. I cannot expect an organization to give it to me. What I do must obviously be of value to the organization, but the total mix of activities is something I, not my boss, should decide. Once I am clear on what I should be doing, I need to choose an organization that will be a good platform.

In choosing my platform, I'd better pick a group I respect, people I like and whose values I share. As a general rule, I should join the best team that will have me. Better to be a mediocre player on a great team than the best player on a weak team. I cannot claim credit for the growth and success of INCAE, Harvard, Bain, Bain Capital, or

Mesoamerica Partners. But the fact that they have been winning teams has directly and indirectly made me more successful. If INCAE had died in the Sandinista period or Bain gone bankrupt in the troubled years, both my bank account and résumé would look a lot different.

When I join a new organization, I need to remind myself that it will take two years to "find the bathroom." I should not assume I understand the culture and way of doing things, so I need time to learn my new environment. Even if I think my way of doing things might be better, I have to earn the right to make changes. I have to be a net contributor before the platform becomes mine to use. Learning the case method à la the business school was not easy when I moved from law to business. Moving from teaching at Harvard to being a consultant at Bain was painful. It took an act of humility to set aside my way of doing consulting and learn how to do it the Bain way.

If I want my organization to support me in activities outside their core business, I have to be a real bargain. At Bain, I was anxious to make sure that I was paid what I had earned, not a penny less. When I was part of the bonus-determining process, it became clear that most of us overestimate our contributions, in part because we are familiar with all we've done, but ignorant of all others have done. The partners we worked hard to keep them happy and in the firm were those that tried to give more than they took.

Even if successful in locating the bathroom and building a powerbase, there often comes a time when my personal mission requires moving on. It's important to do so in a way that does not destroy valuable relationships. When I left INCAE to teach at Harvard and then to work with Bain, I stayed linked with INCAE through giving regular seminars in Central America each year and accepting a position on the board. When I felt my personal mission required me to move to Costa Rica, it was not at all a part of Bain's strategy, yet we figured out creative ways whereby I could continue making a contribution through serving on governance committees, doing training, so Bain supported my work in Latin America.

Not severing important ties sometimes requires audacity as well as creativity. In 1980, less than two years after joining Bain, I asked for a two-year leave of absence to help INCAE though its crisis. Ralph Willard, the Bain partner who had recruited me, was upset. He believed my plan was stupid and that it was dangerous to take my family down to war-torn Nicaragua. He was also sure that Bill would be unwilling to give me an unpaid leave of absence after all they had invested in me. "Bill will kill you, Harry. If you insist on this path, my suggestion is that you sneak out the back door and just send him your letter of resignation."

Instead, I asked to see Bill, and once there, told him I was coming to ask for three things. I explained the situation with Sandinistas in Nicaragua and the strategy we'd developed. In spite of a year of searching for a rector, we had been unable to find anyone to lead the rescue effort. If I didn't undertake the assignment, the board felt it would have to shut down the school. My requests were first, a two-year leave of absence to help implement the strategy. Second, I wanted him to serve on a committee that included a Republican governor of Minnesota, a leading businessman in Boston whose last name was Cabot, and the Dean of the Harvard Business School. This group would be committed to raising "holy hell" with President Reagan if the US cut off aid to INCAE or if I were imprisoned, and each member would give us their home phone number just in case. Finally, I asked him for a donation of $10,000 to INCAE. Bill thought a moment and on the spot agreed to all three requests. I returned to Bain two years later.

FAMILY LIFE

JOYS OF FATHERHOOD

My scrapbook of memories of Sarah and Ken's growing-up years has many more stories than I can fit in this book: digging with them in the sand at Pochomil, the two riding Sammy our big German shepherd, piñatas and costumed birthday parties, learning to swim at the INCAE pool, singing along with John Denver on our car trips, a Club Med vacation when they were young teenagers, holiday meals around a table, gifts under the tree, and on and on. That they brought much richness into my life is a huge understatement.

Gender Neutral

Deirdre and I wanted to raise Sarah and Kenny without gender stereotypes. Deirdre, influenced in part by her interest in feminism, wanted to raise Sarah differently than she had been raised. I concurred. I wanted Sarah to follow in the footsteps of the strong, independent women in my family. In order to toughen her up, I'd get down on the rug and try to get her to wrestle with me or throw her high in the air and hope it would delight her. These tactics weren't very successful. I tried playing catch with her early on, but the sight of a ball coming toward her was scary, and she'd turn away.

Sarah was very sensitive. If I scolded the dog, she cried. (And we had three dogs by this time: Daisy, a galloping stupid Great Dane we'd inherited from the Austins; Sammy, a gentle German shepherd, who let the kids ride his back and pull his ears; and Pelusa, a little spaniel that Sarah loved to cuddle.) Among her favorite activities was playing with her dolls and serving them tea in the doll house.

On the other hand, Kenny loved rough-housing. He banged around the house like a football player, daring the furniture to tackle him. He was forever climbing to places from which he couldn't get down. Deirdre made a valiant attempt to expand his interests, getting him non-violent toys like a boy doll that peed, instead of buying tanks or guns.

A friend, who thought we were going a little overboard, was delighted one day to see Kenny out in the back yard playing with the doll. He'd taken off all the clothes and filled him up with water. Turning the doll upside down, he was using him as a gun to charge Sarah's tea party and shoot water at her dolls.

This unexpected turn of events, among others, began to teach me some humility. I started fatherhood very opinionated and convinced that children were the product of their upbringing, having been raised in the "nurture" camp of psychology. "Bad" children reflected deficient parenting. As I came face to face with the children's strong wills, however, I moved fairly quickly into the "nature" camp, convinced that each child is really is a unique personality and not nearly as malleable as we think. I had friends who were excellent parents struggling with difficult children, and I became aware how lucky I was that my own gave me so little trouble.

Rocking Chair Stories

One of my favorite memories from the early years in Nicaragua was making up stories with Sarah, and later with her and Kenny. We'd sit together in a rocker on the front porch looking down on Managua and the lake or lie in a hammock on the back porch overlooking the garden.

"Once upon a time there was a little girl whose name was . . ." Here I'd pause and Sarah would generally say, 'Sarah.'

"One day this little girl was rocking on her front porch when she heard someone crying. She said 'Who's there?' and turned to look on her left." (Here we would both elaborately turn to look over the left side of the rocking chair.) "But no one was there!"

"The crying continued so the little girl looked to her right." (By now Sarah was very much into the story) "But No One Was There!"

"'Boo hoo, I'm so sad!' the crying continued, so the little girl got out of the chair and went around to look behind it." "BUT NO ONE WAS THERE!"

"So the little girl finally asked, 'Who are you?'"

(With sobs) "I'm the rocking chair."

"But why are you crying?"

"Because I have no friends and no one ever comes and plays with me."

"So the little girl felt sorry for the chair and thought and thought about how she could help. She decided . . ." Here I would pause and Sarah would come up with some wonderful solution for the chair, or depending on the story, the animal or the tree or the dwarf.

In this fashion, Sarah, Kenny, and I had many adventures. For instance, behind the bush in the garden we discovered a passageway into a subterranean world inhabited by dwarves and elves, as well as strange, magical animals that talked.

Before some of my long trips, I even started recording stories that Deirdre would play while I was away, though these were never as satisfying as the ones we discovered interactively.

About this time, I read somewhere that young children have trouble distinguishing reality from fiction and therefore shouldn't be read fairy tales, but rather real life stories. This struck me as terribly wrongheaded. I believed (and continue to believe) that one of the most important things is a good imagination. The ability to make movies in your mind, to visualize events in time and space, is an important part of creativity and judgment, and a cornerstone of leadership. Even if some future research proves me wrong and it turns out a good imagination is not that functional or important for work, I don't think I'll change my mind. My own life from childhood through adulthood has been greatly enriched by the imaginary stories I heard and by the elaborate daydreams I've spun since very young.

Discipline and Consistency

Deirdre was definitely the "A" parent. She invested heavily in all aspects of our children's lives, reading to them, teaching them, organizing play groups, even getting involved in starting up "INCAEito," a preschool and kindergarten for faculty and student children. I never developed her ability to see the fascinating development and patterns of growth going on in them.

Making up stories with Ken and Sarah]

Our different philosophies of parenting created a certain amount of friction, and it took us some time to integrate them into a coherent approach. For instance, when it came to discipline, I believed in strictness. I thought it was okay to lay down rules "because I say so," and I felt no need to explain everything. I also believed, however, that it was important to limit rules to the fewest possible, partly to avoid having rules you couldn't truly enforce. I'm a believer in avoiding legislation that is only going to increase my work load.

I also had no philosophical problem with corporal punishment, though I felt it should be proximate to the crime. I believed "consistency" was terribly important. If you promise, deliver; if you threaten, follow through.

Deirdre was opposed to corporal punishment. If there was misbehavior or fights to break up, she forced each child to go into the bedroom for a "time out." I came to like this punishment technique much better than spanking. She believed in explaining rules and allowing kids the right to re-negotiate them. She didn't see consistency as good logic for following through on a bad decision. She had the energy and patience to make many rules, but did not feel bound to follow through if they didn't seem appropriate, though she felt it was important to deliver on promises and to be predictable.

Gotcha

In spite of our different approaches, the priority that united us was raising our two children, loving them well, and helping them get a good start in life. After two years in the Soldiers Field Apartments of the Harvard Business School, we bought a house in the suburbs of Boston where Sarah and Ken could be in good primary public schools. Deirdre did a lot of research on school districts, and we decided the Pierce School in West Newton was the right place for them. We found a house within a couple of blocks of the school, and then, in the inflating housing market of that period, upgraded to a bigger house nearby the following year.

We were both aware that the world could be a dangerous place for children, but we tended to have different philosophies on how to deal with that. Deirdre's natural inclination was to protect. Mine was to focus on developing skills to cope with danger. In Nicaragua, when Sarah was tiny and prone to squirm on the changing table, I let her roll off several times—catching her before she hit the floor of course—so she'd learn to be still. This horrified Deirdre and her friends when they found out.

If Kenny wandered off in a mall, Deirdre's response was to call him back or chase him down if he didn't respond. This strategy seemed to stimulate him to wander even further afield. My tack if he didn't respond to my call was to walk nonchalantly off in the other direction until he came running back looking for us. Deirdre was certain that this was creating deep inner insecurities that would have to be dealt with in later years in extensive therapy, and that I was not so much teaching our kids that they were capable of taking care of themselves and landing on their feet, as of making them feel the world was unsafe.

On the front lawn of our Newton home: Sarah,
Harry, Deirdre and Ken

Our house in West Newton was on a busy street, and we discussed how to protect the kids. Deirdre suggested a rule prohibiting them from playing in the front yard or crossing the street without an adult. I preferred a different approach. We invented a game where we went out to the street and looked carefully both ways. You lost if you started to cross the street when a car was coming in either direction. Winning involved both waiting for a clear view and crossing the street quickly. Once they understood the rules of the game, I tried to trick them. If I saw a car a block or so away I'd say, "Okay, let's cross!" and if they stepped off the curb, I'd laugh and say, "Gotcha! See that car?" We played this until I could no longer fool them, and they took great pride in their mastery. For years afterward, if I stepped off the curb to cross the street with a car in sight, they would gleefully shout, "Gotcha! You lose!"

Allowances and Finances

One of our objectives was to raise children who knew how to live within their means. We wanted them to save and manage money well and to be generous without being spendthrifts. Even before primary school, Sarah and Ken got small allowances they could use for special treats. We encouraged them to save part of the money for things they might want in the future. As they grew older, we increased both their chores and their allowances, so that by middle school, they were covering their school supplies and clothing, as well as movies and other entertainment.

At one point, to Deirdre's consternation, Sarah began buying her clothes in a second-hand store that sold them by the pound. The conflict between being frugal and being presentable was resolved by agreeing that Sarah have at least one dress that both she and Deirdre felt was appropriate for elegant occasions.

Ken's expenditures focused on high-end, top-quality purchases. For one of his birthdays in high school he asked for an expensive watch. I argued that he should do what I did, namely, buy inexpensive ones that could be replaced cheaply if lost or broken. He insisted that, unlike his father, he did not lose his good things and would take care of them. His argument won, and he still has that watch, although it has been replaced now by a nicer one.

We also had the kids participate in our annual August planning and budgeting exercise. The plan always included choosing a special treat like a new TV, sound system, Jacuzzi, vacation, or car, and it was based on my earning a good bonus and the family staying within our budget.

One morning I was having breakfast with a good friend who had stayed overnight. We were talking about how wealthy families should manage money and inheritance so their children were not spoiled, and he described a billionaire in Texas who had told his four children that his wealth would be divided proportionate to the amount each one had earned and saved by the age of thirty. If one had made $1,200,000 by thirty, another $600,000, a third $200,000, and the fourth nothing, then the first would get 60 percent, the second 30 percent, the third 10 percent, and the fourth nothing.

Ken, who was in middle school at the time, listened attentively to our conversation. A day or so later, he came to me and said, "Dad, I've been thinking about that inheritance plan, and I don't think it's a good idea. If Sarah decides to do social work like Mom while I go into business, I'd get most of it and that wouldn't be fair. I think a better system is . . ."

I don't recall his suggested plan, but I do remember feeling enormously pleased that he had thought about the problem and come up with a solution, and most of all, that he'd been concerned about his sister's well-being.

When Sarah and Ken were in high school, I told them I wasn't planning to leave them a large inheritance. I wanted to be able to take care of my own retirement and become financially independent enough to take a job that did not require me to earn a salary. I did plan to cover their college education, but didn't want them ever to ask me for extra money if they hadn't stayed in their budget. I would set aside the savings for college while they were still in high school and together, we would invest it. The income and principal would then be used to pay college expenses. Anything they earned or saved was theirs and could be used for graduate school or as a down payment on a house. We would adjust the amount up or down depending on the actual cost of education for the schools they selected, as I didn't want finances to determine their choices. They should go to the best school they could get into.

Both put most of their college fund in Bain Capital and did very well. While in college, they prepared annual budgets, and we'd reinvest what was not needed for that year's expenses. They managed their money well, never asked for extra money, and graduated with small nest eggs.

Early in Ken's time at Georgetown, I visited Washington D.C. and invited him and five friends out for an expensive meal. I noticed that his friends seemed careful not to order anything on the menu that was too expensive, even when I urged them to "live it up," saying this was a special treat. Afterwards, Ken explained to me in private that his roommates assumed we were not well off because he was so frugal. He knew I made more than any of their fathers, but they didn't, and they'd been nervous about running up a big bill. I was delighted that he was being thrifty and also that he felt no need to appear wealthy.

Teenage Years

As Sarah and Ken moved into their teen years, graduating from Pierce and then moving through middle and high school at Buckingham Brown and Nichols, our family life in West Newton was enriched by the arrival of extended family, the first being my sister Cathy, her husband, Marc, and their two children, Robbie and Anni. Marc was teaching at the Kennedy School, and they bought a home a block from us. Soon afterwards, we welcomed John and Normita Ickis, colleagues from INCAE, with their daughters, Lisa and Katie. They also bought a home in the neighborhood, and suddenly, Ken and Sarah had younger cousins, two wonderful aunts and other homes to visit when Deirdre and I were traveling. Five of us six adults had jobs that took us out of town, so we covered for each other and often met for potluck meals at one or another of the houses.

Sarah and Ken during teenage years with parents

On the weekends there were sports or social events that mixed friends from INCAE, Harvard, and Bain with visitors and extended family. We had several guestrooms and invited friends coming through town to stay with us. It was something of a joke that Deirdre and I might or might not be there, but Sarah and Kenny were great hosts.

The kids were comfortable with adults, partly because we had preserved a Nicaraguan custom we liked. Upon entering a room with adults, they were expected to go up to each person and either shake hands or kiss them on the cheek. When they left the room, they repeated the gestures.

Each year we hosted a summer social for my Bain teams. The party often had a Latin flavor—margaritas, piñatas, dancing, and favors. Ken and Sarah were not only invited to come, but to serve as co-hosts and to ensure people met each other. I also began to take them with me on "recruiting dinners" that involved interviewing potential consultants. Besides having one less evening we were separated, it gave Ken and Sarah a chance to meet young people who had been successful in college and graduate school, potential role models who were near their ages.

Before these dinners, I'd tell them about the five or six recruits we'd be with and ask for their help in evaluating them. Ken and Sarah took these assignments seriously, and would give insightful reports on those they had talked to during the evening.

Positive Reinforcement

From the beginning, Deirdre and I agreed that there's no such thing as "too much" love or affirmation. While our own parents were good role models, both of us had felt a bit starved for attention and positive feedback. We wanted to be more generous in praise and more open about our feelings than we remembered from our upbringing.

That was our intention, but I'm not sure it was our kids' experience. Just as my father failed to create a different pattern with me than he had experienced with his dad, so I fear Sarah and Ken have experienced me as a far more critical and absent parent than I wanted to be. There are patterns handed from generation to generation that are very hard to change, often because we aren't fully aware of them until much later. For my failures, like my father, I'd like them to know that I'm sorry. I want them to understand that I am proud and grateful for each of them and have always loved them deeply, even if not always well.

FAILURE AT MARRIAGE

Virtually all the young people I interact with are surprised by how difficult it is to build a good marriage. The failure of my first marriage surprised me because we had dated for over three years. We were in love and believed we fit together well. Yet from the first year there were tensions that signaled deeper issues, and I have often asked myself, "What were my big mistakes? What did I do that killed love? If a significant part of the problem was simply lack of fit, why did we not see it during our courtship?"

The stories that follow reflect some of my answers, though I have undoubtedly missed important factors. I am well aware that these reflect only my perspective and that Deirdre's interpretations may be very different.

Let me also add that focusing on the mistakes is not meant to ignore the many positive family experiences we shared, the many friends we developed together, the mutual support we gave each other's careers, or the times of real love and intimacy. Every period in our life had its share of happiness and growth. Things have never been all good or all bad. I focus on the mistakes because I feel it was through them that I received the most valuable lessons.

Early Mistakes

Following our marriage in Cambridge, we flew to Spain for our honeymoon. We arrived in Malaga after more than 20 hours of travel, and we fell into bed where we immediately disagreed on whether the window should be open or shut (I can't remember who wanted what). Even as exhausted as we were, I argued my point and Deirdre argued hers. I ended up doing what she wanted, but then lay awake surprised at the resentment I felt.

Part of my surprise lay in the fact that I had always been attracted to Deirdre's unambiguous expression of her needs and desires. She maintained an order in her life that I did not. Now suddenly, I was bothered by the fact that her wants conflicted with mine. I was largely unaware of my need for control and thus began to feel that our give-and-take was unequal.

I didn't handle this resentment in a constructive way. When Deirdre got carsick driving up the Malaga coast, I was more passive-aggressive than sympathetic. I did not share her enthusiasm for Granada and became withdrawn. Rather than making an attempt to talk things through, I kept quiet and nursed my resentment.

After the honeymoon, we went to Stuttgart where we had an apartment "on the economy." Deirdre wanted to go down to the corner store and get some groceries, and she asked me to go with her since she was still feeling insecure and knew no German. I was working on moving in and told her that she'd be fine going on her own. She insisted I go with her, and what I saw as her dependency touched an unconscious nerve. I dug in and refused to budge, convinced this was manipulative.

So she went on her own, but I can imagine that she was shaken by what seemed to be a lack of love, care, and dependability. She must have wondered if I really loved her since I seemed unwilling to meet her needs.

Many years later, I read a book that suggested a way of understanding what had happened, and it clarified the mistake I made in that first year of marriage. The theory of the book was that people often fall in love with someone who reminds them of a caretaker who has wounded them. They believe that the beloved will heal the past. I experienced my mother as a strong-willed yet dependent person who relied on me to be "the man of the house" and whose dependency made me feel inadequate. My marriage seemed to pull me back into this same experience. Perhaps I reminded Deirdre of someone in her life who had let her down by being distant and refusing to respond to her needs. Whatever the case, we unconsciously set up a very negative pattern, one we would struggle with for years.

The book argued that the road to healing lies in each partner's willingness to try to become the partner the other needs. Rather than "protecting my autonomy," I should have tried to better understand what Deirdre needed and wanted. The paradox is that perhaps with deeper understanding of both our struggles with dependency, I could have chosen more healing patterns and helped both of us. Had I been aware of why dependency, however mild, pushed such hot buttons in me, perhaps I could have found more creative ways to communicate the underlying love and safety she needed.

The Rio San Juan Fiasco

Early in our stay in Nicaragua, I made friends with a nephew of one of Nicaragua's leading poets. José Coronel Urtecho was internationally renowned and lived in the area of the Rio San Juan. Though he was Nicaraguan, he had built his ranch across the border in Costa Rica in order not to live in Somoza's Nicaragua. His nephew, when he learned of my interest in literature, asked me if I'd like to meet him. "Definitely, yes!" was my enthusiastic reply.

He arranged for us to fly down to San Carlos where we would take a boat to the ranch. The invitation was for a weekend during which they'd also be having a mini-family reunion where I would have a chance to meet his sons and daughters as well. Unfortunately, the timing of the invitation was for a weekend shortly after Sarah was born.

I was so entranced by the opportunity that I couldn't imagine turning it down, so I informed Deirdre of my decision, told her that with her friends and the maids she was in good hands, and flew off for the weekend.

It was a wonderful trip, but on returning home, I discovered I'd done great damage to the marriage. Deirdre was deeply hurt that I had chosen to leave over being with her and our newborn daughter. It was the most dramatic example yet of how insensitive and undependable I could be, and years later in marriage therapy, she said this was the turning point in our marriage.

Pulling Back from the Brink

Deirdre and several INCAE wives and their friends formed a women's group that discussed literature and feminist books. The participants were focused on their young families, and some were missing the careers for which they had been trained. Many were angry that their husbands weren't sharing more equally in the child-rearing, that they traveled so often, and that even when not on the road, they worked long hours. One result of this discontent was a decision by several in the group, including Deirdre, to rewrite both the explicit and implicit marriage contract.

My reactions to Deirdre's unhappiness and criticism varied. If I did something inconsiderate, like the Rio San Juan trip, and felt she had a valid point, I'd apologize and promise to try to do better. But I found myself becoming increasingly angry. I felt we'd made a joint decision to come to Nicaragua, and that we had agreed she'd focus on starting the family while I took responsibility for earning a living. My workload was enormous, with teaching, consulting and writing a dissertation, and each responsibility entailed travel. Deirdre had a lovely home, a full-time live-in maid and guard. It seemed to me she had plenty of time for personal needs, her friends, her work as case writer for INCAE's family planning program and as a volunteer in rural health programs.

When the idea of rewriting the marriage contract was broached, I resented it. "Fine, I agree, but if it's not a contract that makes us both happy, let's call the whole thing off."

Talk of divorce led us to join several other couples in crisis to organize couple's therapy. We had no outside professional guidance since several members of the group were psychologists. We met once a week and quickly settled into a pattern of devoting each meeting to one couple. The couple "on the mat" would talk to each other directly about what was bothering them. The rest of us participated by asking questions or rephrasing things so that each one was forced to hear the other.

The sessions were enlightening. Other people's downward spirals were blindingly obvious, their failures of communication apparent, and it was sobering to realize that our patterns must be equally obvious to them.

We read the book *I'm Okay, You're Okay*, which suggests that the secret to good communications is to talk about one's own feelings rather than to attack the other's character. "You're so selfish insisting on your way" is much less effective than saying, "When you insist that we go to your restaurant rather than mine, I feel diminished and get resentful." Though the new language often felt contrived, it was a good reminder that I really only knew what was happening inside of me. It also made me pay attention to the behaviors that were triggering my responses, and it forced me to label my feelings.

The group only lasted six months, and half of the couples were divorced within two years. Whatever insights they'd gotten hadn't saved their marriages. Deirdre and I, encouraged by our improved communication, pulled back from the brink and decided to try to rebuild our marriage.

The Broken Lattice

Ten years later in 1983 in the U.S., we once again approached the brink. In spite of the space we gave each other and better communication, our demanding careers created tensions. We had different perceptions of family roles and responsibilities. We disagreed about whose job was more demanding or important. Each perceived the other's expectations to be unrealistic and selfish. We also had very different approaches to money and financial priorities. I continued to be driven by the objective of financial independence and therefore wanted to allocate most of my salary to savings, whereas Deirdre felt we should take advantage of our good incomes by sending the kids to private schools and living more comfortably. She felt I was over-controlling on expenditures. I felt my financial objectives were sabotaged by her overspending. We were at an impasse.

We discussed divorce, but two things brought us back from this second precipice.

First, we modified our August planning process. We each shared our list of the career decisions and issues we were facing and the options we felt we had. We shared the pros and cons of each option. Then each of us took the other's decision and wrote up, not our own plan, but the plan we would choose for the other.

When we shared the results, Deirdre had chosen for me what I would have chosen for myself, and likewise, I made the choices for her that she wanted. Stepping into each other's shoes dramatically changed our appreciation of the situation, awakened a desire to give the other support, and increased our empathy.

Second, we came across a study of forty families pre—and post-divorce that greatly impacted our thinking. This research measured the impact of divorce on the well-being of each member of the family. The well-being questionnaire was administered to each person in the period before a divorce had split the family and then again about two years after the divorce had occurred.

The results were striking. In about 20 percent of the cases, both husband and wife were better off after the divorce. In about 20 percent, both were worse off. And in about 60 percent, one was better off and the other worse off. However, in over 90 percent of the cases, the children were worse off after the divorce—and the negative impact on the children was uncorrelated with whether it was better or worse for the parents.

The study concluded with a metaphor that caught my attention. "A pea vine needs a lattice to grow on. Even a broken lattice works better than no lattice at all." Putting our school age kids through a divorce would almost surely be bad for them. While Deirdre and I could hope to better our lives, the children would be worse off. We parented in a coordinated fashion, treated each other decently, and kept up a good couple front. It seemed selfish to sacrifice our children's well-being when they needed a lattice, even if it was a broken one. The study did not persuade us that we belonged together for the rest of our lives, but it did persuade us to stay together at least until Sarah and Ken were in college.

POTHOLES, EPIPHANIES, AND TRANSITIONS

INSIGHTS ON THE JOURNEY

In this chapter I'd like to back up chronologically and talk about "Aha!" experiences that gave me important insights—experiences I now think of as part of my spiritual journey, though I'm not sure I would have labeled them as such while they were happening.

After law school my active religious life ebbed. I gave up the practice of daily Bible reading and prayer and only sporadically attended church. Yet I remained fascinated by other people's spiritual experiences and continued to read books about religion and faith. Among the ten or so books I was reading at any time, there were always one or two on religious themes, many from other faiths.

I continued to have experiences, often unexpected, that filled me with awe and made life meaningful, which helped me be more effective and healthy. Often these were provoked by "potholes"—adversities that brought me up short and made me look at my life more closely.

Stranger in a Strange Land

Let me start with one that happened toward the end of my third year in law school. Lon Fuller, the professor I most admired, in his seminar on jurisprudence, assigned a reading, "The Role of the Stranger in Society." This article by a nineteenth century sociologist, Georg Simmel, argued that from the earliest times, strangers have had a key role in society. In the Bible when Joseph was made prime minister, he was playing one of the traditional roles of a "stranger" in Egyptian society. Not belonging to any of the main families, he could earn the trust of all.

This article hit me hard because up until that moment, I'd always felt I belonged to no group among whom I lived. As a little boy in Costa Rica, I was a "gringo," different from most of the children in my classes. I was light-skinned and easily sunburned. Since we moved frequently back and forth to the United States, I didn't speak Spanish particularly well. The sports I preferred were those played in the United States—baseball, basketball, and American football. The books I loved to read were in English, not Spanish.

But I didn't belong in the United States either. We were "Christians" who didn't go to movies, didn't drink, didn't play cards, and didn't dance. We were poorer than those around us. My clothes were out of style. I knew next to nothing about TV and popular music. It did not help my sense of belonging that I attended so many different schools or that when I arrived at a new school, I was always smaller than any boy or girl in my class.

This sense of "stranger-ness" was different from an inferiority complex. I did well in school, always had friends, and was proud of my parents. It was more that "this world was not my home," that in some important way I would always be a stranger. As I progressed through high school, college, and law school, nothing happened that changed that feeling. Selling in the summer convinced me I could be successful in the secular world, but it did not make me feel I belonged.

So when I read this article about the role of a stranger in society, light bulbs went on in my mind. *Aha!* I thought, *That's what I am, a stranger. My role in life is going to be a bridge between the worlds in which I have been raised, perhaps between the U.S. and Latin America.*"

This not only gave me a role to play, but had a very nice "I'm okay, you're okay" twist to it. I could honor both the gringo and Latino inside of me, neither being superior or inferior. Each culture had many positive aspects that I could affirm and incorporate into my personality.

In spite of my new paradigm, when I went to Nicaragua after the doctoral program, I feared I might not have the personality to be successful in Latin America. Besides my poor Spanish, I might be too reserved, too Anglo-Saxon. At a party in that first year, I discovered a "Latin Harry" inside of me. No one had warned us that typically, dinner wasn't served until close to midnight, so the alcohol beforehand could build up to lethal levels. As people got happier and louder, they began the entertainment. Everyone was expected to sing a song or recite some dramatic poetry. Initially I resisted, but finally I climbed up on the table that served as a stage, and with a borrowed guitar, sang "At the End of the Rainbow." Later I recited a speech from "My Fair Lady." It surprised me as much as the Nicaraguans to discover an extroverted Harry who thoroughly enjoyed this sort of party. They responded warmly, and though I wasn't fooled into believing I fully "belonged," the positive reinforcement convinced me that I could live and work effectively in Latin America.

Almost everyone feels what I so acutely felt as a teenager—that they don't belong. Even if they live in the town where they grew up, have success at work, positions of responsibility in church, wear similar clothes, and drive the same cars, they know, deep down, that they are out of place.

This feeling isn't totally false. Each of us is unique, and by and large we have to go through life alone. The mistake is believing that we're the only ones who feel that way. If we are lucky, though, as I feel I have been, we discover a role we can fulfill that makes us a part of the larger whole. We learn to be strangers and accepting of all the strangers around us. Paradoxically, when we are comfortable as strangers and with strangers, we generally find that we really do belong.

Melanoma's Gift

In 1978, approaching my late thirties and teaching at the Harvard Business School, I applied for additional life insurance to protect my young family. During the required medical exam, the doctor discovered something on my right upper arm that looked suspicious to him. It turned out to be a melanoma that had begun to penetrate below the skin. The doctor scheduled surgery for the following morning at Mass General, and Dr. William Wood, the head of the Cox Melanoma Clinic, removed the melanoma, taking a shark's bite out of my arm and grafting skin onto the wound.

Bill Wood was a college friend who had come to Harvard Medical School from Wheaton about the time I was going to Harvard Law School. After the surgery, when the melanoma had been measured and classified, I met with him and asked, "What are my odds?"

"You don't want to know, Harry," he replied.

"Bill, I need to know. I have two young children, virtually no insurance or net worth. What are the odds for someone in my situation?"

He reluctantly answered, "The statistics suggest you have only one chance in four, a 25 percent probability, of living two years or more."

"Is there any special treatment I can take to improve the odds?" I asked. The answer turned out to be yes, and this led to my participation in his immunotherapy study for the next two years. Thirty years later, it appears that the surgery and the immunotherapy were effective. While in the hospital, I had an epiphany that may have contributed to my longevity; it has certainly enriched my life.

In the Harvard infirmary where I convalesced, I was still in denial, determined to keep up with my work and commitments. The day after surgery, I had my secretary bring over a pile of reading, and I organized my space so I could sit on a chair and use the food table as a desk.

As soon as my head was clear of the medicines, I woke up early and started reading back issues of the *American Economic Journal*. It wasn't long before I came across an article that I thought was excellent and for a while was filled with delight with its elegant analysis. Then I thought, *"If I had had a good math background in high school, I might have become a good economist and written something like this, but now it's too late."* Filled with a deep sense of failure, I put the article to one side, unfinished.

Later that morning in a waiting room for some tests, I picked up a *New Yorker* and started reading a short story that immediately captivated me. I thought, *What a great story! In college I wanted to become capable of writing something like this. But I never developed that talent and now it's too late.* Once again I felt a wave of failure sufficiently severe that I didn't finish the story.

Back in my room in the middle of the afternoon, I sat down to write a journal analyzing the two incidents. In the midst of writing I thought, *I've written about this in my journal too many times before, and it hasn't changed a thing. Each new incident still sinks me into the same depression. Damn it! Enough! I'm not going to rise from this makeshift desk until I get an insight that changes the pattern.*

Initially I wrote in my journal with a lot of energy and a great sense of hope. I traced the drive toward excellence back to my desire to emulate and please my father. I suspected that the burden he felt in his responsibilities for the mission was the root of the cancer that killed him, and here I was, repeating the pattern. Understanding the source of my sense of failure, though, was not a solution. Without a solution, my inspiration dried up. I sat looking at the blank pages and was tempted to quit the whole effort.

The story of Jacob came to mind. He wrestled all night with an angel saying "I am not going to let you go until you bless me." Stubbornly I decided to sit and think and write until such time as I got some sort of resolution. My only concession was to the doctor's order that I get up every two hours and walk in the hall for purposes of circulation. I did as asked, rolling beside me the stand with bags of solution and their attached tubes.

When Deirdre visited at the end of the afternoon, she was surprised to see me at the desk, but I didn't explain. She left. I was served supper and still did not get back in bed. Visiting hours passed and the floor became very quiet. About 11 p.m., bone dry of insight, I still sat at the makeshift desk. I finally got up for my last walk of the night to the end of the hall and a big window that looked down on Elsie's Sandwich Shop. It was still full of students. Rain was streaking the window; colored lights glistened on the black road. Normal life had continued without me.

As I walked back up the corridor, I passed a door that until that point had been shut. Through the open door, I heard a weak voice saying, "And as Henry James walked the streets . . ." I peeked in and saw a white-haired woman about seventy sitting in the corner chair taking dictation. On the bed with the sheet up to his chin, lay a frail ancient man with papery skin. His head was on the pillow, and he was looking at the ceiling while dictating.

I was immediately filled with an enormous sense of admiration. *Here,* I thought, *is a ninety-year-old professor emeritus trying to finish his book even as he dies. No self pity. No quitting."* The thought moved me to tears.

Then I thought, *And here I am moaning and groaning about my situation.* A wave of depression headed toward me like a tsunami, but this time, instead of giving in to feelings of failure, I thought, *Now I see the pattern. I am presented with excellence. I recognize it and see how high the bar is. Then I look at where I am relative to that bar, and I see the gap. The truth is that no matter how high my performance, there will be always be a gap. No doubt the economist in the American Economic Journal and the writer in the New Yorker see the imperfections in their work. But this ever-present gap sends me into tailspin. I get depressed and stop trying. What's the solution? I need to realize that excellence is rare enough that when I have the privilege of seeing it, I should focus all my attention on it. I should notice how it's done; watch it as closely as possible. I should rejoice in the privilege of seeing it. Who knows, with enough exposure, perhaps some of it will rub off on me.*

This insight was liberating. I imagined my dad applauding. It also worked. On the many occasions since in which I've been in the presence of excellence, I've generally been able to focus on it and feel gratitude for the example. I haven't let myself get depressed.

Sunday School Cases

During our years in the army, the doctoral program, and Nicaragua, Deirdre and I gradually stopped going to church or participating in formal religious life on a regular basis. When we moved out to the Newton suburb, we decided to try church again. Our young children were a major reason. Recognizing how important Bible stories and Christianity had been in our lives, we believed it would be good to expose them to the same heritage.

I also felt that, even though questioning my childhood faith and letting go of many of the practices associated with it had been a source of positive growth, that vein of ore was largely exhausted. The benefits of "rejecting" beliefs had largely ended, and it was time to start "affirming" and determining the values to which I was going to commit to in my life. The stimulation of church might help.

We started with a visit to the Presbyterian Church of Newton. That first Sunday the pastor, Rev. Monty Burnham, greeted us at the door on the way out. When he heard my name, he asked, "Are you any relation of Ken Strachan?" It turned out he was a graduate of Fuller Seminary, had taken classes from my father during his last illness, and had adopted him as a mentor. He and his wife Betsy immediately asked us to join a small discussion group with them and several other young couples. We became good friends and drew even closer as Betsy faced her final bout with cancer.

Monty proposed that I teach an adult Sunday school class, and my immediate reaction was "No, thanks—I have far too many doubts about the teachings of Christianity." But he persisted. So I finally said, "Monty, I've often wondered what it would be like to approach Bible teaching by the case method. The typical sermon takes a piece of scripture and the minister chooses real life situations that he feels illustrate the passage. But life comes at people with specific situations or problems that, in my experience, are sufficiently complex that different, even conflicting, scripture might be relevant. The right answer is much less obvious than people think. If you want, I'll be happy to bring 'real cases' and lead a discussion about them. But if you want a 'Christian' solution to the case, you'll have to find someone else."

He thought the idea was great. The class was scheduled, and we were assigned a small corner room on the second floor. Six or seven people appeared for the first session.

Every week, I'd search for a true life problem that would serve as a good case, perhaps an incident from work, or from a troubled marriage, or one that presented itself in childrearing. Then I would write out a one-page description of the case. It was important that it be a real case, but I felt free to disguise it or combine several cases into a composite. I also made sure the case required some sort of action or response. For example:

> You are sitting in your kitchen having tea with a good friend who was a missionary earlier in her life. Her husband was killed in a tragic accident. She has had to raise a son and daughter on her own. They are great kids.
>
> She tells you that she's distraught. Her son returned home from college last night for a short vacation and told her two things. First he has discovered that he is gay. Second, in spite of that, he feels that God is calling him to be a minister.

The discussion followed the same format each week, to which the class quickly became accustomed. First, they would ask any questions to collect data they felt was needed to more fully understand the situation. Then, we worked our way through three questions.

What is really going on here? What are the issues at stake?
Does the Bible have anything relevant to say? What?
How are you going to respond? Do it!

I'd write the various answers on the blackboard as the class developed them. When we got to the last question, I'd try to find a way to force role playing. We encouraged disagreement, but tried to create an open, nonjudgmental atmosphere. No one was allowed to shut down others with statements like, "That's heresy!"

Amazing things happened in the class. People were surprised at how many different ways it was possible to interpret the same external facts. It was rarely obvious what was really happening. Many different scripture passages might be relevant. But the most surprising discovery was the way "humanity" trumped "dogma" when people were forced to decide the implementation of their positions. Some, who had been dogmatic in the discussion of the Bible's position on a specific situation, switched their responses when forced to role play.

In the case of the missionary's son, one middle-aged woman had taken an adamant position that homosexuality was a perversion and sin (remember this was back in the 1980s when homosexuality was still illegal and something most gay people hid with shame.) "You have to tell your son that his homosexuality is a sin, that he cannot be a minister and certainly not an effective one, if he persists in it. Make clear to him that in refusing to treat it as sin, he is endangering his very soul." She was aggressive and eloquent in marshalling scripture behind this advice.

I cut her off in the midst of her advice and pulled a seat up in front of her and said, "You're now the friend and I'm your son, do what you're advising her to do." I forced her to visualize me as her son and talk to me. She started haltingly, and in the midst of her prepared speech, she suddenly broke down in tears and sobbing said, "Oh, my son, my son! I love you so much . . . Oh, my son!" The mood in the class changed dramatically and several people wept with her.

I don't know what was behind her tears and changed approach. But it seemed to me that what she had actually done, rather than what she believed orthodoxy required of her, was more the way Jesus dealt with the people of his time.

Word of this unusual class spread, and it quickly grew in size. We moved to bigger rooms. Doctors and lawyers and even two professors from a theological seminary nearby joined the group. Dealing with tough personal issues required people to share more of themselves than was usual. This in turn led to a genuine sense of mutual caring. Soon someone suggested we have a class party some Saturday night, and other parties followed.

The class did little to make me more orthodox or change my thinking. It did, however, make me aware of how much we need community. Like it or not, we all face difficult situations in which we need guidance, strength, and hope. We need spiritual support.

Being at Cause, Acquiring Mass

Bain regularly brought in outside trainers to help us partners become more effective in our selling or leadership, and some of these sessions were life-changing for me.

In one seminar the instructor asked, "How much of what goes on in Bain, in all Bain's offices around the world, can you directly influence?" We were asked to place ourselves on a continuum that ran from 0 percent to 100 percent. Most of us wrote down a number significantly below 50 percent, feeling our range of influence as junior partners was quite limited. In later sessions the instructors persuaded us that the right answer was 100 percent. Anything in the firm, for that matter in the world, which we chose to directly influence, was within the zone of our impact. It was important to recognize this and "be at cause," not victims of things beyond our control.

In another session we were asked to answer the question, "When an airplane is on autopilot, how much of the time is it on course? When your body is healthy, how much of the time is your body temperature at 98.6 degrees?" We all assumed the answer was some very high percent of the time, above 80 or 90 percent. The right answer, though, was somewhere around 5 percent. Both the plane and the body were almost always veering off course or off the ideal temperature. What made them work was that they were constantly monitoring, and as soon as they were off course, they recognized and self-corrected.

Most of us are not "at cause" because we avoid recognizing we are making mistakes. We stay off course until it's so obvious that we can't avoid seeing. We need to learn to reward ourselves when we recognize we're off course, and encourage ourselves to recognize this quickly so we can self-correct before the damage is too great.

In another session on selling, we asked the trainer for gimmicks we might use in our sales presentation. He refused to give us any. Instead he made a point that immediately clicked for me. "When you are sitting across from a potential client, or for that matter, anyone, they are taking a measure of your 'mass.' We all have experienced people that on the outside were quiet and unimpressive, but like Gandhi, projected huge mass. We've all been in the presence of tall handsome salesmen that came across as insubstantial lightweights. People experience you as person of substance or a lightweight. If you have no personal heft, it doesn't matter what words are coming out of your mouth."

Listening to him, I realized that I wanted to become a person of mass. I also began to think about what it was that produced personal mass. I suspected it had something to do with authenticity and was similar to what Jung was talking about when he talked about "integration."

From sessions like this I took away the following conclusions: If I was to be "at cause" regarding the conflicts at work or problems in my marriage, I needed to start asking how I was contributing to them and what I could do to make a difference, not looking for someone else to blame. I needed to be much more proactive at recognizing my mistakes. I couldn't let my fear of failure get in the way of recognizing them. Finally, it was important in all my planning to recognize that *who* I became was as important as what I said or did. In fact, becoming a person of mass was critical to being an effective leader.

Your God Is Too Small

On a trip to Buenos Aires, Argentina, in the 1980s during my years at Bain, a colleague and I met with the Latin American executives of a multinational gathered for divisional meetings. After our presentation, we agreed to join several of them for dinner. When we arrived at the bar where we were meeting, they were starting on their second drinks and sitting with two attractive women in their late thirties, dressed in tailored suits.

It turned out that they were not wives but people they had met at the bar and invited to join us for dinner. Both women were friendly, but one in particular struck me as having an unusual aura about her. She drank very little, followed the conversation closely and seemed self-contained. She reminded me of the Mona Lisa.

We went to a nearby restaurant and were soon seated around a table for eight. In a lull in the conversation, after some talk of religion, I said, "I'll tell you a story that my brother told me, and I'd like for each of you to tell what you think really was happening." They encouraged me to go on.

I told them that my bachelor brother, a psychologist, lived in Utah and had a group of buddies who loved to ski. On the weekends they skied hard and partied hard. A day on the slopes was followed with drinking, dancing, meeting girls, skinny dipping in the Jacuzzi. Late one Saturday evening when he'd not joined his buddies on the slopes, one of his friends showed up at his condo. My brother immediately knew something had happened to him. This is the story the friend told him.

> We got to the ski lodge on Friday and had one of our regular wild Friday nights. The next day, Saturday morning, I went out to ski as usual but, by mid-afternoon I felt sick and tired of the whole thing. I decided to skip the rest of the weekend and go home. Driving down the slope, I came to a fork in the road where I always go left. Some invisible hands twisted my steering wheel right and sent me down a road I'd never taken. Near the bottom of the mountain, I noticed one of those gospel tabernacles with lights blazing. The same invisible hands turned my steering wheel up the gravel road and into the parking lot. It was beginning to fill up with people coming for a service.
>
> Once parked, I suddenly felt paralyzed and couldn't get out of the car. The service began with music and preaching I could hear, but could not make out clearly. It ended several hours later with me still sitting frozen in my car. The cars began to leave and when the parking lot was empty, a voice from my

back seat ordered me to go into the empty tabernacle and to walk down to the front. I was told to lie down on the floor in front of the altar. I began to weep and weep although I didn't know why. After some time, feeling completely cleaned out, I felt free to leave, and I came here. What happened to me? What does it mean?

Most of my table companions suspected that my brother's friend came from a religious background and was feeling guilty about his wild life style. He was hung over on Saturday and therefore not up to skiing. They didn't think a supernatural force had taken the steering wheel from his hands, simply that on impulse, he had taken a different road. Another impulse had drawn him to the tabernacle, and his tears were a release of pent-up guilt.

One of the men put the idea in more technical language. "This is not an unusual type of hysteria. His unconscious broke through, taking temporary control. In the weeping and on the floor, he experienced a catharsis."

I noticed during the telling of the story that the Mona Lisa woman had begun to lean forward and become more excited. "Oh, no," she said, "I think it was God or an angel who took the steering wheel and led him to the service. I think it was a voice from God that ordered him in to the tabernacle. And it was his experience of God's love and forgiveness that left him feeling so clean. I've had a similar experience."

As we returned to the taxis, the woman walked up beside me and asked if I would rescue her from the attentions of one of the more tipsy clients and take her home. She got into the back of the taxi with my colleague and me, while another of the clients sat with the driver. After dropping the others at the hotel, I rode with her to her home about twenty minutes away, and she began to tell me about her experience of God. She had been born and raised in Europe. She and her husband and their two children had joined a church group. In a dramatic experience, God told her to divorce her husband and take her two children to Argentina. She now lived in a commune on the outskirts of Buenos Aires with other like-minded people. The taxi pulled up to the darkened compound of her commune, and I waited in the cab until she had let herself in through the gate and returned to my hotel wondering how to make sense of her story.

My client meetings ended the next afternoon, and I was leaving the day after for Brazil to visit my sister Clare and her husband, Tom. I decided to invite the woman to dinner. She accepted, and we talked in greater detail about her past and more importantly her spiritual practices. She described how the happiest time of her day was in the morning after her children left for school. She would read the Bible and pray. "While I'm doing that," she said, "I feel so enveloped in God's love. He tells me what to do." She was reluctant to say much about the commune except that in these "the last days," part of the reason they were in Argentina was because they expected a nuclear devastation in Europe.

Besides her strange story, I was struck by her passive, childlike faith. I did not feel she was trying to witness to me or save me. She did not proposition me sexually or ask me for money. It was as if she was floating down the river of life in some sort of happy spiritual bubble, so absolutely certain of God's love and forgiveness that she didn't have to worry about anything. He was taking care of her.

The next day in the interior of Brazil, I was talking with Clare and Tom, who headed up a major facility for handicapped and Hansen's disease patients in Bauru. I told them about this strange woman. Tom said, "Oh she's probably one of the 'Prostitutes for Christ'!" When I expressed surprise, he assured me that this phenomenon actually existed in several Latin American cities.

The next morning, alone in the house, I listened to some of Clare's records, one of which was Mahalia Jackson singing gospel songs. One hymn in particular, "His Eye is on the Sparrow," caught my attention. I opened up a book lying on the table next to the record player called *Your God is Too Small* and started to read it. I almost immediately put it back down, put off by its religious language and dogmatic message, but the title of the book struck home.

I thought to myself, *Harry, you get angry with the picture of God that fundamentalists advance, yet you have also put God in a very small box. You are certain that God would never tell a woman to divorce her husband, go to Argentina to avoid a nuclear holocaust, or make love to someone not her husband. If there is a God, which you doubt, you think you know exactly what He is like and wants. Your God is way too small! Admit it—if God exists, He or She or It is beyond anything you can imagine, and as the Bible suggests, capable of asking people to do all sorts of crazy things.*

That night, I flew high above the Amazon jungles back to Boston, seated in the darkened airplane cabin next to the window. Suddenly I heard a perfect rendition of Mahalia Jackson singing, full orchestra and piano, without the scratch of the vinyl records,

> Why do I feel discouraged?
> Why do the shadows fall?
> Why is my heart so heavy?
> And long for Heaven and Home

Unlike the way the song continues, I realized that I was not "happy and free." I felt deeply sad and began to weep, not knowing why, only feeling that my tears were coming from some place very deep inside. After a while the music in my head stopped, and my weeping ended.

I arrived back in Boston the next morning feeling neither enlightened nor particularly cleaned out, and I continued to be perplexed by the woman's story, as well as what had happened to me. All I knew was that any box I put around reality was far too small. How could I imagine understanding God if I didn't even understand myself?

I quickly buried the experience I had on the plane and resumed my busy life. In hindsight, I suspect that was a big mistake. Several years later, painful setbacks forced me to confront that deep inner sadness. In an important visualization, I found myself back in the interior of Brazil, sitting on the edge of the Iguazú Falls, water pouring through my chest, cold and carrying the grief of the world. Perhaps if I had confronted the sadness earlier, I could have avoided some of the setbacks.

THE TRANSITION OF 1989-1992

Before . . .

At the start of 1989, from the outside, my life looked quite enviable. I had had two uninterrupted decades of success at work, first in teaching with INCAE and the Harvard Business School, then in consulting with Bain & Co. I had a smart, beautiful wife with her own doctorate and career, two attractive children doing well in school, a big supportive extended family, and a great set of friends. I lived in a huge house in West Newton, earned an almost obscene salary, and had built up enough savings to be close to financial independence.

Then I hit some big "potholes" in my body, my work, my finances and my marriage.

My body, which I had always thought of as a trusty donkey, taken for granted and abused, broke down on me. My left hip had to be replaced, and I had frequent gout attacks. When I stopped taking the heavy dosage of aspirin for the hip, I had my first heart attack and several years later a triple bypass.

Bain, where I was now a partner, began to implode. A decade of meteoric growth and profitability ended as the economy entered a recession. As growth slowed and the terms of an ESOP (Employee Stock Option Plan) were revealed, conflict between the active partners and the founders came to a head. The founding partners had paid themselves a very high price for their shares and loaded the firm with debt. The slowdown and the debt now coming due meant that bonuses were significantly reduced. When the ESOP debt levels were revealed, many of the partners felt betrayed and began to leave the firm, some even setting up competing companies. As a recently promoted Executive Vice President, I was supposed to provide positive leadership, but I was powerless to change a financial and governance structure I felt was unfair. Neither remaining in my job nor quitting in the crisis felt right. On top of that, I felt the time had come to start my third career of public service.

Our family financial portfolio, which should have given us financial independence for any subsequent career, took a big hit in the recession. The securities of Bain that I owned melted away as the value of the firm evaporated. To make matters worse and against my better judgment, we had significantly increased our standard of living, buying a house in West Newton that was double the value of the one we had lived in for nearly ten years. In the depressed housing market, a sale of the new house would result in a huge loss.

My marriage was in equally bad shape. Deirdre and I had grown apart. In the aftermath of the heart attack, we faced the failure of our marriage, and began to consider divorce as our kids entered college.

Evidence-based Medicine and Logical Solutions

Much of what I did during this transition period is what you'd expect of a management consultant. I tried to analyze the challenges I was facing and their root causes. I imagined options and actively explored them, keeping my boat moving, as I had learned in earlier periods of planning. I investigated jobs like teaching that might involve less travel and be compatible with the heart disease. I also let myself flesh out my dream of a third career in Central America by traveling back into the region and even teaching for a month at INCAE. On these trips, I met with close friends, shared my options with them, and sought their advice. An elaborate financial analysis quantified our losses and compared the cost of continuing in our expensive house or selling at a loss.

On the health front, I accepted advice from doctors that was founded on "evidence-based medicine." Doctors did a balloon angioplasty to open up the arteries. They put me on a low-fat diet, enrolled me in an exercise program, and suggested I take a course on stress management that used techniques based on yoga and meditation. The stress management course made me conscious of the external stimuli that triggered a "fight or flight" response and the self-talk that aggravated it.

When the angioplasty failed, rather than more invasive interventions, I spent a month at the Pritikin Institute in California, undergoing an even more drastic regime of diet, exercise, and yoga. The doctors were impressed by how much weight I lost, my exercise regime, and all the books I was reading. They even suggested I might be going overboard attacking my disease.

When I told my cardiologist my plan to change my personality from an aggressive Type A, prone to heart attacks, to a more laid-back Type B, he laughingly told me, "You know, Harry, we doctors have a saying. 'There is only one person under more stress than a Type A personality—that's a Type A trying to be a Type B.' Take it easy, it could be genetics."

Dream Work and Therapy

Recognizing that he might be right about my heart problems being inherited and just something I had to live with, I nevertheless decided to take seriously an idea I found in a book I was reading. Illness may be the body trying to tell you what is wrong with your life. Instead of trying to make the symptoms go away, try to hear the messages your body is giving you. It seemed to me I was getting a pretty consistent message from a number of sides. There was much wrong in my life, and I needed some humble soul searching.

Therefore, without abandoning the healthy practices recommended by the doctors, I began "inner work," guided in great part by Jung's thinking and example. Jung believed that each of us has multiple personalities in our unconscious that influence our behavior. Besides my "persona" (my self-image), there was my "shadow," many of whose characteristics I disliked and projected on to others. There was also my anima and animus, the neglected feminine and masculine parts of myself and perhaps other pieces formed in forgotten childhood traumas.

My health, energy, and effectiveness, Jung suggested, required me to become conscious of these multiple facets and to integrate them. Rather than trying to kill or suppress the hateful and needy parts, I needed to acknowledge them and put my arms around them, so to speak. The transition process, if I was to go through it successfully, was not likely to be the linear logical solving of a mathematical problem. It was more a journey that required me to mourn the past and say goodbye, even to things I wanted to leave behind. I had to take the time for the muddled, messy middle period of confusion while things worked themselves out in the unconscious. Only if I took this journey would I come to a successful new beginning.

One of the ways I did this inner work was through a more disciplined analysis of my dreams. Awakening, I would immediately write down the dream, using the present tense as if still in it. Then I'd jot down any associations with the characters and settings. I'd treat each person in the dream as if they were a part of myself. Those who showed up with some frequency might be fragments buried in my unconscious. Finally, I'd complete the sentence "My dream is telling me . . . ," writing down whatever came to mind.

After investigating some alternative types of therapy, I began to do "awake dreaming," namely, visualization therapy. Earlier experiences of more traditional therapy had not helped much, since I felt I went off on head trips designed to fool both the therapist and myself.

Early in the transition, shortly after my hip replacement in 1989, I had a dream in which the doctor made it clear that I not only needed to learn to walk correctly, but also to live right. In visualization, I traveled down an artery and talked directly to my heart. It told me that the underlying problem was not my heavy work load, but the lack of love in my life.

Dreams and visualizations also introduced me to buried parts of myself: a 5-year-old ragged urchin with a deep need for the affection of his parents; his 10-year-old caretaker sister; a young idealistic knight encased in armor, rigid and judgmental. Dreams revealed lots of buried hostility, anger, and sorrow and suggested these might be the source of the cholesterol clogging my veins.

The Gulls, the Carcass, and Bain

The main focus of my journals in late 1989 and early 1990 was on the deteriorating situation at Bain and my anger with the founders. At times I felt like the monkey caught with his hand in the jar, unwilling to let go of the "peanuts" and take the radical step of leaving.

In the midst of the conflict of partners and founders over equity and governance, I had the following dream:

> We are at a big roast of a pig or cow on the sloping lawn in front of a large building of white sandstone that reminded me of Blanchard Hall at Wheaton. A large group of white gulls have gathered around. They carry the carcass up into the air and onto the roof of the building. I notice that they don't get the carcass all the way up on roof but only onto the ice that has formed over the gutters.
>
> Sure enough, as soon as the gulls stop flying and settle down to pick at the carcass, both the carcass and the gulls come tumbling down. I expect to see the gulls fly off the carcass like a cloud of mosquitoes, but most don't. The carcass with about

seven or eight gulls hits the ground rolling over and over down the hill. I awake convinced the gulls have been killed.

The hanging ice represented a real danger for me, falling icicles that could pierce my brain. But the ice was also a good metaphor for the values of our firm, cold and ultimately not solid enough.

The dream also told me that the key thing was to keep the birds flying and make sure that the meat was placed on the roof of the building, on solid values. I should join with others to try and save Bain. But if we could not get a financial and governance structure that permitted us to build the type of firm we believed in, we should all be ready to leave.

Meeting Smiley

When I began to do "guided visualizations" with a Jungian therapist, my unconscious surprised me with vivid pictures, amazing characters, and Delphic advice. The first session was typical of many that followed. My therapist suggested that we go down and find my inner guide. After a period of guided relaxation, she sent me down a set of stairs that would take me into safe place.

I started down, noting the stairs were of good wood. They were very steep. At the bottom they led into a paneled library with a fireplace. I sat in a high-backed winged easy chair facing the fireplace. To the left of the fireplace was a leaded window looking out on a walled garden.

When I was comfortably seated, she told me a special guide would appear, a wise helping figure would approach me. I thought I saw a tall beautiful woman in long regal white robes, but this figure never came into sharp relief, and I figured it must be the lace curtains blowing in the breeze. Outside a robin sat on the branch with its head cocked to one side looking at me. When I asked the robin if it was my wise guide, it just continued to look at me with cocked head.

As I waited for the guide, a hunchback old man in gardener's overalls came around the corner. He had a crinkled smile on his face. The therapist suggested I ask him his name. "People call me Smiley."

I thought "This is ridiculous. What a stupid name for a spiritual guide."

She suggested I ask "What do you do?"

He answered, "I am responsible for the garden, making sure the birds are happy, the sun has a chance to get in, the dampness doesn't get in the house."

He asked me "What do you do?"

I felt a wave of confusion. "I don't do anything worthwhile. I am just sitting here looking at the garden, feeling sad."

She suggested I ask him for help. He handed me a shovel and took me to a corner of the garden where there was a rose bush bed and said, "I'm going to help you pull up the grass your dad wanted you to pull out of the flower bed which you couldn't." (I immediately knew he was referring to a painful incident in my early childhood. I was weeding in a flower bed with my father. I tried to pull out the grass, but the blades broke off in my hand. My father exasperated said, "Harry, come on, pull it up by the roots!" I knew I was failing, my hand was cut and raw, I felt terrible.)

With Smiley's guidance, I stood on the shovel top, felt it cut through the grass and sink into the ground, and then when the shovel was half buried, I leaned back and rode the shovel down while it tore up the grass. Then I reached over, pulled up the grass quite easily, and shook the dirt from the roots back into the bed. I felt childlike and happy. This was not hard work; it was fun. I quickly finished my job and sat down on the bed in the sunlight. I felt good and a little tired.

The therapist suggested I ask him one more question about my current life. "Why am I so sad and depressed and fearful? What is down there?"

He gave me a big hug; I felt tears on my cheek, and he answered, "You're the only one down there." His next remark I didn't quite hear. It was either "You don't have anything to fear," or "You have only yourself to fear!"

"What should I do?" I asked.

He answered "You can never untangle down there where it's all matted. You're going to have to use a sharp knife to cut it. You'll be surprised how easy it is."

I interpreted this as advice to be more drastic in my approach to the marriage and the other issues I was facing. The therapist wondered if perhaps I was being advised to "cut to the core," go down even deeper.

The White Stallion

As I approached the end of the transition period, I began to develop an ambitious picture of what I hoped to do in Central America. It was not clear, however, that I had the body and health capable of the travel and effort it would require. I approached my friend Dr. Bill Wood, the surgeon who had given me the odds for an earlier bout with melanoma. I asked him what my odds were now, given my history of cancer, heart disease, and hip problems. What sort of work load was it reasonable for me to undertake?

He answered, "I'm not going to give you odds, Harry. Let me say that your three diseases are not multiplicative; they are independent. In other words, your arthritis doesn't increase the severity of your heart disease. I'm going to give you scenarios and suggest that you make your plans and decisions as if any one of them could turn out to be your reality."

In one of his scenarios I lived twenty years with good health and full energy. In another, I had a stroke after eight years and lived another ten as an invalid. In the last, I had a heart attack and died after two years.

My health and capacity for work was thus on my mind when I had the following visualization:

I am walking down a stream bed in the mountains of San Jose on a farm that reminds me of the orphanage. I turn left and come up on a large field. A handsome white stallion gallops over to me. I grab his mane and swing up on his broad back.

He wheels and begins to canter across the field. I am delighted, filled with a sense of well-being.

Then he starts to gallop up the mountain. I begin to get apprehensive and then panicked at the thought that he is galloping far too hard and is going to have a heart attack, (This is similar to my father's experience on Boy, the white horse that galloped up those same hills, had a heart attack, and died under him.)

I try to slow him down, but he doesn't respond and just charges ahead until we come out into a meadow overlooking the valley. I slip off his back, trembling from my fear. The stallion leans over and says, "Harry, don't worry! My heart is strong! I can carry more than a full load! You don't have to fear."

I took this as a confirmation that my heart, which in the various attacks had suffered surprisingly little damage, was still capable of a full work load. If I got my life right, I didn't have to worry about my body.

Smiley's Final Advice

The last and toughest issue in the transition had to do with my marriage. The kids were off to college, and Deirdre and I had still not closed the gap between us. We had not learned to be good friends, cultivating activities we enjoyed together. My heart attack scared Deirdre and made her realize how little she could count on my being around for her after the kids had left home. It also woke me up to the unsustainable nature of our marriage.

Sharing the heart visualization with Deirdre put the failure of our marriage on the table. As Deirdre opened up about her feelings, I realized with surprise that she was as unhappy as I. However, she felt we should exhaust all options before making a final decision about divorce. We agreed to couple's therapy and to jointly make our ultimate choice. Discussions with a therapist brought many of the wounds of the past to consciousness. It made us aware of our downward spiral, the implications of a divorce for the kids, our conflicts over finances, and my desire to return to Central America and hers to stay in Boston. The process dredged up painful and angry emotions. For over two years, we went back and forth, sometimes convinced we should divorce, sometimes hopeful we could rebuild a satisfying, intimate marriage. But we were rarely on the same page at the same time.

I don't know what finally crystallized things for Deirdre. For me it was one of my last conversations with Smiley:

> I go into a time machine and type on the console, "Please take me to the time and place to get what I need for my journey." I shut the door behind me. I sit down in the pilot's chair and strap myself in. I take a deep breath and hit the red button.
>
> There's a whirling, gray mist at the edges of the cabin. The green light goes on. I don't have any sensation of having gone forward or backward. I unbuckle myself, get out of the chair, and come out.
>
> I find myself up on a bluff next to the seashore. There's a bracing wind blowing and waves are dashing down below. I sit down on the grass facing the ocean, cross-legged in a lotus position, and take some deep breaths. I want to recapture the sense of happiness and freedom I had on my previous trip into the future, but I can't. I remind myself that the only place to be is right where I am in the present, to be aware, to be detached from the past or the future. There are some birds wheeling in the sky. It seems to be early morning and I must be facing southeast. The sun is rising in front on my left side.
>
> When I'm ready, I cross a pasture and go through some woods. I come to a macadam road and take a right. A pickup truck comes along behind me and pulls over. The driver is Smiley, who asks if I want a ride.
>
> I clamber into the truck without saying a word. Finally I say, "OK Smiley, where are we? Where are we heading in this pickup truck?"
>
> "We're heading to a town in the interior of Brazil."
>
> We come to what looks like a new town cut out of the jungle with wide roads, wooden houses, lots of mud, and high sidewalks. I am totally baffled at what we're doing here. He pulls up and we go into a little restaurant to get some

breakfast—gallo pinto and huevos a la ranchera (rice with beans and fried eggs).

Smiley sits across the table looking at me with an impish grin on his face, waiting, as if a big joke is about to happen. I find his high spirits irritating. I say, "What are you looking at? You're supposed to be helping me figure things out."

He says, "Look around. What do you see?"

"I see a little restaurant in what seems to be the boondocks of Brazil. Smiley, I give up. I have no idea what this is all about."

"What would you like to talk about?"

"I'm worried about my health, my marriage, my work. I'm feeling pressure to make the right decisions. If anything, I am feeling more confused than when I started out."

"One of the reasons I brought you here is to give you some sense that your little world isn't all there is. There's a lot happening in the big world. Maybe you're taking things too seriously."

"That's easy for you to say."

"Well, have some patience; let's pay the bill and get in the truck again."

We get into the truck and start down a road, going deeper and deeper into the jungle. After a while he stops the truck, and we start walking into the jungle. Suddenly we come out into a clearing where there is a waterfall. It's the Iguazu Falls where in a previous visualization I had sat on a rock, the water flowing through my chest, and felt the sadness of the world.

He asks if I recognize the place. I say yes. He opens a canteen and fills it with water and passes it to me. I start to drink it. I splash some on my face and hands. It feels very cool and sweet and clean, but there is still an enormous sadness in it, an impersonal sadness.

Smiley says, "Part of what you have to do, Harry, is sit in this water a lot more. Feel it down your back, on your head, feel it going through your body until it goes right through you without obstruction."

I ask Smiley if he knows where the water is coming from.

"Harry, if you look at the amount of that water, you know it's not just one thing. It's not one night on the bathroom floor in Asheville feeling humiliated. It's not one trip of your dad's. It's not being humiliated at being so small. You are just a part of this river. You can't love because you can't feel. You can't feel because you're so micro-focused on just yourself. Learn to feel for others, not just for yourself. Don't treat the boundaries between yourself and others as so permanent. Don't be afraid of the sorrow."

I ask Smiley, "What's your secret of always being in high spirits and happy, as if life is a big surprise party?"

He starts laughing, "It is! Life is a surprise party! Just think of it, I got to drive with you today instead of working in the garden."

I ask him if he has any idea where the garden where I'm supposed to work is located. He tells me it's a much bigger garden than the one at the foot of the stairs. He waves his arm, it seems to me, over all of Latin America.

"Smiley, do you know what I ought to do about Deirdre?"

He looks down at the ground and becomes very pensive. He resists answering, but when I insist, he finally says, "You've got to learn to love her and leave her."

His words shock me, but I sense they are exactly what I need to do. I ask him what he means by that—is it to love her and not need her in some psychological sense, or to make her feel loved, but to separate from her?

"I don't know," he says. "I just feel you've got to learn to love her and leave her, but I'm not a pro in things of love." He continues, "We'd better hurry back or the time machine will leave you."

We walk back, get in the truck, and drive to the bluff. The sun is now at our backs. It seems to be about four in the afternoon, although it doesn't feel as if that much time has passed.

"Smiley, before I go back, is there anything I should have asked you?"

"You should have asked me, 'How do I learn to love?'"

"How do I learn to love?"

He laughs, "I don't know, but that's the question you should be asking."

The therapist closed our session saying very quietly, "It's all there!"

. . . and After

I ended the transition making four tough decisions: I changed my job, moved my residence, simplified my life style, and separated from my wife, all decisions that reportedly create the greatest stress in life.

Deirdre and I jointly agreed on a separation and went on to divorce. We communicated the decision together to both our families, urging them not to take sides and to stay in touch. We've continued to co-parent and to jointly celebrate key events like graduations, birthdays, and weddings.

We sold the large house and furnishings at a loss and greatly reduced our belongings. I moved to Costa Rica with two suitcases, radically simplifying my life. I set up daily routines that included eating healthily, doing regular exercise, and practicing good stress management. I continued to start each day with a habit developed during the transition, namely, a quiet time of meditation and inner listening.

I remained a director of Bain and participated in the group of partners who took control after negotiating a buyout from the founders on favorable terms. My role in the firm's new governance structure frequently took me to Boston and over to Europe and Asia. The firm, though, agreed to let me focus my consulting work on Central America and supported me with a small new office in Costa Rica. We experimented, modifying Bain's "tool kit" to the needs of the region in hopes of helping family groups become globally competitive.

Though unsure of what I should do, I made several promises to myself: I would only work with people I liked and respected—tension and hostility were not good for my arteries. I would not try to push rocks up a hill. I'd let the market help me decide where to focus my effort. If there was not an immediate positive response to my ideas, I'd set them aside.

There were two markets I would monitor. Both had to send positive signals. There had to be "demand"—schools that really wanted the teaching, companies that really wanted the consulting, investors that really wanted to invest. But, equally important, there had to be "supply"—a talented group of young professionals eager to help me do the work. If a heart attack took me, there had to be people who could deliver the results.

These decisions turned out to be exactly right. The Costa Rica office was successful beyond anyone's expectations, and our client list grew to include the leading family business groups of the region. A course I taught at INCAE on "Leadership and Competitiveness" received the highest ratings. The private equity investments were profitable. And the Strachan and Mesoamerica Foundations, fed by the profits of the consulting and investments, grew in size and scope.

After the transition—a new beginning in Central America

I also found the community I sought, a wonderful group of close friends. We worked together, played golf and poker, discussed books and ideas. We shared investing tips, initiated philanthropic projects, and tried to figure out how to achieve sustainable development in our part of the world. With some of these closest friends I formed a father-son group that gave my son and my nephew five "uncles" and me twelve new "nephews." And I even found a new love, which I'll describe later.

The fifteen years following these decisions have probably been the happiest and most successful of my life.

Why It Worked

One of the questions in my mind as I sat down to write about the transition was why it had been so successful and which of the many things I tried really worked. Uncertain of the answer, I decided to reread the eight notebooks written in that four-year period. Going through the journals was painful, but I reached the following conclusions:

Part of the answer was that the decisions I reached were the "right" ones. They were right because they were reached in a participative process that helped me better understand myself—my hopes and fears, my goals for the future. I was able to achieve consensus with those affected by the decision.

If I'd rushed unilaterally into divorce, it is likely that the divorce would have been acrimonious, the property settlement contested, the kids and family forced to take sides. By doing therapy together and by agreeing to make the decision when each was ready, we laid the groundwork for an amicable divorce.

This was also true of the Bain process. It took a deep two-year recession before the founders were willing to turn over the firm to the active partners and remove the major debt load. Had I left Bain at the start of the period, my only option would have been to resign and sever ties. By staying involved through the difficult negotiations with the founders, by trying to play a constructive role in the crisis, I was able to make a small contribution to the turnaround, which in turn earned me Bain support for my efforts in Costa Rica.

Similarly, my visits to Central America during the transition period when I taught for a month at INCAE, helped me better understand the challenges of the region, and my discussions with close friends helped me clarify my vision, all of which ensured a warm reception when I moved down.

Decisions are rarely black or white, right or wrong. What makes them right is how they are fleshed out, negotiated, and then implemented. Rarely is that process quick and sharp. Getting things right takes time, requires creative solutions to obstacles that arise.

But there is another part to the answer. The process also changed me in important ways and created conditions for later success. I'm convinced that the dream therapy and visualizations helped me become more integrated. Discovering and putting my arms around the buried people in my unconscious and getting Smiley's advice was deeply healing. As a result of being more accepting of all the parts of myself, I became less angry and hostile, more tolerant and healthy. No longer feeling obligated to push rocks up a hill, I was willing to accept the leadership of the market and of others.

This integration also probably gave me more mass, made me more effective in playing my different roles. In no area of life was this integration more important than in following Smiley's advice and learning to love.

LEARNING TO LOVE WELL

KEN AND SARAH

Divorced, I was acutely conscious that my relationship with my kids was now 100 percent my own responsibility, no longer a shared relationship with Deirdre. My medical problems and the divorce had been painful for them. We all knew we shouldn't presume I had unlimited time. My living in Costa Rica required a conscious effort at regular communications.

Ken and Sarah with Dad enjoying the CARE Ball

We began to talk at least once a week by phone and to plan an annual vacation together, in addition to as many holidays as didn't conflict with Deirdre's plans or (when they were older) time with the families of their significant others. That first year in Costa Rica both Sarah and Ken made a special effort to come and live with me.

During the summer, Ken came down to help me establish the Bain office and get settled. Besides his job in tourism, he helped me locate an apartment in Bello Horizonte. He also got to know his Roberts cousins better, organizing nights of horror movies and junk food.

On one of my trips out of town, I left him with the task of buying me a car. "I don't want anything that advertises wealth or status. I want it to be second-hand. I want it to be comfortable to ride in and totally reliable."

When I returned I was surprised to find he had bought a used Toyota Four Runner—a four-wheel drive SUV, bright red with a stripe running down the side. I teased him that he had bought a car for himself, not for me, a staid businessman. He said, "No, Dad, think about it. This is a very reliable car. The only available one was painted red, but you can change that if you want. The roads of Costa Rica are full of potholes, and this car is high enough to ride over them without scraping the bottom. It's safe and dependable, perfect for explorations on dirt roads."

It turned out he was right. I fell in love with the car. Three years later I replaced it with a more powerful, six-cylinder version, but this time a nice, quiet gray. As I write this, eleven years later, the car, though dented here and there, still serves me well, is reliable, non-ostentatious, safe, and comfortable, both in town and in the boondocks.

The three-bedroom apartment in Bello Horizonte was on the fifth floor with full length windows looking out on the southern mountains. I equipped it with comfortable, well-built wooden furniture; I wanted a solid masculine feel that didn't suggest the resident was ascetic. I had a king-size bed, and the living room was furnished with comfortable sofas and easy chairs and side tables with lamps. For the dining room, I chose glass cabinets and a matching sideboard. Friends recommended a rectangular expandable dining room table for six to ten guests, but, with Ken's support, I decided that it would be round, big enough for a poker game of eight. There were going to be many more poker games than dinner parties.

When Ken returned to school that fall, Sarah, newly graduated from college, came down to live with me in the apartment. She had raised money for a project teaching art to children in some of the poorest barrios of the city. She worked in the daycare centers of *Roblealto*, the organization founded by my grandmother and a project to which my mother had dedicated much time. Through art, Sarah hoped to enhance the creativity and self-esteem of the third to fifth graders. Components of her program included training the staff in non-traditional methodologies for teaching art, organizing the painting of murals at the centers and in the community, field trips to museums, and the children's own art show.

Living with Ken and then with Sarah marked a turning point in our relationship. They passed from being my children to becoming adult friends. Both were good housemates. Each of us had a full busy life, our own set of friends and activities, but we enjoyed each other's company. We often went out to dinner together. Sometimes we entertained their friends in the apartment, other times mine, sometimes both at the same time. On weekends we might go with a group down to the beach. I felt their love and care for me and sensed that part of their motivation in choosing to spend time in Costa Rica was to make sure I was okay.

They both returned to the U.S., Sarah to San Francisco and then Seattle to a career in web design and art, and later to marriage and the raising of two grandsons. Ken got his law degree, moved to Boston, married another lawyer, and began a family that has produced three more grandsons.

In 1998, when I had a serious heart attack, both Sarah and Ken dropped what they were doing to come down and spend time with me in the hospital. At that time they became my partners in finances as well as philanthropy. We reorganized the Strachan Foundation, whose endowment had grown, and they joined the board. Ken with Rob Lindenberg, Mark and Cathy's son, began to work with Rio Fuerte, the family investment company that manages the endowment of the Strachan Foundation, my own wealth, and the savings of many of my relatives. They encouraged me to put much of the wealth Mesoamerica was generating into the Strachan Foundation and to include in my inheritance plans gifts of stocks to all my brothers, sisters, cousins, nieces, and nephews.

This past year both Sarah's and Ken's families came to Costa Rica for a week and we inaugurated "Camp Strachan." In a beautiful rural area on a working farm, the grandsons learned to milk cows, ride horses, pick coffee, and saw how sugar and coffee are processed. In the evenings they created stories with their grandfather about brothers who discover a hidden valley where they help a talking stallion defend his brood of mares and colts from wolves and other scary dangers.

Camp Strachan 2010: Sandy, Zephyr, Ken, Liam
Amanda, Granddad, Asa, Sarah, Ari and Nate

Over this period of fifteen years, the "taking care" arrow has steadily been switching direction. Now they are taking as much care of me as I of them.

DATING AGAIN

When I decided to separate, I had little confidence in my ability to be successful in a long-term intimate relationship. I also knew I was vulnerable. Friends warned me that before rushing into another relationship I needed to understand how I had failed in my marriage. Otherwise I'd end up repeating the same mistakes over again. So I promised myself a period of three years in which I would not embark on any "spousal" relationships. I envisioned living alone, or with Sarah and Kenny, in an apartment that I furnished to my own tastes and managed on my own.

Among the things I needed to understand was the source of the near panic in certain lonely situations, my approach/avoidance with intimacy and dependency. I needed to know what my heart as well as my head wanted in a mate. I considered but then discarded chastity and decided to explore whatever attractions I felt. I wanted to learn more about my anima by watching how it was reflected in the women to whom I was attracted, whether or not these women fit the preconceived mental pictures I had picked up from my parents and friends.

In these relationships, I determined to only get involved sexually where it was really mutually beneficial. I would care about the welfare of the other person; try to make them feel attractive and positive about themselves. So long as our objectives were parallel and things remained good for both of us, we would be "lovers and friends." I wanted to be unselfish and sensitive to them, but was determined not to let another's desires or needs push me into commitments that went beyond what I wanted.

Like many "recovering spouses," I was negative on the institution of marriage. Not so facetiously, I would say, "Marriage is a pernicious institution designed to kill love!" I mainly meant that you often marry expecting that your spouse is taking a vow to make you happy and that you are making the same commitment; therefore if they are unhappy, it's your fault, and if you are unhappy, it's their fault. This is a source of a downward spiral of resentments. Before I got into a committed relationship, I needed to take full responsibility for my own happiness and not require anyone else's affirmation to feel good about myself. I needed to learn the subtle difference between loving another well and taking responsibility for their happiness.

I also promised to use the lonely periods to explore my fear of aloneness. If on a weekend or evening I became fearful of solitude, rather than running to a singles' bar or calling up a girlfriend at the last minute, I'd walk into my loneliness, go down into my fears, and seek to understand them.

One night sitting on the couch looking over the lights on the southern hills of San Jose, I felt loneliness approaching me in all its horribleness; it came sweeping toward me as a black roiling cloud that I imagined full of monsters. Rather than running away, I walked toward it, awaiting it at the window. To my surprise, the cloud arrived and passed over me. Inside the cloud, I found that it was not dark black, but a light gray mist. The sorrow and grief inside the cloud was not only bearable, it was almost healing. With time I learned to be capable of happily spending a night alone; I learned that my loneliness was manageable and exploring it a source of insight.

Another rule I made for myself was not to date women significantly younger than myself or out of a need to build up my self-esteem. It seemed to me, perhaps inaccurately, that these relations were psychologically unequal, perhaps early on in favor of the older man, but inevitably later in life unequal in the opposite direction. I encouraged myself to look for women with nice personalities and interesting minds and not to focus on physical beauty. I didn't have illusions about my own handsomeness and wanted to date equals.

I promised myself no lies. If each of us was to take responsibility for determining what was "good for us," each needed an accurate understanding of the true situation. Therefore, I determined to practice honesty even if it killed the romance. I would not try to seduce a woman with false promises. If I knew or sensed that because of her religion or personal history, making love outside of a committed relation would make her feel soiled, I determined I would not sleep with her. I'd date, enjoy her friendship, but stop there.

As a result of my travels and work, I didn't have a lot of time for social life, but friends' wives introduced me to a number of attractive women. I had never before dated Latin women and quickly realized I didn't understand the way the game was played in that part of the world. So I was careful and cautious about giving offense. Initially, most women encouraged my flirting, but were baffled by my honesty and unwillingness to even pretend commitment. This scared them, and I began to wonder if my refusal to play the romantic game was in some way a form of "cultural imperialism" that was going to condemn me to undesired celibacy. I decided, however, to stick by my guidelines. If I didn't practice ruthless honesty, I would get confused and make mistakes. I was also discreet, because I did not want to scandalize society, my kids, or my extended religious family.

SANDY

Meeting at the CARE Ball

When I left Boston for Central America, my brother-in-law Marc Lindenberg and sister Cathy moved to Atlanta. He took a top management position with CARE, a large non-profit involved in development work, in order, in part, to help it adapt its strategy to new funding constraints. He asked me to help him by serving on CARE's finance committee and by teaching in the management seminars he organized for CARE executives.

About two years after my separation, with the divorce process underway, my sister Cathy told me that there was a woman who worked with Marc that she thought I might enjoy meeting. She was recently divorced, and Marc considered her "the best facilitator" he'd ever known. Cathy suggested the CARE Presidential Ball, a black-tie gala affair held in Washington D.C., as a great place to introduce us, and also a convenient time as one of the board meetings was to be held the day after the ball.

I agreed, and Cathy invited Sandy Conant Powell, as she was then known, to go to the ball with a blind date, without explaining that I was her brother. Sandy's first reaction to the invitation was, "No thanks, I am not into dating." Knowing that Sandy very much enjoyed dancing, Cathy told her that the man she had in mind liked to dance. Sandy said, "Well, in that case, since I have to be in Washington for the board meeting the next day, let's do it."

Immediately Cathy's inspired plan began to run into obstacles. Since Marc's table at the ball held about fourteen people, I suggested that we invite son Ken to join us. He was studying at Georgetown and loved diplomacy and black-tie affairs. He quickly accepted. When Sarah heard about the event and his invitation, she persuaded Cathy to give her an invitation as well. When Deirdre heard both of them would be there, she decided she'd like to come. A blind date at which your ex-wife and children will be present didn't strike me as a good formula for impressing a woman. Fortunately, Sandy backed out due to some problems with her daughter.

At the last minute, Cathy herself cancelled but then Sandy's situation with her teenage daughter was resolved, so Marc asked her to come and be the hostess at his table. Since she had to come to DC for the following day, she agreed. We were introduced but, for obvious reasons, didn't get to spend much time talking. She did get in a lot of dancing, but mainly with Ken.

The next day, I had the opportunity to sit near her at the board meeting and I started to get to know her during breaks. She claims that one of my first questions was, "What is your marital status?" I don't remember asking that and can't imagine doing something that "un-cool." I did invite her for a walk after the board meeting, but she had other commitments, so the best I could do was to get her to agree that we'd have dinner together during an upcoming trip to Atlanta.

Two weeks later, I visited Cathy and Marc for the weekend and asked Sandy for a date that Saturday. We spent the afternoon walking through Stone Mountain Park. As we walked and talked, I became fascinated by her story. After college she had left a conservative Texas home and spent most of her adult life working in community development, initially in the slums of Chicago and then all over the world. Her organization reminded me of the mission family in which I had grown up. Its formal name was the ICA (Institute of Cultural Affairs), but insiders called it "the Order," as it functioned similarly to a Catholic order. Its religious roots were deep in theologians like Bultmann, Niebuhr, Bonhoeffer and Tillich. People lived in community, often among the poor and in slums, sharing what they had, while they focused their efforts on the felt needs of the community. Sandy's first job with them had been as a teacher in a daycare center.

I had known nuns, monks, and evangelical missionaries whose conservative theology had led them to take vows of poverty and to give their lives to service, but I had never known anyone motivated by a liberal theology willing to make similar sacrifices. To my prejudiced way of thinking, "liberal Christians" were people who had lost their faith, but were unwilling to admit it. As Sandy described her own faith, it sounded much more like what I had come to believe. I realized how real and meaningful it was to her and thought, *Here is someone with a lot to teach me.*

Walking among the trees, we shared something of our inner journeys as well. She had also had important life-changing dreams.

My crazy visualizations made enormous sense to her. We talked easily and laughed frequently. The way her mind worked fascinated me. I sensed that her EQ (emotional intelligence) was off the charts and that she was smarter than I. The thoughts she expressed came from her own experience and often had a unique slant to them. She was a great listener. If there was a moment I fell in love with Sandy, it was probably walking among the trees at Stone Mountain Park sharing our dreams.

For dinner that night I proposed we find a country western honky-tonk with line dancing. I didn't know how to dance country, much less how to line dance, but over the years I had moved from despising maudlin country music to finding that the best of it captured feelings I shared. I had never been to such a "down-home" place, but thought it would be a fun experience and not something she'd expect of a businessman who normally wore a suit to work. Sandy was game and helped me find something that looked like what we wanted.

The food was greasy, but the margaritas were great. We arrived early for a class in line dancing. Though I never picked up the circular two-step, we got a lot of exercise and had a great time talking as we watched couples in matching shirts and boots circle the floor below us. It was a wonderful first date, and thereafter, we began dating as often as we could get together, never apart for more than two or three weeks at a time.

One weekend Sandy's work for CARE brought her to Central America, and we spent several days at a hotel up in the mountains. On another occasion we met in Miami and discovered the Thai restaurant where years later we had our wedding dinner. One time we took a weeklong vacation in Cozumel with friends of hers.

Two months after we met and still in my self-imposed three-year period of staying uncommitted, I was at the lake house of good friends Roberto and Celina Kriete in El Salvador. They asked me all about Sandy, and I told them that I thought she was the perfect one for me. I even read them a journal entry which explained why I was falling in love. It waxed effusive about Sandy's many traits, how she brought out the best in me, and why I felt there was such a good fit between us.

When I was finished describing my infatuation, they told me the story of their own whirlwind romance, how Roberto had literally stolen Celina from under the nose of her boyfriend. His categorical advice was, "If you don't know within a month that she is the one, then she isn't." Celina agreed, "This sounds like the one. Go for it!"

An Unusual Proposal

Emboldened, I wrote Sandy a proposal. She's since teased me about it, saying that it sounded like a consultant's document, beginning with an "Introduction and Summary," and ending with a job offer. I still think it was romantic and, in hindsight, amazingly prescient.

Introduction and Summary

I have "fallen in love" with you. This is a new experience for me I have not yet understood fully. That makes me cautious.

My past experience has led me to feel that just about everything I was taught to expect and believe about love and marriage was wrong. In my marriage we got into a doom loop because we started with "expectations" for each other that we had absorbed from society around us. So I don't want to buy off the shelf someone else's definition of what it means to "fall in love" or "live together."

But I have "fallen in love" and I want to bring you fully into my life. I have enjoyed just about every minute I have been with you. From the beginning it has felt to me that we were an almost perfect fit. When we talked about our dreams that first afternoon, I felt we were soul mates. When we danced it felt like we belonged in each other's arms. When we kissed and made love, I thought our bodies were designed to fit together. When Cathy and Marc described your personality and skills, I thought, "What a great helpmate."

When I saw you moving so comfortably among my Latin friends at the INCAE reception, I thought how well you would fit in all my different worlds: the Latin and Gringo, the wealthy and poor, the intellectual and practical, the religious and secular.

When you described your spiritual beliefs and journey, talked about God's immanence as well as transcendence, I felt we were on the same wave length spiritually. What's more, it seemed to me that you would be able to understand my fundamentalist background. You were already further down the path I am taking.

When I visited your apartment and saw how you had decorated it and we talked about attitudes toward money and things, I thought, I will never feel out of place or have things that are tacky in my apartment. We will never fight over money. There is not a part of my life that I can't see you fitting comfortably into.

In the morning I find myself wanting to share with you the cool air of Costa Rica along the path I walk. In the evening I dream of margaritas while we watch the sunset. Throughout the day I find myself thinking, I must remember to tell Sandy about this incident or she would enjoy this joke. I often think, I would love her advice on this decision. I look around the apartment and wonder how it would look with your tasteful, warm decorations. I visualize small dinner parties in our dining room. I won't mention what I see going on in the big king size bed or how I ache at night to curl up around you.

I would be happy to have you just as a roommate while you pursued your own career and work. But I also have a vision that goes beyond that. I see us as a team doing some wonderful things in this part of the world and you compensating for some of the deficiencies that I've not been successful at solving on my own.

I see me contracting you to be my coach and support system in the diet and on meditation. I can't wait for your help in "managing" our home. I would love to help you build a consulting practice for non-profit entities. I would love for you to help me build the Strachan Foundation and find social entrepreneurs we can help.

I see us some day building a compound around a swimming pool, tennis court, and Jacuzzi where many of our closest friends and relatives could live. Our house would become a social center for these and many other friends. People would drop by for drinks. We would organize fun parties. We would have more serious groups for watching movies or discussing books or even worshipping together and sharing spiritual experiences.

I see us inviting the young professionals of Bain, the students and young faculty of INCAE into our home, befriending the Peace Corps and missionary types coming through Costa Rica, and in the process, becoming "mentors" and "cheerleaders" who help them believe in their potential and set high goals for themselves.

I see our home as a way-station for nieces and nephews. managing a trust fund that helps them in their education and supports them in their career start-ups.

I see us traveling through Central America, becoming friends and confidantes of a group of business people and leaders, helping them set up think tanks and networks that help them understand more of what is going on around them, affirming their aspirations and visions for using their wealth and talents in the service of their countries and the peoples around them.

As this vision of us together has run away with me, a part of me has looked on with anxiety. It says, Wait! This relationship with Sandy is too good to be true. At other times I've thought, Cool it. If you overload it, you will burn it out! Two friends, however, have in one way or another told me recently, "Seize the day!" "When it's right, you know it within thirty days." "Go for it." "Nothing ventured, nothing gained."

So . . . . my proposal is . . . come to Costa Rica, let's live together as soon as possible, and let's try to learn to love each other in the fullest and best sense of the word. Let's try together to build a balanced life of fun, worship, and service . . .

Sandy was touched by my invitation, but not yet ready to make the move. She tried to let me down gently. "If we're still in love one year from now and your divorce has come through, I'll consider joining you."

Diamond Promises

One year later we were still in love. My divorce had finalized. We had both committed to an exclusive relationship, even if we were not yet ready to get married. At the end of a trip that included a vacation on the Florida Panhandle with many margaritas and some key lime pie, and then a week in Boston, she moved to join me in Costa Rica.

My central promise to her and to myself was to try to "to love her well." We found a ring that captured our promises to each other. It had five diamonds. The central diamond represented the promise of loving each other well. The four flanking diamonds were to remind us of the four elements of love. One diamond stood for "passion," making love frequently and creatively, but also showing physical affection in little ways. She asked me to always give her a good-bye kiss when I left the house for work.

Another diamond represented "humor, fun and friendship." We wanted to make sure we kept the laughter in our relationship. Little things would get us giggling, and we remembered these as among our most intimate moments. We felt it was important to cultivate a friendship that kept us in touch, and early on, more by accident than design, we got into the habit of playing gin rummy after dinner. While playing cards, we'd often talk about things that happened during the day. We also started a breakfast ritual in which one of us would read a poem or short piece, often from a spiritual tradition. Then we would share a reflection or intention for the day.

The third diamond represented a commitment to "mutual support." I wanted to support Sandy in her work, whatever she felt it to be. Her career had been as a consultant and facilitator mostly in non-profit organizations. At CARE she was head of management development. One of my biggest fears was that having given up this prestigious work, she'd get bored. In Costa Rica her plan was to keep doing consulting assignments, particularly those that might take her back to her beloved Africa, but she felt she was ready to move on, perhaps into coaching, writing, and hobbies like painting. I succeeded in persuading her to be the executive director of the Strachan Foundation.

It was important that Sandy not be torn between loving me and doing her work. I hoped to help her in the entertainment that went along with her work by making our home a welcome place for her colleagues and clients.

The last diamond was a very practical one. It represented a commitment on my part to make sure that Sandy was financially well taken care of should something happen to me. I wanted her to both feel and be financially independent. If things between us didn't work out, she should feel free to leave without having financial problems. We had learned from prior relationships that it was healthy to keep our finances separate and important to have our own money to spend without the other feeling resentment. We agreed that I would pick up our joint expenses and that anything Sandy earned, including her salary as foundation director, would be for her personal expenses and savings.

Keeping the promises and implementing the dream

Vows

After seven years as "recovering spouses," we became convinced that we could risk marriage. It was not likely to kill our love, and it would have several important benefits. My heart attack in 1998 had revealed how complicated it was for Sandy to be legally empowered to make medical decisions on my behalf if we weren't married. We also wanted to eliminate any obstacles to members of our families and good friends from fully accepting our life mates.

As anticipated, marriage didn't change our commitment to each other, but it did give us a new opportunity to articulate our love for each other. We each wrote, in secret, the vows we shared on the beach the afternoon after our civil wedding at Coral Gables. Sandy had chosen Valentine's Day for the wedding so that I would have only one romantic day a year to remember and so that everyone in the world would be reminding me of it.

My vows were engraved in gold on a green stone tablet:

> Dearest Sandy,
> My Vows to You
> This Day of Our Marriage

> To love you well, so that you feel always as smart, as good, as beautiful and sexy as I see you today.
> To support you in your life's work—you have so many talents that the best is still to come.
> To make sure you are financially secure and never fear again being a bag lady.
> To be a good friend, a good listener (most of the time), with whom you laugh frequently and share the daily richness of life.
> And finally, to be diligent in the maintenance of our love, so that only death ends up parting us.

> Harry Strachan
> Valentine's Day 2002

Her vows to me, written on parchment, reflected her more romantic and poetic personality. She began by thanking the two couples who had joined us for the weekend ceremony, Gary and Linda and Don and Barbara, then continued:

> As I stand with you, my life partner, my soul mate, I celebrate our dance. We have learned many steps in the past, and we will

learn new ones in the future. We have danced through peaks and valleys. We have moved from the giddy rhythm of early love to a quieter, more confident ballet. As time goes on, we will deepen our ability to anticipate each other's moves and move with them.

Forever" isn't ours to give. But I can commit each day to laugh with you, to support you in your work and play, in sickness and in health, to listen and respond. I promise a joyful & willing fidelity. I promise to be honest & trustworthy in all aspects of our life together.

And though at times our steps will falter and our toes get stepped on, it will not mar the beauty of this dance. We will recover and move on. Two partners, each unique and independent, bound together by the music of our love and our commitment to growth and grace.

This ring symbolizes the dance of our lives—a uniting of two entities who, in coming together, create a third reality that cannot exist without them. They do not lose identity, but rather enlarge it. Only our shared commitment to the creation of something larger, to lifelong learning, spiritual and personal growth gives this covenant its form. This ring is an outward and visible symbol of my love and a promise to participate wholeheartedly in that creation.

God brought you into my life. I pledge to steward the wonderful gift of **you**, each day renewing the promise to love you well.

We put serious thought into our commitments, and we have continued to practice good habits of marriage hygiene, like addressing estrangements before going to bed. These learned behaviors have no doubt contributed to our staying in love. But my words could easily give the impression that learning to love well has been hard work.

The truth is just the opposite. Loving Sandy has felt wonderfully natural and effortless. Only rarely have I felt I had to do something that I'd rather not. Sandy has encouraged my work, as well as my golf and poker and my activities with my men friends. And I encourage her painting, writing, and friendships. While we both prefer to be together, neither of us feels that trips apart will damage our relation. We go to bed together, get up in the morning together, and have meals together. Our rituals, like the gin rummy, happen comfortably. Neither feels obligated to entertain the other. In the words of the song, I "love her just the way she is," and it has been incredibly healing to feel that she is delighted with me just as I am.

CONCLUSION

REVISITING THE SUMMER OF 1965

This last chapter is written in my sixty-eighth year. It has taken me three years to complete a first draft, and it will probably take another year of rewriting before it's ready to share. I'm still living in Costa Rica in a condo overlooking the twinkling lights of the central valley of San Jose.

Writing these stories has forced me to examine them closely, in some cases even to correct facts and dates that letters and journals showed as "mis-remembered." I now ask myself, *What do I believe was the real story? What truly happened on the journey?*

My story for forty years was that in the summer of 1965, I lost my faith, realized that I would never be a missionary, and faced the daunting task of finding a work that would fit my talents. Deeply angry, I had returned to Boston convinced that my father's death was an unmitigated disaster for everyone in the family as well as the mission.

Nothing in subsequent years caused me to change my mind. As I saw it, a very talented brother dropped out of college and experimented with drugs. My mother, though she heroically developed a new career, never got over her sadness. Convinced she'd been a failure as a mother, she died four years after my father. The mission splintered into multiple independent ministries. The assertion that "all things work together for good," especially in relation to Dad's death, struck me as worse than false, almost insulting.

Was Dad's Death an Unmitigated Disaster?

I recognize today that I have had a wonderful life and have been exceedingly blest, to use a word from my childhood. I've had interesting work, financial rewards, a wonderful group of colleagues and friends. Yes, I have had my share of trouble—medical potholes (including cancer, heart attacks, and hip replacements), job setbacks, failed investments, and a failed marriage. No one gets through life free. But in spite of the medical adventures, I have lived fifteen years longer than my dad and am still going strong. My life has been fun. Things have turned out far better than I could have imagined, in work, in marriage, and in a family that now includes five wonderful grandsons. My life has been far from a disaster. And I realize that somewhere, I have lost that deep anger.

It's still hard for me to see how my father's death was good for the mission or my mother or my brothers and sisters, but with a shock, I see that perhaps it was good for me. Dad's death, in a strange way, freed me. Had he and Mother lived and stayed with the Latin American Mission, it would have been much more difficult for me to take the road I did. Paradoxically, both his living with integrity and his death made it possible for me to find much more suitable roles and work than if I had followed the family tradition and gone to seminary.

The values that have worked for me—perhaps even been the secret of any success—are amazingly similar to those of my grandparents and parents, to what I learned in childhood, HDA, and Wheaton. They are values and attitudes I have tried to share with my classes at INCAE and Harvard, in training sessions at Bain and Mesoamerica, and in the forums where I am asked to speak. Colleagues and friends joke that I'm just a missionary in disguise. I have a gospel, and I preach it.

I now see Romans 8:28, which was such an offense at my father's funeral, as a profoundly adaptive attitude toward life. Everything that has happened in my life was a potential source of growth. Believing that every experience could be a means of learning encouraged me to creatively transform bad into good. As the saying in Spanish humorously puts it, "what doesn't kill you, fattens you."

. . . and the Romance?

And how do I see the romance of the summer of 1965 and my subsequent marriage? That is a tough question. My first marriage failed, yet both Deirdre and I have continued to grow. She has had a great career, found love, lived a good life. We were an effective team as parents; we had two children that have turned out great. We shared many good friends and taught each other much. We even found a way to divorce amicably and continue to help each other. Afterwards, each of us had a successful second marriage.

The summer romance of 1965 has taken on a new meaning in the light of what I've subsequently learned about love. Perhaps the intern was sent into my office that night to give me the opportunity to realize that far more than a "helpmate," I needed a "soul mate," someone to talk and laugh with.

I even see the "making out" differently. At the time sexual passion seemed to be a dangerous drive that was only going to get me into trouble. Had I recognized it as an aid to intimacy, to caring, perhaps it would have helped me learn much earlier how to love well. Perhaps I'd have recognized that our sexuality, our need for intimacy and love, are really offshoots of our deepest spiritual impulses.

WHERE I'VE ENDED UP

Claiming the Blessing

In 1986, before I had permanently returned to Central America, my father's only sister Aunt Grace, our guardian, was dying of cancer. We all knew the end was near so we organized a family reunion on the INCAE Alajuela campus during the Christmas holidays. The twelve Strachan and Roberts cousins, my cohort group, each with our spouses and our children, along with some other cousins and aunts, descended on campus.

Day-trips were organized to visit places with powerful childhood memories, like the *Roblealto* farm and the *Clínica Bíblica*. There was a regular afternoon soccer game involving old and young, male and female, where it became clear that the competitive spirit was alive and well in the next generation. In the late afternoons we had a series of one-hour seminars where family members shared their special knowledge.

A Strachan Roberts family reunion circa 1993

The seminar hour was followed by cocktails. After dinner there were games and conversation. Word games like Scrabble were popular with one group. I led another group in a low-stakes poker game. By popular demand from his younger cousins, Ken resurrected his evening of horror movies and junk food, no parents allowed. There was much joking and laughter. The closing New Year's Eve party ended in dancing, and even Aunt Grace took a final twirl on the dance floor with Uncle Dayton.

I recall at one point in the reunion recognizing how much I enjoyed my extended family, how proud I was of the way each one of them had made it through their education into by-and-large successful careers. My kids and nieces and nephews were bright and attractive, most of them already on successful trajectories. No one had had a free ride, but we'd all had better lives than I feared would be the case after Dad's death. Though we were aware that about half of the family considered themselves active Christians squarely within the family legacy of faith, and the other half had left this legacy behind, this difference did not keep us from caring about each other.

One evening, Aunt Grace invited my generation and our spouses, without children, to Cathy's house nearby in La Garita. She wanted to share with us, not the outward story of her life, but her inner spiritual journey.

Over the course of her life and service, Aunt Grace had become a legendary figure in the mission and the evangelical community of Costa Rica. Older men told me she was drop-dead gorgeous as a young woman, her natural blond hair and blue eyes being particularly striking in Latin America. Her gifted piano playing and high spirits only added to her fame. A family rumor was that in her late teens, Grandmother Susan sent her away to Wheaton Academy to break up a romance with the scion of a prominent Catholic family.

In mid and late age when I knew her, she was still strikingly attractive and now known for her public speaking and missionary service. The story was that after Wheaton Academy, while at Columbia Bible College, she found the Lord and her calling. (Incidentally she also met my mother then, whom she later introduced to her brother.) She married Dayton Roberts, a Wheaton and Princeton Seminary graduate with missionary roots in Korea, and they returned as missionaries to Costa Rica and Colombia. Uncle Dayton became an LAM director, and Aunt Grace, among many other initiatives, was the moving force behind the *Caravanas de Buena Voluntad* (Goodnews Caravans) where doctors, dentists, nurses, agronomists, and others provided critical services to needy rural areas.

On a personal level, she was known for her generosity even when it damaged her own family's finances, and she was famous for her impassioned interventions with the government, the church, or mission if she felt someone was not being treated right.

In our gathering at Cathy's, she sat in a big easy chair in front of the fire and talked to us mainly about her spiritual journey. If I remember correctly, the most important experience occurred when she was in her fifties, after thirty years of missionary service. It involved the charismatic healing of a shoulder, an inner cleansing, and an experience of the Holy Spirit that dramatically changed her view of God.

When she finished, someone suggested a period of prayer. This was a custom in the mission, but within the family it highlighted the range of differing beliefs among us. The most fervent participants in the prayer meeting were the "insiders" who had remained staunchly evangelical. Several prayers attributed my dad's death to the devil and the subsequent loss of faith of many in the family as a great victory for the forces of darkness. One prayer even suggested that in this way the devil had blunted the family's potential contributions to Latin America.

During the praying, I watched the group. It seemed to me that several couples who considered themselves "outsiders" were visibly uncomfortable. For example, Marc Lindenberg was Jewish, his wife Cathy, agnostic. Yet I felt strongly that they were exemplary in their demonstration of the family's legacy of service, he as rector of INCAE and a leader in CARE and she through her nursing with the World Health Organization and her efforts with teens at risk.

The same was true of Evie and Michael Goslin. Both had doctorates and successful careers, he as a college professor, she as therapist in advocacy work with children. Their two sons, Michael and Neill, were among the six older nieces and nephews, outstanding students and already on clear success trajectories. Evie and Mike did not talk about their beliefs, but I sensed they had long since left their early faith. Yet, based on the "fruits of the spirit" in their vocations, their generosity and care of family members, they lived the Christian virtues of honesty, discipline, and compassion.

I found myself thinking how ironic it was that some who felt like "outsiders" in fact participated equally in our family heritage of excellence and service, albeit not as practicing Christians. The categorization of "insiders" and "outsiders" felt deeply wrong, based as it was on a false interpretation of history. The truth was that there was not and never had been "one faith" that was shared by our ancestors. Yes, they all affirmed the statement of faith that begins "I believe in God the Father Almighty, Maker of Heaven and Earth . . ." But for each of them the experience of God had been unique, dynamic, changing, and personal. Grandfather and Grandmother Strachan had been anti-Catholic and ardent about the victorious life. My father stopped preaching the victorious life and became much more ecumenical. My mother, late in life, came to believe in universal salvation and wondered whether she should resign from the mission because of this shift in thinking. Uncle Dayton was writing books on the need for ecology and sustainable development, new passions that not only put him out in front of most of the Christian community, but had probably never occurred to my grandparents. And here was Aunt Grace admitting that her experience and concept of God had changed dramatically in her fifties, thirty years after starting missionary service. Her charismatic experiences and healing would have worried her parents.

The family legacy was therefore not one of unchanging Christianity, but rather a set of attitudes and values that each member embodied and applied in their own unique way to the unique circumstances of their time in history. As I saw it, each of us was on a distinct spiritual journey, and so far as I could judge, was genuinely seeking to know the truth, love others, and do good work. I could, without hesitation, affirm both the outsiders and the insiders.

I thought of Johnny and Bary who had been young rebels, "wandering in the wilderness" for a while. Yet each, with their special and wonderful wives, Dama and Cynthia, had come back to a Christian faith. They had successful careers and raised families of beautiful, smart kids. They were active in their churches.

Yes, every member of this special clan had a unique story. Each had a life in which there was much to admire. There was evidence of grace, acts of service and compassion, commitment to society and its neediest members. This was the legacy to which all of us could legitimately lay claim.

Sibs approaching retirement look back on good lives:
Marie, Clare, Harry, Cathy, John, and Robert

With these thoughts flashing through my mind, I impulsively said something like, "Aunt Grace, I'd like to interrupt the prayers. Though I'm one of those who is an "outsider," no longer considered a Christian, I feel I am also a true descendant. Like others, I have continued the legacy of the family. Before you die, I'd like to ask for your blessing."

She knew what I was trying to say. Perhaps she too recognized the falseness of the divide. Struggling out of her chair, she shuffled over, stood behind me, put her hands on my head, and gave me a beautiful blessing. I don't recall her exact words, but I felt a deep affirmation of my own life, as well as an affirmation of everyone else in the room. We were all custodians, in our own way, of the family legacy.

My Faith

I still jokingly describe myself as the "black sheep of the family." I love rum and Cokes, and my main hobbies are golf and poker. I'm not a part of any local church. I am careful not to pretend to be a practicing Christian, though I have renewed and treasure my friendships with the *evangélicos* and missionaries with whom I grew up. I think of them as "my people" and believe we share more of the same faith than they recognize. I support, both with consulting and foundation grants, many of their social outreach projects, including some that my grandparents and parents founded, like the *Clínica Bíblica, Roblealto,* and *Colegio Monterrey.*

While I am agnostic on many traditional doctrinal planks in the Christian statement of beliefs, it's something of a surprise to recognize that if faith is defined not as what you believe in your brain, but as the beliefs on which you bet your life, then I have come to a faith that takes the spiritual and moral dimensions of life seriously.

I have adopted my mother's practice of an early morning quiet time. I start most days with a reading from some religious tradition and a period of meditation or listening. I feel like C.S. Lewis's pilgrim, still on the journey of trying to understand life, to find out what makes for successful living. I'm still looking for "evidence of the divine" in the world around me, but now with fewer preconceptions of what I will find.

My quiet time often ends with a prayer written in my journal, such as, "God, I don't know if you exist or if you're hearing this. If you exist, I suspect you are beyond anything I can imagine. Today, though, as I go out to my life, with all respect, I need your help. In the meetings I have this morning, please help me listen well to . . . Remind me to encourage . . . . Give me wisdom for . . ." (and I list decisions or problems I'm struggling with)."

I also try to widen my circle of concern. "These friends and family . . . also need your help. And all of us on this planet have some big problems with violence, poverty, and climate warming . . . What should I be doing about them?"

And it works! Almost always in these quiet morning periods, my awareness widens, creative solutions and ideas come from somewhere as a gift. I don't worry about whether they're coming from my unconscious, or the Spirit of God, or perhaps Jung's "collective unconscious." I'm just grateful they come.

Today I like to imagine that in that summer of selling on that dark night in Kentucky, God was standing beside the bed while the tears were rolling into my ears. He was hoping I wouldn't give up. I like to think He was delighted when I got angry and announced I was going it alone. Perhaps the coincidence of sales of $501 per week was a small hint of His presence.

I also have a new appreciation for the missionary aunts and uncles whom I interviewed. Yes, they were all too human but, when you think about it, there is something "divine," almost miraculous, in the struggles of people to love and help each other and in their ability to grow. With all their limitations, they strove to put their faith into action, to help others find their way. They have been "God's hands" in much of their work. I am surprised at how frequently I meet people whose lives their efforts dramatically helped.

What about the potholes, setbacks, and painful lessons?

I wouldn't wish them on anyone else. But knowing how hardheaded and hardhearted I tend to be, they are probably the only way I could have learned what I needed to learn. Life has given me many second chances and the years to take advantage of them. Come to think of it, aren't second chances a great example of grace, and isn't that grace "evidence of the divine?"

For many years I saw the summer of 1965 as a turning point that sent my life off trajectory and away from the faith of my fathers. Late in life, but not too late, I have come to a place where I can claim the inheritance of my grandparents and parents, be thankful for their values, their legacy of faith and service. I have asked for and accepted their blessing. I have tried to add my little contributions to this family legacy and pass it on to the next generation.

The island of faith I have found feels spacious. To some it may appear different from that of my childhood, but it feels to me very much like a home I share with my grandparents, my parents, siblings, uncles, aunts, and cousins. And it has plenty of room for the children, nieces, and nephews who follow.

Let me end with a quote from Wendell Berry's main character, Jayber Crow, in a novel by the same name. He's reflecting on his life but I feel the same could be said of mine:

> If you could do it, I suppose, it would be a good idea to live your life in a straight line—starting, say, in the Dark Wood of Error, and proceeding by logical steps through Hell and Purgatory and into Heaven. Or you could take the King's Highway past appropriately named dangers, toils, and snares, and finally cross the River of Death and enter the Celestial City.
>
> But that is not the way I have done it, so far. I am a pilgrim, but my pilgrimage has been a wandering and unmarked. I have been in the Dark Wood of Error any number of times. I have known something of Hell, Purgatory, and Heaven, but not always in that order. Often I have not known where I was going until I was already there. Often I have received better than I have deserved. I am an ignorant pilgrim, crossing a dark valley.
>
> And yet for a long time, looking back, I have the feeling that I have been led—make of that what you will.

Now you know what I mean when I say I feel "blest"!

Acknowledgments

I owe the richness of my life and many of these stories to friends from all the different phases of my life, my school years, time in the Army, years at INCAE, Harvard, Bain, and Mesoamerica. It would be impossible to thank all of them individually but I do feel gratitude for their contributions to my stories and life.

I would, though, like to thank by name a diverse group of friends who offered to read the first draft and give me honest reactions. Within the limits of my capabilities, I have tried to take advantage of all their useful comments. I know their suggestions have improved the book and shortened it by almost a third.

So a big thanks to what I think of as "my focus group:"
John and Doris Stam, missionary "uncle and aunt" for their many comments, new stories about my folks, and for their own inspiring lives

Ernesto Fernandez Holman and **Barry Hershey,** two successful businessmen, also true intellectuals, for their encouragement and cautions

Wickham Skinner, my mentor in so many areas, for pushing me to both shorten and improve the book

George Masselam, playwright and father of my daughter-in law, Amanda, for his perceptive and encouraging suggestions

Beau and Leslie Conant Thorne, niece and nephew through Sandy, for sharing a screenwriter's cumulative wisdom and identifying their favorite stories

Robert Lindenberg and **Erica Strachan,** great representatives of their generation in the family, for positive encouragement as well as questioning certain stories

Cathy Lindenberg, Evie and Mike Goslin, sister and cousins, for steering me away from mistakes and for detailed suggestions on where to shorten

Erv Snyder and **Sara Lotz Powell**, friends since high school with better memories than I, for corrections, good suggestions, and encouragement

John Stanham, Mesoamerican partner for his enthusiasm for the stories and his help in identifying those most useful to people like himself

Gabriela Poma, a teacher of literature, for her encouraging reactions and for her commitment to our region

Stace Lindsay, fellow CALI moderator for his probing questions and for all he is doing to help Central America.

Gregory Wolfe for his publishing advice and my groups at the **Image's Glen Workshop, 2007 and 2010,** in Santa Fe, one led by **Ann McCutchen**, the other by **Lauren F. Winner,** gave me useful advice on a sample story for point of view, voice, tone, and pacing. Their advice carried over to other stories.

In many respect this book has been shaped by the father-son group in which **Ken Strachan, Rob Lindenberg,** and I have participated these last 10 years. The fathers—**Ricardo Poma, Ricardo Sagrera, Stanley Motta, Archie Baldocchi,** and **Jose Ignacio Gonzales**, great friends—encouraged me to devote time to the project, and their stories validated my own experiences. Their sons, my adopted nephews—**Alejandro, Fernando, Alberto,** and **Andres Poma; Marco Baldocchi; Ricardo Jr., Arturo** and **Marco Sagrera; Alejandro** and **Carlos Gonzalez;** and **Carlos Motta**—have been part of my mental audience. Their positive response to stories in oral form has been a great encouragement. Thanks to them and also all the **CALI young leaders**, whose energy and idealism gives me much hope for the future.

Sarah Strachan, my daughter, and **Deirdre Dunn Strachan**, my first wife, helped find, scan, crop and organize the pictures. Sarah also worked hard on the cover art. Thanks for this, not to mention the many other ways over the years they have supported, cared for, and enriched my life.

Elaine Cummings of Bain & Co, who edited *Bain Stories from the Early Years*, provided constructive advice for the book, the cover, and its publication. It was, though, her enthusiasm for what was written that I most appreciated.

Clare Strachan Frist, my sister and our family historian, for her generous editing and proofing of the manuscript.

My greatest thanks I owe to **Sandy Conant Strachan**, my wife, my soul mate, and now my editor. From the beginning when I was ready to quit, she encouraged me to keep at this long project. She used her high EQ and skill as a writer to advise on many of the decisions: what to keep in and what to leave out, and how to make the final draft more readable.